Going Dutch in the Modern Age

Going Dutch in the Modern Age

Abraham Kuyper's Struggle for a Free Church in the Nineteenth-Century Netherlands

JOHN HALSEY WOOD JR.

OXFORD
UNIVERSITY PRESS

OXFORD
UNIVERSITY PRESS

Oxford University Press is a department of the University of Oxford.
It furthers the University's objective of excellence in research, scholarship,
and education by publishing worldwide.

Oxford   New York
Auckland   Cape Town   Dar es Salaam   Hong Kong   Karachi
Kuala Lumpur   Madrid   Melbourne   Mexico City   Nairobi
New Delhi   Shanghai   Taipei   Toronto

With offices in
Argentina   Austria   Brazil   Chile   Czech Republic   France   Greece
Guatemala   Hungary   Italy   Japan   Poland   Portugal   Singapore
South Korea   Switzerland   Thailand   Turkey   Ukraine   Vietnam

Oxford is a registered trademark of Oxford University Press
in the UK and certain other countries.

Published in the United States of America by
Oxford University Press
198 Madison Avenue, New York, NY 10016

© Oxford University Press 2013

Library of Congress Cataloging-in-Publication Data
Wood, John Halsey.
Going Dutch in the modern age : Abraham Kuyper's struggle for a
free church in the nineteenth-century Netherlands / John Halsey Wood, Jr.
p. cm.
Includes bibliographical references and index.
ISBN 978-0-19-992038-9
1. Kuyper, Abraham, 1837–1920.   2. Church.   3. Netherlands—
Church history—19th century.   4. Netherlands—Church history—20th century.
5. Church and state—Netherlands.   6. Public theology.   I. Title.
BX9479.K8W66 2013
284'.2092—dc23
2012018349

ISBN 978-0-19-992038-9

1 3 5 7 9 8 6 4 2
Printed in the United States of America
on acid-free paper

For Marne
sine qua non
(without her, nothing)

Contents

Acknowledgments

THE PUBLICATION OF this book owes a great deal to several people besides me, foremost my wife, Marne, who was determined to see me finish this project. An excellent wife, who can find? She kept chaos at bay so I could work, a task usually assigned to divine power and virtually impossible when four children are involved. Moreover, despite how much I enjoyed writing this book, I am also glad that she found things besides Abraham Kuyper and ecclesiology to talk about over dinner. The dedication is not a gift; it is her just deserts.

This book brings to completion work that I began as a doctoral student under Dr. Michael McClymond at Saint Louis University, and I wish to thank him for his wisdom on the research and writing of historical theology from the beginning of this project till now. He also guided me through the paths of the academy, ways that are not always friendly or obvious to the uninitiated. I trust that he is as pleased as I am to see this work finished.

I am grateful to several other colleagues at two institutions who read and commented on parts of this work at various stages: Saint Louis University—Dr. Belden Lane, Dr. Angelyn Dries, Dr. Kenneth Parker, and numerous members of the modern history seminar in the Department of Theological Studies; and Free University of Amsterdam—Dr. George Harinck, Dr. Jasper Vree, Dr. Martien Brinkman, and Dr. Eddy van der Borght. Beyond lending his expertise in Kuyperianna, Dr. George Harinck's hospitality made my stays in the Netherlands so pleasant, and he traveled all the way to St. Louis, Missouri, to ask the first and most difficult question of my doctoral examination.

Financial support for this study came from the Institute for International Education through a Fulbright scholarship in 2006–2007, and the *Stichting De Honderd Gulden Reis* sponsored further research trips to the Netherlands in 2008 and 2009. I wish to thank both of these organizations for their generosity. Chapter 6, "Theologian of the Revolution," appears slightly revised under the same title in *Kingdoms Apart: Engaging the Two Kingdoms Perspective* (Ryan McIlhenny ed., Presbyterian and Reformed). The images in this book are provided courtesy of the Historical Documentation Center for Dutch Protestantism at the Free University Amsterdam. Hans Seilhouwer graciously found all of the requested images and sent electronic copies. Thank you to Oxford University Press and Cynthia Read for accepting my manuscript and seeing it through publication, to the manuscript readers for their supportive comments, and to Dr. David Steinmetz for having my work in such an excellent series.

Finally, I attribute my interest in the Christian church to two sources: my parents, who took me to church, and the pastors and churches that have served me and my family. Since this is a book about the church, it seems fitting to thank them as well: John and Melissa Wood, Rev. Bill Hay and Covenant Presbyterian Church, Rev. Craig Troxel and Calvary Orthodox Presbyterian Church, Rev. Jeff Meyers and Providence Reformed Presbyterian Church, Rev. Chris Smith and Resurrection Presbyterian Church, as well as Rev. Britton Wood, Rev. Lanier Wood, and Rev. T. J. Wolters. A pastor's salary is not the reward for his work, Abraham Kuyper said. It is a necessary provision for living. A pastor's reward lies in the future. May it be great.

Going Dutch in the Modern Age

I

Going Dutch in the Modern Age

WHEN ABRAHAM KUYPER arrived at the New Church in Amsterdam—the cathedral of Dutch Protestantism—on January 5, 1886, he found the doors to the consistory chamber, where the elders and pastors met, locked. It must have been surprising for him to find that his keys did not work. He was, after all, a member of the consistory and a regular in that hall. But the doors were now secured with new locks, installed exactly to forbid him entrance, and that delayed him a few hours. Kuyper came back the next morning better prepared, this time with lawyers and locksmiths. This formidable showing was necessary since the door had also been reinforced with metal plates and a guard had been set, all with the suspicion that Kuyper might try something drastic—as of course he did.

The *panel-sawing* (*panelzagerij*), so called after Kuyper removed one of the door panels to gain entrance, was the culmination—nadir, some would say—of his efforts to reform the Dutch national church, the Netherlands Reformed Church (Figure 1.1).[1] Intertwined with it were disputes that Kuyper had waged for years over the church's doctrinal and liturgical practices as well as the church's role in modern Dutch society. The outcome of the panel-sawing and these tangled disputes was Kuyper's suspension and his final deposition from ministry in the broad Dutch Protestant church that dominated public life in the Netherlands. This end also marked the beginning of a new confessional Reformed church founded by Kuyper and his allies, though undoubtedly he wished for a more auspicious start.

The panel-sawing incident stands at odds with the common perception of Abraham Kuyper as a creative public theologian with an expansive vision for Christian cultural engagement. So broad is the influence of Kuyper's public theology that historian Mark Noll says, "The only Protestant system currently at work in twentieth-century America that can even approach the intellectual depth, breath, and sanctity of neo-Thomism is the Dutch-American cultivation of the Calvinist theology of the Dutch

Figure 1.1 Panel-sawing (*paneelzagerij*) cartoon. From *De Nederlandsche Spectator*, January 9, 1886. Collection Historisch Documentatiecentrum voor het Nederlands Protestantisme (1800-heden) VU University Amsterdam.

activist and politician Abraham Kuyper (1837–1920)."[2] Kuyper hardly seems like the Calvinistic separatist that his actions at the New Church and his exit from the national church implied and of which his opponents accused him.

Moreover, Christianity's public role was just one of the conundrums that the panel-sawing raised for Kuyper. It also embodied the tensions of his beliefs about the church. In his 1898 *Lectures on Calvinism*, for which Kuyper is best known, he wrote that the church is the

> *regenerated and confessing individuals,* who, in accordance with the Scriptural command, and under the influence of the sociological element of all religion, have formed a society, and are endeavoring

to live together in subordination to Christ their king. This alone, is the church on earth—not the building—not the institution.³

If the church was not the building or the institution but the believers, why did Kuyper go to such extremes to get control of the New Church?

Theologically, the panel-sawing symbolized challenges Kuyper faced pertaining to the church, such as how the institutional aspects related to things like believers' faith and participation. It also raised questions about how Christianity could relate to society at large once one withdrew from the national church, the church with the strongest and most enduring connection to Dutch public life. In view of the tensions and challenges represented in the panel-sawing incident, this study examines Kuyper's ecclesiology, which was a lifelongtheological concern of his and certainly an earlier one than his much discussed public theology. Ecclesiology bookended his professional career as a theologian, from his master's thesis and doctoral dissertation to his final theological study, "Concerning the Church," which ran sixty-eight chapters and was brought to an end only by his death.⁴ In the nineteenth century, Kuyper judged that the "church problem" was "none other than the problem of Christianity itself."⁵

Of course, Kuyper's church problem was not the product of just one peculiar incident on a cold morning in Amsterdam. It was a problem created by the cultural upheaval of the nineteenth century. The pressures of modern society, especially the separation of church and state, democratic trends, and changes like societal differentiation, religious toleration, freedom of conscience, and religious pluralism, impinged on all churches. Cumulatively, these pressures undermined the Dutch national church's heretofore taken-for-granted status. Historians Fred van Lieburg and Joris van Eijnatten explain: "Orphaned by the withdrawing of the state and no longer obvious symbol of the existing order, [the church] needed a new legitimation."⁶ The church would no longer be underwritten by the state, and it could not presume upon the automatic support of the Dutch people. Consequently, the church would have to provide its own legitimation and not depend on public sources such as a state or nation for it. Dutch Protestantism faced the unprecedented prospect of "going Dutch," so to speak. From now on it would have to pay its own way, figuratively and in some ways literally. Kuyper provided the *new legitimation* through his free-church ecclesiology, which reconceived the nature of the church and its social position for the modern world.

Kuyper's free-church ecclesiology was a work of improvisation. There was no obvious or preprogrammed solution for dealing with modern changes such as the separation of church and state. Claude Welch notes that by the end of the nineteenth century most European theologians, Protestant and Catholic, still believed in the unity of church and state.[7] Undoubtedly, Kuyper dealt with this issue before other theologians because the Dutch churches faced disestablishment much earlier than their neighboring European peers. (Disestablishment occurred in 1848 in the Netherlands compared with 1905 in France and 1949 in Germany. Søren Kierkegaard's Denmark has an official state church to this day.) Consequently, Kuyper's ecclesiology did not spring forth fully formed but grew and developed in fits and starts as he dealt with concrete events in the Dutch church and experimented with various remedies.

It was especially the church's institutional structures that the emerging social situation had thrown into question, yet until Kuyper accepted the legitimacy and necessity of the institutional church there was little need to defend or explain it. Not that he ignored the church: it was his earliest theological interest as a young theological student and church historian, but the institutional church was more a matter of historical curiosity than devotion for him. He accepted the notion common to many in his day that the church was only a temporary and provisional necessity in the advance of humanity's maturity. Kuyper first came to appreciate the church as an enduring institution and something more than a spontaneous gathering of believers when as a pastor he was challenged by two varieties of mystics: the Calvinistic conventicles and theological modernists (Chapter 2). Thereupon he developed an ecclesiology that maintained externals like sacraments and the church's teaching office but equally insisted on the personal commitment of the members.

From this point on, the challenge of Kuyper's ecclesiology was to reconcile the internal and the external aspects of the church. As part of his plan to reform the Dutch national church, he explained these two aspects of the church as existing in a reciprocal relationship, using Pauline metaphors of the church as body and building, organism and institution. With this ecclesiology he intended to reform the national church in both respects (Chapter 3). Kuyper's early free-church ecclesiology was sacramental insofar as the institutional form of the church was an essential, God-given means of grace for believers.

Kuyper's plan of reform struck at the core of the national church; its distinguishing trait was neither theological orthodoxy nor theological modernism but a spirit of accommodation that comprehended both orthodoxy and modernism at once. A fissure opened between Kuyper and the national church that could not be bridged. That precipitated Kuyper's reconsideration of the external, institutional forms of the church. It was necessary to delegitimize the national church, especially the outward forms that he had defended so vigorously, to justify leaving it. Yet that had to be done without abandoning the institutional aspect altogether, the way some modernists had done (and Kuyper himself almost did). Kuyper's solution was a new construal of the relationship between the inner organism and outer institution, wherein he no longer considered the institution essential to the church.

Instead, the inward "organism" was the essence of the church for which the institution was only coincidentally and "conventionally" necessary (Chapter 4) and could be reformed, even broken if necessary.[8] In contrast to Kuyper's sacramental ecclesiology, this was a believer's church ecclesiology, wherein the external forms declined in importance and the inward aspect took supreme priority. The development of Kuyper's baptismal theology followed the same pattern, from an initial account of the instrumental efficacy of the sacrament to his later doctrine of presumptive regeneration, wherein the external sacrament followed the internal work of grace rather than preceding and preparing for it (Chapter 5).

While this development in ecclesiology and sacramentology is interesting enough in itself, doubly so is the coinciding development of Kuyper's thinking on the church's public significance. The withdrawing significance of external forms and heightened importance of inward aspects of the church accompanied a change in Kuyper's understanding of the church's social standing. Previously, he had attributed to the institutional church an indirect but nonetheless public function and responsibility—seed (*kiem*) and caretaker of the nation (Chapter 3). After his break with the national church, Kuyper's secession church could no longer claim any obvious custody for the nation, since only the small portion of it remained in the pews. In response, Kuyper offered a radical new vision of church, state, and society, one that overturned traditional Dutch Reformed thinking and, moreover, the historic European settlement. He outlined a religiously plural society characterized by the continuing dominance of Christianity in the public sphere but no longer by a single dominant church (Chapter 6).

That required some explaining. Kuyper's secession church looked like a sect except for one obvious fact: its leading light was "Holland's Foremost Citizen" (as one American brochure called Kuyper).[9] The task of

Abraham Kuyper's public theology, of which so much has been made, was to make this church, which had withdrawn from the public life of nation and state and which was grounded in the inward and therefore private aspects, somehow public again (Chapter 7).

A Brief History of Church and Society in the Netherlands

Abraham Kuyper's ecclesiology makes sense only within its historical context, and for a historian like Kuyper that context stretches back to the Reformation era. In the sixteenth century, the Reformed Church (Gereformeede Kerk) won its freedom at the same time the Dutch Republic did. Against Catholic Spain and Philip II, William of Orange (or William of Nassau) led the Netherlands to independence in the 1570s and early 1580s, and he was Reformed. Historians now refer to the privileged Reformed Church that grew out of these events and continued through the eighteenth century as the *public church*. The public church was public in the privileges it received from the civil magistrates, the privileges the magistrate claimed over it, and its broad responsibility for the Dutch people. The Reformed Church received support from the government for the payment of ministers and the upkeep of buildings. It also had unique rights, such as the right to public worship, not shared by other groups like Catholics. In return, the government demanded oversight of ministerial appointments and the church's acceptance of everyone to the sacraments, especially baptism. As a matter of preserving Dutch solidarity, the magistrates required that anyone who wanted to be baptized or have his or her children baptized should be able to do so. The Reformed Church accommodated this request by loosening its original rationale for baptism. Baptism of children was said to be based on their membership in the covenant, as Isaac's circumcision was, and the public church accommodated the demands of the magistrates by stretching the idea of covenant to include the whole of the nation including Roman Catholics and those not members of the Reformed Church.[10] The public importance of the church was apparent in other areas as well, such as education when the first university in the Netherlands, in Leiden, was founded for the purpose of preparing ministers.

There were already tensions in this compromise that remained until Kuyper's time and that his ecclesiology set about to solve. Its confessional particularity combined with its broad public appeal gave the Dutch

Reformed Church an "ambiguous" character, say van Eijnatten and van Lieburg: "on the one side she held as tight as possible to her Reformed identity; on the other side as much as possible she granted general religious services."[11] There was also tension between the church and the civil magistrate over control and independence. It was not a state church, insofar as it was not an organ of government, and the Reformed Church had a history of independence. Yet the church's own confession, the Belgic Confession, charged the state to "protect the sacred ministry, and thus remove and prevent all idolatry and false worship."[12] Finally, dissident groups like Catholics were permitted to exist, though the Reformed Church enjoyed obvious privileges. Thus, Peter van Rooden calls the Dutch Republic a "confessional state" yet "an example of enlightened toleration."[13]

Through the seventeenth and eighteenth centuries the Dutch Reformed Church retained its public position, but the French invasion in 1795 and the subsequent Napoleonic battles in the next two decades upset the social-religious situation. Until that time the church had operated more or less like the Republic did, with relative autonomy for local communities and authority and control based in local elites. But the French Revolution, Napoleon's invasion of the Netherlands, and the Netherlands' own internal Batavian Revolution led to the formation of a centralized state and then to the Kingdom of the Netherlands in 1815. In 1816 King William I turned what had been a de facto establishment into a de jure one, and he named his new church the Netherlands Reformed Church (or Nederlandse Hervormde Kerk, NHK), which came to be known in the nineteenth century as the national church, or the *volkskerk*.

Whether to call the Netherlands Reformed Church a national church is a matter of debate; however, if properly defined, that is the best English equivalent to the common Dutch term, *volkskerk,* used to describe this church. The *volkskerk* was not a state church in the traditional sense of being the sole church privileged and sanctioned by the state. In fact, a group of smaller church communions was also sanctioned by the state in 1816 by William I, though his ideal had been to combine all these churches into a single administrative unit. Nevertheless, the Netherlands Reformed Church was clearly primus inter pares. It enjoyed superiority of numbers and influence in Dutch society in the nineteenth century. According to church historian and theologian Karel Blei, "A *volkskerk* is characterized by breadth and plurality. It coincides with a particular *volk*, or at least understands itself especially responsible for and related to the whole of the people."[14] The Netherlands Reformed Church aspired to be just that, and it was the only church that could and did plausibly make such a claim. Even after the separation of church and state, the NHK still hoped to be the church that could unite all Dutch Protestants.[15] Hence, the NHK is best described as a national church, not a state church, though it never achieved the dominance that other national churches did (e.g., those in Scandinavia).[16]

Key to this definition of the Netherlands Reformed Church as a national church is the distinction between nation and state, a distinction unfamiliar to many today, especially Americans. The Dutch nation was a people group constituted by a common language, history, and, in the eyes of Kuyper and others, even a common religion. The Dutch nation was not necessarily considered to be bound to a particular state. While the state changed from a republic to a kingdom, for example, the nation remained constant. Thus, the national church, in spite of its ties to state, was not and is not a state church because it is neither an organ of the state nor would it cease to exist even should the state do so. Ernest Gellner gave the classic definition of nineteenth-century nationalism as the political principle that the political and the national unit should be congruent.[17] Measured by this standard, Kuyper did not qualify as a nationalist since, though he was firmly committed to the Dutch people, he was skeptical of the imposition of the centralized bureaucratic modern state, a crucial point paralleled by his antipathy toward the synodical hierarchy of the Netherlands Reformed Church.

The boundaries of the national church were broad, coinciding almost completely with the Protestant majority of the population. Membership in the church and membership in society were virtually indistinguishable, illustrated by the fact that until 1811 baptism records were the only registration of newborn children in the Netherlands. Carrying on the policy of the church of the Republic, even those who were not members of the Netherlands Reformed Church could and did have their children baptized in the church. But separation of church and state upset the simple equation of church and nation that defined the national church. In the 1850s, a new category of membership was added: the *birth-member*. This meant that children born to members of the national church were members of the church for life, regardless of whether they were baptized or made a public profession of faith, thereby preserving the national church's broad reach after the separation of church and state.[18]

The synodical hierarchy was the creation of William I. The unified state called for a unified church, but since the sixteenth century the Dutch church had not been a strict hierarchical institution. Instead, the Reformed Church consisted of a rather loose group of ecclesiastical bodies, the key to which was the local congregations. The congregation (*gemeente*) was the church of the city and the most basic unit of the church in classical Dutch reformed polity, though it might be broken further into parishes. Every congregation had only one governing board of elders and ministers, the consistory. The next body was the classis or classical board, a regional gathering of representatives from a group of congregations. Above that was the provincial board, representing an entire province, Holland or Utrecht perhaps. Finally, the synod was the highest ecclesiastical gathering of the Dutch church, a body representing the entire Dutch Reformed Church. During the Republic, although the synod had the broadest representation, it did not have much power. Instead, it was a place for corporate discussion and counsel, but lower bodies were not subject to its authority. The 1619 synod of Dort is remembered for its canons against Arminianism, but equally important for Dutch religious and social life was the church order or polity (i.e., canon law) it promulgated. That was the church order that Abraham Kuyper sought to reintroduce: article 84 stated, "No church shall have any authority over other churches, no minister over other ministers, no elder or deacon over other elders or deacons."[19] And even the church order of the synod of Dort was not adopted by all of the congregations, though this lack of full agreement did not lead to dissention. Thus, classical Dutch Reformed polity had been a form of connectionalism between local units but not a hierarchy of courts in English Presbyterian style.

In 1816 William I literally overturned this localist polity. Empowered by a new constitution to intervene in religious affairs, he introduced a hierarchical system of church courts with the synod at the top. He would have most preferred a single, unified Dutch church, including Protestants and Catholics or, failing that, a common Protestant church including the Reformed and Lutherans. He had to settle for a unified Reformed church, in which the synod was now the highest authoritative body, and he, the king himself, would name the first members of the synod.[20] Looking back, Kuyper and others considered this as un-Dutch as the new centralized state that replaced the localism of the Republic.

Through the nineteenth century, several processes began to erode the national church's dominant position. Two are particularly important: the differentiation of society, especially the separation of church and state; and its democratization. The constitutional separation of church and state had its beginnings in 1796 with the new National Assembly, which took on the

French slogan of liberty, equality, and fraternity but which did not accept the French hostility to religion. Rather, it was thought that the separation of church and state would be good for religion, and religion was thought to be good for society.[21] After William I's experiment, in 1848 the separation of church and state was finalized by a new liberal constitution, which also guaranteed freedom of assembly and freedom of press. The Dutch separation of church and state came sooner and was more radical than in almost any other European country, which explains why disentangling the two was so confusing. There was hardly any precedent. There were many questions to work out, such as what—church or state—controlled church property, education, and welfare. In the years immediately following 1848, the church order went through a series of revisions to adapt the church to the new situation,[22] but even then it was easier to put separation on paper than into practice. The government department of public worship continued for several decades more; pastors continued to be paid out of state coffers, and the church order still charged ministers with inculcating love for the fatherland. As James Kennedy explains, "Even after 1848 the churches continued to fill a public role and were seen as indispensible pillars of the public order," an inevitable fact when more than 99 percent of the population was listed on the church rolls (in 1879).[23]

Abraham Kuyper, skilled in oratory, mass communication, and group mobilization, became one of the great populist leaders of nineteenth-century Netherlands and bore an important responsibility for the democratization of church and society. The 1848 constitution made some provisions for a more democratic polity, but the Netherlands remained behind most other western European nations in enfranchisement in the late nineteenth century. Kuyper supported broader enfranchisement and near the end of his life finally witnessed universal male suffrage (1917) and then female suffrage (1919). Van Rooden says, "The Protestant nation of the Dutch liberal elite was destroyed by the emergence of mass politics in the last quarter of the nineteenth century."[24] Newer research, however, suggests something different. Democratic practices did lead to the downfall of the Protestant establishment, but those practices arose first in the church and then spread into politics. Although the Netherlands Reformed Church was still formally a top-down bureaucracy, the laity received an active role in local church government in the 1860s, when article 23 of the church order allowed the laity to choose their own consistory members. Kuyper was a Christian republican, in church and society, from the first, despite his opposition to religious individualism. He supported article 23, calculating that his views held sway, if not in the highest church court, the synod, then with the laity themselves. As it turned out, Dutch Protestants learned to vote in church before they did in civil government.[25]

Traditional religious authority structures also suffered with the appearance of various new religious movements that emphasized individual spirituality and offered alternatives to traditional forms. Some such as Mary Baker Eddy, Madam Blavatsky, and Franz Mesmer worked outside Christian churches, and others within. Decades before Kuyper, the atheistic humanism emanating from France sparked a backlash in the form of religious revivals that spread over Europe. Kuyper struggled to form a consistent opinion on revivalism. At times Methodism, Darbyism, Alexander Vinet and the French Réveil, and the Reveil party in the Dutch church all came in for a lashing for their "one-sided spiritualism" and their neglect of church forms.[26] Other times, especially after his own experience with Robert Pearsall Smith in Brighton, England, Kuyper advocated bringing the revivals home to his fellow Dutch Protestants.[27] The cumulative effect of all these phenomena, from the separation of church and state to revivalism, was the expanding religious pluralism in the Netherlands.

Religious pluralism accelerated in the nineteenth century to such a degree that it may be the dominant feature of the period. The French Revolution toppled the unity of the dominant churches and the state and so opened the way for a variety of religious movements. Historian Hugh McLeod explains, "Pluralism is the key to the religious situation in later nineteenth-century Europe, and...trends towards secularization have to be seen in the context of intense religious competition, whether between rival branches of Christianity or between religious and secular views of the world."[28] The Netherlands participated equally in Europe's growing religious diversity, both between Christians and non-Christians and also among Christians. Diversity meant competition, and competition was hardly more intense anywhere than within the Netherlands Reformed Church, which was "between 1850 and 1880 a hotel for very diverse religious schools."[29] Pluralism and competition were new challenges for the NHK after 1848. The parties in the Netherlands Reformed Church require some account for the present study since they will not be familiar to many today, but to Kuyper they were the competition that oriented and inspired his theological polemics.

Theological modernism in the Netherlands, like modernism elsewhere, attacked the supernatural foundations of historic Christianity and relaid them with this-worldly ones in an attempt to accommodate Christian theology to the naturalistic science (taken in the broad *wissenschaftliche* sense) of the day. (NB Dutch sources speak more often of *modernist* theology and modernist Christianity than *liberal* theology, and that convention is adopted here.) J. H. Scholten was perhaps the foremost modernist theologian of the century, and besides Kuyper his students included Herman Bavinck and Abraham Kuenen. Scholten was educated by the supernaturalist Utrecht theologians but gradually abandoned those beliefs. Initially, Scholten rejected external religious authorities for the internal testimony of the Holy Spirit in the mind and heart, but, later, influenced by the rationalist philosopher C. W. Opzoomer, Scholten abandoned even feeling for pure reason. "The witness of the Holy Spirit is none other than the witness of reason in moral purity."[30] Scholten also abandoned the divinity of Christ and the Bible, but he did come to embrace the Calvinistic doctrines of the sovereignty of God and predestination since he was able to reconcile them with deterministic evolutionary naturalistic science. Scholten bequeathed his higher-critical principles to Kuenen and his commitment to sovereignty and predestination to Kuyper.[31]

Modernists also stripped the church of its supernatural character. One may hear echoes of the early Kuyper in Scholten's view of the church. He denied that Jesus established an institutional church or any fixed doctrinal formulas. The church was the gathering of those possessing the life principle of Christ: independent personal conviction on purely moral grounds, not external sources of authority, like church or Scripture.[32] Richard Rothe's Hegelianism influenced many other Dutch modernists, like L. W. E. Rauwenhoff and Allard Pierson. These concluded that the state, and no longer the church, was the supreme ethical institution of human society and the fullest development of what earlier, less developed generations sought in the church. The modes of thought familiar to Kuyper are apparent in Rauwenhoff's description of Rothe: the state is the organism of human ethical life, and the church is the organism of human religious life. But these two cannot be separated, and eventually the state will take over both aspects of human life.[33] Pierson states, "What actually lays in the beautiful dream of the Kingdom of God on earth can be fulfilled in and through the state."[34] These sentiments occasionally had scandalous implications, such as when well-known pastors and theologians including Pierson, Domela Nieuwenhuis, C. Busken-Huet, and renowned scholar of religion C. P. Tiele made highly visible exits from the church.

Some modernists believed that the church still had a role to play though its days were numbered, while others, like Pierson, believed that the church ought to be abandoned immediately. Common to most of these was the belief that the Kingdom of God would be realized on earth, though in society at large not in the church, and that the church institution illicitly inhibited human freedom, the most basic principle of Protestantism.[35] This inward religious individualism led Kuyper and Troeltsch to see in modernism, especially Rothe's, a form of mysticism.[36] Kuyper agreed with Rauwenhoff on one point in particular: that "the church question" (as Kuyper called it) was the most important one of the day. No wonder, because the question was not simply over the church's nature or mission but whether it ought to exist at all.

As in France and Switzerland, a spiritual revival swept the Netherlands in the early nineteenth century. A loose party including leaders like poet Isaac Da Costa and jurist and historian Groen van Prinsterer (Kuyper's mentor) formed in the Netherlands Reformed Church around Reveil spirituality, which emphasized inner religiosity. Like the Christian Reformed Church (CGK), a group that seceded from the Netherlands Reformed Church in 1834, the Reveil party embraced the Reformed confessions, though not quite so tightly, as illustrated, for example, by Groen's disregard for the Reformed doctrine of election. More importantly, the CGK insisted on a pure church, per articles 27–29 of the Belgic Confession, whereas the Reveil stressed personal piety and conversion. The CGK thought the Netherlands Reformed Church was a false church; the Reveil party thought it was only ailing.

Although the Afscheiding found sympathy among the Reveil party, the groups represented two different social classes. The Afscheiding was composed mainly of a lower class of merchants and farmers, while the Reveil largely arose among the aristocracy and better-educated classes. Groen was aid to the king. Coinciding with the aristocratic color of the Reveil was its social conservatism, and coinciding with that was a refusal to take the radical step the Afscheiding had and to leave the national church.[37] This kind of social conservatism, rather than strict doctrinal conservatism, among Reveil followers in Utrecht and then in Amsterdam upset Kuyper more than the out-and-out heterodoxy of the modernists.[38] Kuyper dubbed those like his Amsterdam nemesis Pastor J. Kramer *irenicals*, a sardonic term for what Kuyper viewed as a weak, peace-at-all-costs accommodation of un-Reformed and unorthodox elements in the church.

Modernism experienced its heyday from the 1850s to the 1880s, but even before that, several parties (or schools of thought, *richting*) already opposed the intrusion of Enlightenment rationalism in theology and church. The

Groningen party arose around Groningen University in the northern province by the same name and led by Petrus Hofstede de Groot. Against the pure reason of the rationalists, these theologians elevated religious feeling, which also set them opposite orthodox Calvinists, who wanted to maintain strict adherence to the sixteenth- and seventeenth-century Reformed doctrinal confessions with their scholastic formulations. The Groningen party did not emphasize the radical rupture in human nature caused by sin and repaired by regeneration; rather, sin and redemption were ethical categories. Redemption and atonement did not deal with metaphysical or forensic problems but with the ethical pursuit of Christ's perfect example of human life. Though it was not antisupernatural, some have called the Groningen theology a "crisis-less" theology.[39]

The church then found its role in forming or nurturing (*opleiding*) humanity to its highest ideal, the full image of Christ, the task that modernists would have attributed to the state. Jasper Vree captures the intersection of atonement and education: Christianity was "God's perfect revelation of love in the person and life of his Son Jesus Christ, an act intended to educate mankind, by the example of His love, to live in uniformity with their God and Father in a reciprocated love."[40] The goal was the civilized or educated Netherlander, as the title of the Groningen periodical indicated: *Truth in Love: A Theological Journal for Civilized Christians*. This coincided with the mission of the church as the book of church order (*Algemeen Reglement*) specified it: for "cultivating love of King and Fatherland."[41] With that mission in mind, the Groningen theologians construed the scope of the church's mission as broadly as the fatherland itself. Rather than a church membership defined by doctrinal commitments, Hofstede de Groot prescribed "a warmer approach to church members but also a broad conception of the confession—as broad as the nation as possible." Christianity and Dutchness; church and nation were tightly interwoven. The University of Groningen sponsored the contest that Abraham Kuyper won as a graduate student at Leiden University with his *Commentatio* on the ecclesiologies of John Calvin and John a Lasco, and Jasper Vree says that the enthusiasm one finds in Kuyper's *Commentatio* for a Dutch national Protestant church owes to Groningen influence.[42]

The Groningen party was not the only party that opposed Enlightenment rationalism. Many people, such as Hendrik de Cock, also of Groningen, and interestingly enough, Petrus de Groot's successor at the church in the town of Ulrum, demonstrated their opposition by returning to traditional Calvinist theology. While De Groot and the Groningen school made peace with higher-critical methods, many like De Cock would not. Some parishioners from surrounding areas did not want their own unorthodox pastors to baptize their children, and they brought their children to De Cock instead. When he baptized them, however, the provincial board suspended and deposed him. This led to a secession, the Afscheiding, in 1834 and the formation of the Christelijke Gereformeerde Kerk (CGK), the Christian Reformed Church. This was the church with which Kuyper's secession church united in 1892, six years after Kuyper's own secession. At that time one of the highest hurdles to the union went all the way back to the 1834 articles of the Afscheiding secession. Therein the CGK had declared the Netherlands Reformed Church a false church, and from then on they regarded it that way.[43] It was then difficult to accept that an orthodox Calvinist party, like Kuyper's, did not leave the national church and join the CGK.

The history of the Afscheiding also shows just how tightly intertwined the national church was in state and society through the 1830s and 1840s (until the separation of church and state was once and for all secured in 1848). One hundred and fifty soldiers were sent to Ulrum to be quartered with secession church members there. Twelve of those were with de Cock, who was eventually imprisoned for preaching, after which time Afscheiding services were forbidden.[44] The national church was a broad church, tolerating a wide range of groups, from rationalistic modernists to (as we shall see) pietistic followers of the Reveil, but while it tolerated diversity it would not tolerate dissent.

The Ethical movement or Ethical theology was an offshoot of the Reveil. Ethical theologians like Daniel Chantepie de la Saussaye (father of famed theorist of religion P. D. Chantepie de la Saussaye), J. H. Gunning, and A. W. Bronsveld sought to capture the ethos of the Reveil and give it intellectual formulation and rigor. Although they accepted the confessional statements of the church, they viewed them as expressions of inner religious life, the center of Ethical theology. *Ethical* thus referred not only to morality but also to life or ethos. This put the Ethical theologians at odds with others among the Reveil like Groen van Prinsterer, the jurist who regarded the churches' confessions as legally binding documents.

Two things especially characterized Gunning's ecclesiology: freedom and sociality, both common concerns for Kuyper. During the early 1860s, Gunning and Kuyper, following Schleiermacher, believed that the basic unit of the church was the congregation, not the individual believer. Gunning conceived of the congregation, however, not first of all in its institutional form but as a freely gathering communion of saints, out of which the institution then came forth. Thus, Gunning put the priesthood of all believers before office (*ambt*), and he refused to answer synodical-oversight questionnaires about the faith and life of officers in the local congregation out of a desire to protect Christian freedom. This position exemplified the curious way Gunning and Kuyper might coincidentally adopt similar positions yet for very different reasons. Kuyper also refused synodical questionnaires, though not out of a concern for freedom but for the opposite reason—because he judged that the synod did not intend to enforce its own standards anyway. Gunning and Kuyper were bound to grow apart, and they did the more Kuyper championed institutional forms of the church like confessions.[45]

Gunning's understanding of the social situation of the church was complicated and perhaps never really consistent. He initially accepted the separation of church and state, though he later accepted an ongoing relation between these institutions (due to the exigencies of pastoral work, as Vree suggests); however, he never lost his appreciation and devotion to the "fatherland-church," the church instituted by God for the Dutch nation. He opposed Kuyper's idea that the church might take plural forms and advocated a unified visible church.[46] Further, he did not support general enfranchisement in civil society, yet he did in the church as a means to break the power of the synod. Apparently his commitment to freedom had its limits.[47]

In lay discussions, Kuyper is often portrayed as a critic of modernist or liberal Protestantism. No less a historian than Heiko Oberman describes Kuyper as "the great critic of liberal Protestantism in the Netherlands," and Oberman plays Kuyper against modernist Allard Pierson.[48] But if this view leads one to believe that Kuyper was therefore a conservative, then it is wholly inadequate—especially regarding Kuyper's ecclesiology and ecclesiastical actions. It fails to explain the mutual regard Kuyper and Pierson had for each other such that Pierson even opened his house to Kuyper, who had made a special effort to stop there while on vacation. What bound Kuyper to Pierson was what revolted them about the national church: conservatism. The conservatism of the national church was the conservatism of a dominant, established church and the elites that controlled it, much as Troeltsch described it:

> The Church is that type of organization which is overwhelmingly conservative, which to a certain extent accepts the secular order,

and dominates the masses; in principle, therefore, it is universal, i.e. it desires to cover the whole life of humanity.... She becomes an integral part of the existing social order.[49]

This conservatism was not strict theological conservatism but was a socioreligious conservatism. It was a social conservatism in their views of the church, its nature and social position, that resisted upsetting the social order. This was the kind of conservatism that characterized most of the aforementioned parties, and its opposite was radicalism, not necessarily liberalism.

Almost all leaders of these various parties were social elites, either by their social class or their position in prestigious universities, congregations, or the government. What Abraham Kuyper recognized (what the Afscheiding found out firsthand when soldiers were quartered in their houses) was that Calvinist orthodoxy was not necessarily conservative.[50] J. C. Rullmann, Kuyper's sympathetic biographer, recalled accusations that Kuyper's actions in the church were dangerous not only to the church but also to the state.[51] What Kuyper shared with certain modernists like Pierson and with the Afscheiding was the willingness to take the radical step of leaving the established church to realize their ideals. Thus, Kuyper and Pierson cultivated a mutual respect, in the midst of disagreement, that was not unlike staunch secularists H. L. Menken's or Walter Lippmann's regard for *doctor fundamentalis* J. Gresham Machen.[52] Liberal politician Joannis Kappeyne van de Coppello, certainly no orthodox Calvinist himself and Kuyper's sworn enemy in the political arena, even wrote legal briefs for Kuyper's breakaway church, so much did Van de Copello despise the establishment conservatism of the national church.[53] What modernists like Scholten, Groningen theologians, Ethical theologians, and (as we shall see) some strict confessionalists like Philip Hoedemaker shared—for all of their deep theological disagreements—was the commitment to a broad national church, as broad as the nation if possible.

Of all the groups in the Dutch church, Kuyper posed the greatest crisis for the confessionalists, who maintained a strict commitment to the Reformed confessions, some stricter than Kuyper. Hoedemaker, for example, who taught theology at Kuyper's Free University until Kuyper left the national church, disagreed sharply with Kuyper over article 36 of the Belgic Confession, which charged the state with overseeing the doctrine of the church, a point that Kuyper rejected but Hoedemaker accepted. These confessionalists had to decide whether to go with Kuyper, whose religious convictions they mostly shared, or stay in a church alongside many with whom they had virtually no shared religious beliefs, though they did share an ecclesiastical heritage.[54] Hoedemaker exemplified the paradoxical situation of these confessional conservatives by remaining in the Netherlands Reformed Church—which he agreed with Kuyper was corrupt but which he yet expected to reform from within (by the very system he regarded as problematic)—because he believed Kuyper had acted rashly.[55] In the present American religious marketplace, this predicament is nearly inconceivable, but Hoedemaker ought not therefore to be dismissed easily. For such Dutch Protestants history had real purchase, and it was not to be bargained away on the cheap. Consequently, many confessionalists went with Kuyper into the new church, but many did not. What the disputes among confessional Calvinists like Kuyper and Hoedemaker also show is that there was not a simple or obvious answer to the question of how to make Calvinism modern. It is by no means certain that Calvin would have sacrificed the church's dominance over society to preserve its doctrinal purity, had that been the choice facing him as it did Kuyper and Hoedemaker.

From the sixteenth century on, the Dutch national church never had the dominance that some other European Protestant churches did because of the large portion of Roman Catholics in the Netherlands and because of the tolerance extended to various Protestant dissenter churches. Nevertheless, it could claim an undisputed hegemony over the Protestant portion of the Dutch people, and it enjoyed a privileged social standing. To retain that hegemony amid growing theological diversity, it had to broaden its theological boundaries and loosen restraints on various practices. Even after final disestablishment of William I's church, his synodical hierarchy remained and, with it, the church's centralized bureaucracy wherein the synod had final say.

Confessional subscription for ministers and baptismal practices were two areas pertinent to Kuyper's history, where the church tried to accommodate emerging differences. In 1827 the subscription formula whereby ministers swore agreement with the doctrinal standards of the church was rewritten in such a way that it was ambiguous as to whether ministers were swearing that they agreed with the church's doctrinal confessions because (*quia*) they were in conformity with Scripture or insofar as (*quatenus*) the confessions were in conformity with Scripture. In the case of *quatenus* subscription the minister's individual conscience remained the final arbiter of Scripture because he decided whether the confession conformed to

Scripture. In the case of the *quia* subscription, the minister agreed that the church through the confession was the final arbiter of doctrine.

Following the religious interiorization of the day, many wanted to reserve ultimate freedom for the individual conscience, while constitutionalists like Groen and Kuyper considered the confessions binding documents that had to be abided by unless officially amended. The synod resolved the conflict for the laity when it affirmed that religious convictions could not be a reason for denying membership,[56] and for prospective ministers it resolved the conflict in 1883 by simply removing all reference to the confessions and even to Jesus Christ from their vows. That was the last straw for Kuyper. According to his own testimony, that was the most proximate cause for the panel-sawing at the New Church and his subsequent secession, the so-called Doleantie.[57] It was telling that prospective ministers pledged to promote the interests of the Kingdom of God (a phrase many considered indeterminate) and the Netherlands Reformed Church while Jesus Christ was not named in their vows.[58] Again, fidelity to a specific church communion, or not, defined Kuyper and his opponents both. (Today the Protestant Church in the Netherlands, or PKN, the successor of the Netherlands Reformed Church, continues the broad church tradition, allowing even self-proclaimed atheists like Klaas Hendrikse to minister in good standing in the church.[59])

The church also accommodated a diversity in practice by demandating the traditional Christian baptismal formula. As the church broadened, a series of synodical decisions in the late 1860s made the Trinitarian baptismal formula optional. Instead of Father, Son, and Holy Spirit, one could now be baptized "into the name of the Father," "into the name of the congregation," "into faith, hope, and love," or "for the initiation into Christendom."[60] Kuyper summed up the result and indicated his own estimate of the importance of correct liturgical forms: "In order to maintain doctrinal freedom the synod abandons Christian baptism."[61] Kuyper did not want a confessional straitjacket, but he did want a measurable set of standards for doctrine and liturgy. "'Fixity but not unchangability of form for liturgy and confession both,' was then and still remains my motto."[62] That is, he wanted an objective touchstone for doctrine and liturgy but not one that could not be adjusted or amended, yet it was exactly this pursuit of doctrinal and liturgical definition that struck at the amorphous national church.

However, as has already been hinted, Kuyper did not start out as a zealous confessional Calvinist. Time and experience, notably pastoral experience more than academic, were what changed his mind.

"I Was Converted": A Very Short Life of Abraham Kuyper

What is known about Kuyper's youth is slight but not, therefore, insignificant. The very earliest scrap available from Kuyper's hand exhibits a sincere and intense religiosity that never abated. He wrote, at ten years old, his short confession:

> It was the tenth of October, 10:30 p.m. that I went to bed and could not sleep for the evil I had done. Then at 11:30 I was converted and made a firm decision to flee the evil and to pursue the good.
> I, Abraham Kuyper, son of J. F. Kuyper
> Middleburg
> 1848[63]

The year 1848 was a year for revolutions, within Kuyper and without.

Abraham Kuyper grew up as the son of a pastor in the Netherlands Reformed Church—humble beginnings that did not portend much. His father did not always have the money to make ends meet, and loans were sometimes necessary. But Kuyper recounted to G. J. Vos (who turned out to be his ecclesiastical foe) that these experiences made him sympathetic to the "little people" (*kleine luyden*) who became the popular base of his Christian school movement, his Anti-Revolutionary political party, and his confessional Calvinist church.[64] Growing up the son of a pastor did not endear the church to Kuyper. He later recalled the "liberal regime" of his father's Leiden church and the "deceit, the hypocrisy, the unspiritual routine" and the distasteful disputes over the city council and the Huiszittenhuis, a charitable organization serving the poor.[65] Perhaps those experiences encouraged his hope as a university student that the era of the church was over.

Besides his youthful conversion, no concern dates farther back in Kuyper's theological corpus than the church. Under the tutelage of church historian N. C. Kist of Leiden University his first serious research examined the development of papal power under Pope Nicolas I (d. 867). Kuyper commended Nicolas for his true Christian piety, his concern for the oppressed, his zeal for justice, and for using his papal power to these ends. Yet the church in external forms such as the papacy was for a humanity underage, one that had not yet reached the spiritual maturity that Kuyper (following Richard Rothe and other Dutch modernists) believed the nineteenth century had attained:

> Religion exerts a mighty influence on the destiny of the world from within through the human heart, and where it fulfills its destiny, then only by that route. On a lower level of development, it works less as an inspiring principle, but manages to intervene in the course of events through the Church as its organ. Thus, the more religion comes into its own, to that degree the Church loses its importance in history. Already in the history of our day the Church has been designated a most subordinate role.[66]

With such a low estimate of the church, it is not surprising that Kuyper, pastor's son though he was, did not worry about attending.[67]

A year later, in his doctoral dissertation on the church in the theologies of Calvin and a Lasco (Figure 1.2), Kuyper was more optimistic about the church as a spiritual community, though he believed that its tangible, visible form was only ancillary. The church was not the cultus but the

FIGURE 1.2 Kuyper at his doctoral promotion, 1862. Collection Historisch Documentatiecentrum voor het Nederlands Protestantisme (1800-heden) VU University Amsterdam.

society of Christians gathered together. Overemphasis, like Calvin's, on the institution hindered human freedom. On the other hand, this was not an individualistic piety, because the church was not a gathering of individual Christians but was irreducibly a society, one of the few persistent points in Kuyper's ecclesiology through all its later developments. Vree attributes this democratic and social ecclesiology to the influence of Schleiermacher.[68]

Kuyper's view of the sacraments exemplified this social ecclesiology. The sacraments promoted Christian unity but lacked any gracious efficacy.

> Baptism and the Supper are actions of a *symbolic appointing*, which in the glorious memory of our Lord advance the unity of the institute of the church, at the same time also pricking and inspiring us, in order that we may embrace Christ with a whole heart and that we may foster the most tender love towards our brothers.[69]

Calvin had incorrectly ascribed a "magical power" and "excessive stability" to the sacraments.[70] He apparently belonged to a lower level of development. As for the church's social position, at this early stage Kuyper already worried that Calvin and a Lasco both gave the state too much control over the church.[71]

Kuyper's personal spirituality helps explain the role of the church in his theology. Kuyper did not have the typical Puritan conversion, the one moment of sublime clarity wherein grace made its claim and the sinner's life was forever changed. He had several of them. After writing the note as a ten-year-old, Kuyper was next converted as a graduate student. In 1859, he had scoured the libraries of Europe in search of a Lasco materials but came up empty-handed, only then to find on the shelves of an old pastor of a Mennonite congregation in Haarlem (who happened to be the father of Kuyper's university professor, Matthias de Vries, at the time) a wealth of a Lasco material unrivaled by Europe's great libraries:

> Yes, I know: such an experience is not to be equated with a conversion. But it is an encounter with the living, acting, sovereign God on life's way. And the impression this almost unbelievable experience made on my heart was so deep and permanent that, by whatever route I go back in memory to recall the searching love of my God, I always return to this miraculous event of the Lasciana.[72]

That was not the last conversion.

Kuyper hardly mentioned his wife, Johanna Schaay, in his professional writing, but she was pivotal for his ecclesiology (Figure 1.3a). Kuyper was always ambitious and, as a young theology student, arrogant too. Kuyper plied his young fiancée with all sorts of theological questions and urged her to more sublime subjects than the theater and concerts and home life that she loved.[73] She, of course, had no answer for the seminarian's interrogation, but in 1863, just before Kuyper entered his first pastorate, she succeeded in introducing him to a novel, *The Heir of Redclyffe*, by the English author and Oxford movement disciple Charlotte Yonge. Following Kuyper's 1873 memoir *Confidentially*, historian George Puchinger says that Kuyper met two things in the novel: first, in Philip de Morville, the antagonist, Kuyper saw a picture of his own egotism; and second, the novel presented the idea of the church as a mother.[74] Kuyper's first sermons at his pastorate at Beesd show that he was not as fully enthralled with mother church as his memoir suggests—"*at that moment* the predilection

(a)   (b)

FIGURE 1.3 The Women of Kuyper's Ecclesiological Career: wife Johanna Schaay and parishioner Pietje Baltus. Collection Historisch Documentatiecentrum voor het Nederlands Protestantisme (1800-heden) VU University Amsterdam.

for prescribed ritual, the high estimation of the Sacrament, the appreciation for the Liturgy became rooted in me for all time"[75]—but still the impression was a lasting one.

Kuyper spoke of one other decisive moment in his memoir, one that also occurred at the instigation of another persistent woman, Pietje Baltus (Figure 1.3b). Baltus represented for Kuyper the pietistic Calvinists—"fanatics"—that he came across at Beesd, who were not as impressed with his university learning as he was. They threw Calvin and the Reformed fathers back at him, and he was forced to deal with these theologians again, now as more than historical artifacts. Puchinger calls this Kuyper's "conversion" to doctrinal Calvinism and to the commoners.[76] Again, the story seems to have been more complicated than Kuyper or Puchinger say, but, nonetheless, *conversion* may not be too strong a term. What Kuyper remembered, the "greatest attraction" of these "cantankerous, proud eccentrics" was that "here was conviction. Here the topics of conversation went beyond nice weather...here spoke a heart that had a history and life-experience...that not only had them but knew them."[77] So these pious Calvinists spurred Kuyper toward Calvin, but they also gave a kind of negative impulse to Kuyper's ecclesiology by refusing him as their minister (the subject of chapter 2).

Perhaps these mystics struck a chord with Kuyper because of his own commitment to personal piety. Besides his theological and political pieces, throughout his life he wrote thousands of devotional articles for his flock. In 1875, he attended the camp meeting of American revivalist Robert Pearsall Smith in Brighton, England, where he received a fresh measure of the Spirit. And if he was given to intense spiritual highs, he was also given to spiritual lows. Some months after his trip to Brighton, Kuyper experienced a deep spiritual and psychological breakdown, which led to his resigning his parliamentary seat and taking a year-plus leave of absence that included stops at Lake Como, Switzerland, and Nice. The pattern established here continued throughout Kuyper's life.

The diversity of Dutch Protestantism, the new situation of the national church, and the twists of Kuyper's life yielded an ecclesiology that was dynamic and developing. Further, Kuyper worked out this ecclesiology in occasional pieces like sermons and polemical tracts that dealt with specific disputed points and therefore did not answer every possible question. Writings from every period of his thought reveal undeniable tensions. His ecclesiology, therefore, did not appear fully formed on a single occasion. Only later in life did he produce the larger systematic works, where he attempted to draw all the threads together. Then he would plead for understanding in the theological searching of his early life:

> Do not forget that I was first brought over from modernist fold into the Ethical circle, and so came into Reformed circles only at a rather advanced age, and then I had to find my own way, little by little, without a teacher, in the middle of a very stressful and eventful life, in order to understand the writings of the Confession of our fathers.[78]

Perhaps the most consistent theme in this pattern was not the answers he gave but the questions he asked.

This biographical sketch exhibits two long-standing concerns—church and conversion—that anticipate the main dilemma of his ecclesiology: how to bring inner spiritual commitment and the outer church forms together in a consistent ecclesiology. In answer to this dilemma, this study argues for a development in Kuyper's free-church ecclesiology from a sacramental ecclesiology to a believers' church ecclesiology.

The Questions Kuyper Raises

Two issues dominate the historiography of religion in nineteenth-century Europe: secularization and revival. Secularization refers to a variety of phenomena including the differentiation of the church from other social institutions, disenchantment with the Christian worldview and its replacement by a strictly immanent frame of mind, and the uncertain status and prospects (if not quite yet the decline) of the traditional institutional churches. Yet the grimmer side of Christendom was counterbalanced by the evangelical awakenings that focused on individual religiosity and that required high levels of personal commitment. Moreover, these two themes, secularization and revival, were not distant antipodes but were in some ways interdependent, as Charles Taylor explains: "Christians in a world which less and less reflects God are thrown back on their own resources."[79] That is, as the traditional social footing of the churches began to slide, it fell to Christians to shore up their religion. Indeed, in some cases it may have been the latter that caused the former. Pierson, Kuyper's contemporary, observed that "liberal theology broke down dogma; *the Reveil broke down the church*" (though Pierson, liberal Protestant, was not the least saddened by it. He continued, "I cannot help but rejoice in this spirit").[80] In broad strokes this was the background of Kuyper's own religious life, and it frames the dominant themes in research surrounding Kuyper—namely, conversion, church, and social ethics.

Puchinger, better than anyone else, shows the importance of Kuyper's various early conversion experiences for determining the course of his life.[81] His multivolume biography was, however, cut short by an untimely death. Recently, Jeroen Koch has taken a similar approach, focusing on Kuyper's conversion experiences as hermeneutical keys to his life. Koch applies William James's concept of conversion as an inner experience and total reaction that reshape one's whole life, but this Jamesian hermeneutic that downplays (if it does not outright ignore) outward institutional religious forms yields some strange results for Koch. He concludes, for example, that Kuyper's conversion to orthodox Calvinism erased the boundary between the public and private domains and that Kuyper "established a church more public than had been the case in the Dutch Republic."[82] James may be a fine theorist, but here he fails the historian. It is a matter of plain historical record that Christianity (never mind Kuyper) has never been purely private. Further, Koch—no theologian—takes Kuyper's appeal to orthodox Calvinism at face value and therefore far too uncritically.

In general, European scholars have given the most attention to Kuyper's ecclesiology and the institutional church therein, whereas Americans and English-language scholars have generally focused on his public theology. In 1946, Petrus van Leeuwen provided an outstanding systematic study of Kuyper's ecclesiology, and the best comparable English study is Henry Zwaanstra's much shorter article.[83] Van Leeuwen and Zwaanstra both deal with Kuyper systematically, and within each topic they occasionally note the changes or inconsistencies in Kuyper's ecclesiology. Yet they offer relatively little by way of historical-contextual explanation for these developments. Vree and Johan Zwaan recently give much more historical texture to Kuyper's ecclesiastical life and particularly his early ecclesiology. Zwaan explores Kuyper's social concern and the hints of his sympathy for modernist views concerning the obsolescence of the church in Kuyper's university thesis on Pope Nicolas I.[84] Vree and Zwaan published a two-volume critical edition of Kuyper's seminal doctoral dissertation on the ecclesiologies of Calvin and a Lasco, the second volume of which is an exhaustive historical analysis of the treatise's context and theology. Vree points out how Kuyper had come to appreciate the church since his earlier work, due in part to the influence of Friedrich Schleiermacher. Yet the church Kuyper received from Schleiermacher's hands, Vree explains, was not

Calvin's institution of salvation but a spontaneously forming social body.[85] Kuyper's first appreciation for the institutional church came at the instigation of several influences and pressures, including the Oxford Movement, the Calvinist conventiclers of his first parish, challenges from modernist theologians, and his own continuing historical research, points made by Puchinger, Vree, and Kuyper's autobiographical remembrances.[86] Vree also details the social and ecclesiastical context of Kuyper's early life as a pastor in Beesd, Utrecht, and Amsterdam (1864–1873) and explains how many of his early ecclesiological pieces dealt with issues in the church.

Vree's studies provide the historical background necessary for any careful discussion of Kuyper's early theology, though Vree has been criticized for not providing an overarching historiographical perspective and for leaving the data points, which are many, too detached from each other.[87] Vree refrains, for example, from any more programmatic assessment of the young Kuyper than "A Brilliant, Enthusiastic Mind."[88] Nonetheless, the contributions of Vree and also Cornelis Augustijn in unearthing the mutability of Kuyper's mind must be the starting point for any future studies of Kuyper's thought.[89] Whether there is an overarching logic to Kuyper's intellectual changes, whether it is a matter of organic development, pragmatic adaption, or shear inconsistency, is still in question.

From the literature on Kuyper's ecclesiology one point emerges clearly: Kuyper's concept of the church as organism and institution is one of his most important and innovative contributions. Henry Zwaanstra says that the organism was the core of Kuyper's doctrine of the church.[90] Focusing narrowly on this distinction, Vree examines its development in Kuyper's thought. He and van Leeuwen uncover important changes, especially the novelty of the visible organism in the 1890s, which Kuyper had previously considered a strictly inward and invisible.[91] In contrast to C. H. W. van den Berg, who says that there was nothing new in Kuyper's ecclesiology after 1874,[92] the present work builds on the insights of Vree and van Leeuwen and contends that the secession from the national church in the mid-1880s was the key ecclesiological turning point. It explains how the dynamic between the organism and institution coincided with a larger adjustment in Kuyper's ecclesiology, thus harmonizing various shifting elements in Kuyper's ecclesiological thought.

Finally, Americans and English-language scholars have devoted most of their attention to Kuyper's social ethics and public theology (two categories that are almost indistinguishable in Kuyper), undoubtedly because of the importance of Kuyper's Stone Lectures at Princeton Seminary. In his yet unpublished biography, James Bratt claims that Kuyper's most characteristic theme was Christian action in the world and speaks of Kuyper's theological fixation on culture and his crusade to reform culture.[93] Specifically, the Calvinistic worldview of Kuyper's *Lectures on Calvinism* and his concept of common grace are remembered as the foundations of his social ethics and public theology.[94] Yet the intensity of interest in Kuyper's public theology obscures a historical oddity, and current interest ought not to be confused with priority in Kuyper's own thought, either priority of chronology or importance. The oddity is this: in his *Lectures on Calvinism* Kuyper described the wrestling of two life systems (or worldviews), Christian and Modernist-pagan, which the lectures addressed as "*the* struggle of Europe...and in which I myself have been spending all my energy for nearly forty years."[95] Yet the *Lectures on Calvinism* were the late harvest of Kuyper's theological labors. In fact, decades earlier, Kuyper had a very different estimate of his theological agenda. The "church question" (not the clash of worldviews), he wrote, "has become presently, through a unique coinciding of a series of factors, *the* question of our day, a question of general European concern."[96] Can any sense be made of these two apparently competing claims regarding church and public theology?

These three themes—conversion, church, and social ethics—absorb a good deal of the scholarly attention to Kuyper. They are themes that arose prominently in Kuyper and generally in theology of the nineteenth century. Welch claims that the principle concerns of late nineteenth-century theology were the interrelated matters of faith, ethics, church, and culture[97] and "a new concern for the social interpretation of Christianity—in its origins, its historical expressions, and its relevance to modern society."[98] Yet in spite of an adequate picture of many of these points separately, their interrelation in Kuyper's theology remains unclear. Ecclesiology is a fruitful avenue for drawing these themes together because it stands at the intersection of all three concerns: faith, church, and social ethics. Ernst Troeltsch's definition of the free church (the controlling definition for this study) bears this out.

> The Free Church system is the destruction of the mediaeval and early Protestant idea of a social order welded together by one uniform State Church....This meant that the question of Church membership now became a matter of individual choice, and that, at least outwardly, the form of Church-order becomes that of a

voluntary association, even though theologically the community which thus comes into being may still continue to be considered as an objective, ecclesiastical institution.[99]

Troeltsch puts his finger on the ambiguity of Kuyper's free church: its dual nature as a divinely given institution and as a voluntary association, thus having both an objective and a subjective basis. The peculiarity of the Dutch churches' modern situation, historian James Kennedy says, arises from this dual nature as institute of salvation (*heilsinstituut*) and voluntary organizations, and he calls for a more thorough investigation of the public roles of the Dutch churches in the modern era, because they were not mere private organizations as commonly assumed.[100] This study examines how Kuyper conceived of the church's public stance and attempts to relate that to his broader ecclesiology, especially his reconciliation of the church's inward aspects (e.g., the faith and commitment of its members) and external aspects (e.g., institutional forms such as sacraments and office).

This study takes its controlling methodological questions from Ernst Troeltsch's *The Social Teaching of the Christian Churches*. Although students now remember it primarily as a foundational work of religious sociology, Troeltsch viewed it as a work of the history of doctrine and church history, one necessitated by churches that had to reevaluate their positions under modern social conditions like democracy, industrialization, and modern centralized states.[101] In a similar fashion the present work is a history of doctrine, but one that keeps the same sociological questions at the fore. Troeltsch's question, and ours, was tripartite: what is the nature and structure of Christian communities? What is the external relationship between the community and its social environment, the world? And how do these two qualities interrelate?[102] Troeltsch went beyond Max Weber, says Welch, in asking about the community's attitude toward the world, and that concern makes Troeltsch's categories useful for examining Abraham Kuyper.[103]

Social had two senses for Troeltsch: the inner relationships of the members of the group; and the relationship of the group with society. The relationship between these two characteristics may be stronger or weaker, clearer or more confused, but for Troeltsch these characteristics were surely in some way related.[104] For the sake of this study, these questions of internal and external group relationships are helpful heuristic questions because they are also some of the most basic questions that any concept of the church, any ecclesiology, tries to answer.

The typology that Troeltsch gave in answer to these questions is now well-known: the church–sect–mysticism distinction. The goal of this study is not to fit Kuyper into any one of these types (as we shall see, Kuyper's ecclesiology does not neatly fit any of the categories) but to use these types as heuristic categories for analyzing Kuyper's ecclesiology. That is, *church, sect,* and *mysticism* are ideal models or types that aid our understanding, not actual entities, not, in this case, actual Christian communities. These types provide a set of questions and issues for exploration. These categories are suitable because the primary subject under investigation here is theoretical and theological, as was Troeltsch's, not a historical manifestation of the church. Rodney Stark and William Bainbridge, for example, criticize Troeltsch's church–sect typology as inadequate for describing religious movements, and for all we know they may be right.[105] Describing religious movements, however, was not Troeltsch's intention; examining their *social teaching* (i.e., doctrine) was. An account of ideal types is useful when the subject under investigation is an idea, yet, as Troeltsch understood, the real may vary greatly from the ideal.[106]

Troeltsch's typology is also useful because it resembles Kuyper's own conceptual schemes, which should come as no surprise since, during Kuyper's lifetime, these ideas were "in the air."[107] These categories do not impose a foreign structure on Kuyper's mind but aid in clarifying elements already present in his ecclesiology. While we must take care not to reify the ideal types, we ought to note that Kuyper did not. If for Troeltsch medieval Catholicism most nearly approximated the church type, and if the sect reached its highest development during the Cromwellian era, Kuyper treated the nineteenth-century Dutch national church and the seventeenth-century Labadists, a kind of Dutch analogue to the Moravians, as virtually perfect embodiments of these types.[108]

Troeltsch's questions and categories are useful for dealing with the prevalent issues of nineteenth-century theology, which Stephen Sykes identifies specifically as the relation between the inward and outward aspects of Christianity and their implications for understanding the continuity and diversity of Christianity. The growing diversity of Christianity raised the issue of the essence and identity of Christianity to crisis level. From Adolf von Harnack's *Das Wezen des Christentums* to *The Fundamentals*, the need to define the true nature of Christianity was pervasive and paramount. In particular, the question of the inner and outer aspects of Christianity, the form and the content, and their relation to the essence of Christianity were in question, Sykes says,[109] and Troeltsch's categories—church, sect, and mysticism—were a historical typology of attempts to reconcile the inner and outer aspects. Beyond Sykes, however, Troeltsch observes that how a theologian relates the inner and outer aspects has implications for not only the structure of the Christian community but also for its relation to the world outside. That correlation is key for understanding the development of Kuyper's ecclesiology.

Troeltsch's church type stresses primarily the outward, objective features of Christianity and the church, such as objective religious truth, the church as a means of grace, tradition, sacrament, and the official hierarchy. "The essence of the church is its objective institutional character."[110] This in turn produces a certain kind of social structure. One is born and baptized into the church apart from any voluntary decision, and in that respect it has a compulsory character and requires relatively little by way of inward personal commitment or holiness. This also coincides with the church type's distinctive approach to its wider social context, its aim at cultural dominance. It wishes to bring the whole of human life under its wings. Consequently, it has a conservative cast insofar as it accepts the secular order and does not rebel or withdraw from it.[111] This is the kind of conservatism that Kuyper railed against when he pitted orthodoxy against conservatism in his pointed parting sermon from the Utrecht congregation ("Conservatism and Orthodoxy").[112] Likewise, Kuyper's criticism of the national church for ignoring the spiritual life of its members and simply presuming their involvement resembled Troeltsch's account of the church type.

Whereas Troeltsch defined the essence of the church as the objective, the sect, in contrast, depended on the inward, voluntary participation of the members instead of the objective institution, and it demanded high levels of involvement and especially personal holiness. The institution was relatively devalued as a means of grace, since communion with God rested on subjective measures.[113] The premium on holiness corresponded with a renunciation of the world and its opposition to the Kingdom of God. "The sect, therefore, does not educate nations in the mass, but it gathers a select group of the elect, and places it in sharp opposition to the world."[114] Troeltsch's categories frustrate later scholars because they do not fit realities of the modern situation,[115] at least not if woodenly applied, and the example of Kuyper shows why. Kuyper desired the strong personal commitment typical of the sect, but he did not embrace a categorical withdrawal from the world, which would have been difficult to do anyway sitting in the parliamentarian's seat, the professorial chair, or the newspaper editor's desk. Troeltsch's categories did not anticipate every possible option for Christian communities in the modern world, but to be fair that was not his goal. In his own words:

> My object will be to pave the way for the understanding of the social doctrines of the Gospel, of the Early Church, of the Middle Ages, of the post-Reformation confessions, right down to the formation of the new situation of the modern world, in which the old theories no longer suffice, and where, therefore, new theories must be constructed, composed of old and new elements, consciously or unconsciously, whether so avowed or not.

A better description of Kuyper's ecclesiological program would be hard to find.

Finally, mysticism focused on inward religiosity and resisted any objectification of religious life through institutions or dogmas or otherwise. It was the supreme realization of what Sykes calls the *tradition of inwardness*. Mysticism in Troeltsch's understanding did not preclude a social group, and it was difficult to draw a line between mysticism and sectarianism. Theodore Steeman explains the chief difference between the two, according to Troeltsch: sectarianism protested mainly against the church's compromise with the world; mysticism protested against the objectification of spiritual life. Mysticism did not necessarily need to withdraw from society, because the world was outside, and religion was inside. The confrontation with mysticism, after his own brief flirtations with it, became the initial reason for Abraham Kuyper to reevaluate the necessity of the institutional church. He recalled that experience almost forty years later writing a tract against mysticism, which he said "estimated the mystical work of the Holy Spirit over the work of Christ, over the Word, and over the Church."[116] (NB Mysticism differed from the mystical aspect of Christianity, which Kuyper affirmed and even made central to his ecclesiology). Once Kuyper had accepted the importance of the institutional church and its forms, the main dilemma was how to reconcile the purity of the Christian community typical of the sect type without giving up its necessary outward forms of the church type.

The history of Christianity can be read as a history of the conflict over how to reconcile the inner and outer aspects of Christianity. Church and sect may be viewed as poles on either end of this continuum rather than as mutually exclusive categories. Dietrich Bonhoeffer criticized Troeltsch's and Weber's sociological typology as too rigid. The church is never strictly a compulsory association (*Anstalt*) but requires cooperation, while many sects in the second or third generation turn into national churches (*volkskirchen*) and are not, therefore, strictly voluntary associations (*Verein*).[117] Bonhoeffer signaled a potential danger: that the types would obscure the true nature of the case if forcibly applied (especially, Bonhoeffer noted, in the case of Protestantism). This warning is timely because one of the main tensions in Kuyper's ecclesiology is between the objective and compulsory qualities of the church and its subjective ones, and Troeltsch acknowledged the existence of mixed types, the free church being a primary example and Kuyper a key proponent of it.[118] Troeltsch regarded Calvin and primitive Calvinism as churchly for their insistence on the church as means of grace, their acceptance of the world, and their close union of church and state, but Calvinism also included an insistence on purity of life, which made it a transitional form between the medieval church and the later sects and free churches.

José Casanova, citing Richard Niebuhr, said that Troeltsch could not have conceived of Christian associations adapted to modern differentiated society, a point others continue to repeat.[119] Niebuhr's own typology given in *Christ and Culture* attempted to remedy this, but two caveats are in order here. First, even if Troeltsch could not have conceived of the vast differences of American denominations (and it is doubtful that Niebuhr could have conceived of the vast differences between the religious forms now available), Troeltsch's free church was precisely a type of Christian community adapted to a differentiated society. The free church was a mixture of aspects of the church and the sect, evolving out of Calvinism and having a bond and affinity with democracy.[120] Casanova says that the denomination is the form of religious organization adapted to a differentiated society and that Troetlsch could not have anticipated it.[121] Kuyper's free church was similar to both Troeltsch's free church and Casanova's denomination: a negotiation of traditional Calvinist ecclesiological forms (the churchly aspects of Calvinism) and Calvinist piety (the sectarian qualities of Calvinism) and an adaptation of the Calvinist church to modern society, including democracy and differentiation. Indeed, Kuyper claimed democracy and differentiation as the inheritance of Calvinism.[122]

Second, the subject of Niebuhr's investigation was not the same as Troeltsch's. Niebuhr's "Christ" was not necessarily the Christian social body. Lewis Mudge explains:

Even H. Richard Niebuhr, who saw his *Christ and Culture* as linked to Troeltsch's work, was in fact pursuing something different. Niebuhr gives us a brilliant typology of theological visions, but he does not wrestle in Troeltsch's way with "the social question." And in his reluctantly written final chapter Niebuhr tries to graft the social dimension onto a fundamentally Kierkegaardian, and hence individually focused, understanding of faith.[123]

George Marsden lodges a similar complaint against Niebuhr. He sees Niehbuhr as focusing on a "more abstract 'Christ,' rather than on the church or Christianity."[124] Troeltsch, then, still offers something useful when it comes to questions of the concrete social structure and social relations of the Christian community.

Permit it to be repeated that the goal of this study is not to fit Kuyper's ecclesiology into any one of Troeltsch's categories. Troeltsch's questions are ours but not necessarily his answers. This study inquires into Kuyper's theology of the nature and structure of the church, and while a consideration of whether and in what ways Kuyper's church was a compulsory society or a voluntary association is important, that is not the only point of interest in ecclesiology. Bonhoeffer cautions that those social categories are not fully adequate for dealing with theology and the church.[125] In particular, they focus on the human side of the church and neglect its divine constitution. That is, categories like *Verein* and *Anstalt* by themselves are religiously and metaphysically sterile. Nonetheless, Troeltsch's questions and categories do provide a conceptual map and heuristic categories that make it possible to compare elements of Kuyper's ecclesiology with those of his contemporaries and also to chart some of the changes in Kuyper's ecclesiology.

Following Troeltsch, this is a history of doctrine, but it focuses more exclusively than Troeltsch on ecclesiology. It takes other cues, therefore, from Roger Haight's recent work in historical ecclesiology, and like Haight it aspires to a historical-contextual account. It sets Kuyper's ecclesiology in its historical context and shows how Kuyper's ecclesiology dealt with its context. Although it draws out the principles of Kuyper's ecclesiology, it does not treat them as abstract timeless principles, but principles developed in response to specific conditions and challenges. It applies what Haight calls a *method of correlation*, which

means that theological understanding arises out of the conjunction of theological data or sources with the context or situation of a particular culture in order to bear meaning and relevance for that culture. In other words, our present situation enters into our understanding whether we are aware of it or not.[126]

Kuyper was keenly aware of it, and he explicitly aimed "to bring Reformed theology into rapport with human consciousness as it has developed at the end of the nineteenth century."[127] This study argues neither that Kuyper's theology was a product of his social situation (as Marx might say) nor that the church as it was realized concretely was the perfect embodiment of Kuyper's ideal. "The point," as Robert Wuthnow puts it, "is not that theology is *only* a reflection of social circumstances. It is rather than religious beliefs and practices *articulate* with these circumstances."[128]

Further, following John Austin, John Searle, and Quentin Skinner, the goal of this study is not merely to understand what Kuyper was saying but also what he was *doing* in his ecclesiology. Understanding what an author is doing can be accomplished only by understanding the context of the text. Critiquing an approach that regards texts themselves as self-sufficient objects of inquiry, Skinner explains, "Any statement is inescapably the embodiment of a particular intention on a particular occasion, addressed to the solution of a particular problem, and is thus specific to its context in a way that it can only be naïve to try to transcend."[129] Since the goal here is to understand how Kuyper's theology answered particular occasions and context, this study is not purely thematic, nor does it seek comprehensiveness in Kuyper's theology in general or even his ecclesiology in particular. Specifically, the question is how Kuyper brought Reformed ecclesiology into rapport with principles and realities of the modern world, such as the differentiation of society, religious pluralism, democratic tendencies, the new nation state, and the antimetaphysical strains of modern science.

This study partakes of elements and themes of both Haight's historical ecclesiology and his comparative ecclesiology. The basic goal is the same: to account for the theological understanding (in this case, Kuyper's) of the *nature* and *mission* of the church. In doing so, this study attends to many of the modern developments that Haight does, including historical consciousness, pluralism both among churches and other religions, secularization and individualism, and the relationship of the church to the world in the sense of culture, society, and state.[130] The present study is also comparative insofar as it makes some systematic comparisons between elements of Kuyper's ecclesiology at various stages and occasionally between Kuyper and other theologies.[131]

Yet this study differs from Haight's in several significant ways. Haight's main typology of church from above and church from below fails when applied to Kuyper because Kuyper's ecclesiology was simultaneously both. Kuyper's church was an ahistorical, Mystical Body of Christ and a historical institution that had to be adapted to modern realities. Haight takes these two ways of thinking—from above, characterized by theological reflection, and from below, characterized by empirical, historical, "in-church" concerns—as contrasting. But why should this be so? Over against Haight, James Ginther says that ecclesial experience and theological reflection need to be considered in tandem.[32] That is especially the case with any theologian who had to break into his own church, for being locked out of the church is bound to change your ecclesiology. Further, the goal of this study is not to draw out a set of ecclesiological norms from historical ecclesiology, as Haight's goal is (if history-transcendent norms are possible within the frame of an ecclesiology from below).[33] There are positive theological lessons to be learned from the history of theology, but they must wait until the concluding pages.

Panel-Sawing Redux

Political cartoons are a measure of social significance. The more cartoons a person garners in a lifetime, the more important, for better or worse, they are or were to society. That probably explains why theologians have received so few caricatures since newspapers and their cartoonists became widespread in the nineteenth century. The nineteenth century saw technological advances that permitted faster and cheaper printing and, in the Netherlands, a repeal of newspaper taxes, all of which put newspapers and their cartoons in the hands of more and more readers. At the same time, other developments, notably the separation of church and state and the methodological atheism of modern science, began to push Christianity and the church toward the shoulders of society's main street. Political cartoons gained public importance just when the church began to lose it.[34] Abraham Kuyper, however, received a great deal of attention from comic satirists because, besides social significance, he also elicited in abundance the other absolutely necessary ingredient for a good cartoon: ill will. Most of the Kuyper cartoons relate to his political career, not a religiously insignificant one to be sure, but cartoonists did not ignore Kuyper's ecclesiastical career since it affected virtually the entire Protestant majority of the Netherlands. The church and religion were still very public concerns for Kuyper and all the Netherlands in the nineteenth century, hardly something that people did only in their solitude—the opinions of A. N. Whitehead and William James notwithstanding. So when Kuyper came to the New Church in Amsterdam on the morning of January 6, 1886, with lawyers, locksmiths, and the police, the scene was ripe for a parody (Figure 1.1).[135]

As told at the beginning of this chapter, Kuyper arrived at the New Church accompanied by the church custodian, F. L. Rutgers, and the jurist (and member of the Dutch national parliament) A. F. de Savornin Lohman. A pair of guards under charge of the Classical board (the regional church board that had suspended Kuyper and Rutgers from ecclesiastical office several days prior) met them there and refused them entrance to the consistory chamber, where the local board of church officials usually met. After some squabbling all agreed to send for the police, but the police agents were unable to make any peace between the feuding parties. So the police agents went up the chain of command and called out Inspector Marchand, whose words were as futile as the agents' had been. Finally Lohman and Rutgers went to see Police Commissioner Stork. Stork, who did not want to get involved, suggested that they return to the church and use inspector Marchand as a go-between, a suggestion that Lohman and Rutgers then turned to their own advantage. They went back to Marchand and handed him an order to bring to the guards. The order asked the guards to leave, which they obeyed, coming as the order did from church warden Rutgers and now in the hands of Inspector Marchand. When the dismissed guards reported back to G. J. Vos, a member of the Classical board and Kuyper's opponent, Vos was furious. He went over Stork's head to the mayor, and then events unfolded in the reverse order. After Vos went to the mayor, the mayor went back to Stork, and Stork went back to Lohman and Rutgers. Lohman and Rutgers seemed to shrug. They had not tricked the guards; they had simply followed Stork's own advice.[136]

For Lohman, Kuyper, and Rutgers, still waiting at the church, the delay caused by the charade with the guards (from about 9 a.m. to 10 a.m.), provided just enough time to accomplish the main task: seizing the consistory chamber. Possessing this meeting room held symbolic and real importance, as Vos later explained:

> If one actually possessed the sacristan [i.e., the consistory chamber], then one possessed the New Church, and therefore the *archives* of the consistory, as well as those of the Ecclesiastical Commission, the Classis, the Provincial Board, and the *fire safe* with all the funds

of the churches and the Diaconate present therein. One possessed
the chief citadel with everything necessary for war. The opposition
had *nothing*, and moreover in view of procedures, one was actually
in possession [of the church].[137]

Getting in, however, required more than ecclesiastical right or the
mayor's favor. Kuyper knew that, because when he visited the church the
night before (January 5), he found the door to the consistory room locked
and impossible to unlock. His keys did not work because another member of the Classical board, A. J. Westhoff, had changed the locks (legally
or illegally, depending on whom one asked), a precaution in case the
guards failed. So when Kuyper arrived at the New Church the next morning, besides church warden Rutgers and de Savornin Lohman, he also
brought a locksmith. But Westhoff was still one step ahead. Not only had
he changed the locks, he had armored the doors with iron plates. So far as
Westhoff could help it, no one was going to church that day. Kuyper, however, turned out to be the more determined, and he came with "carpen-
ters," "panel-sawers," "lock-cutters," and "the French Revolution in heart,
vulgarities on his lips, and a pry bar in hand," said Vos.[138]

The events at the New Church that morning illustrate just how confused
and ultimately comedic the situation of the Netherlands Reformed Church
(the Dutch national church) had become by the late nineteenth century. For
starters, in 1848 the Dutch constitution had officially separated church and
state, yet now the civil authorities were called upon to parse ecclesiastical
law and decide who really owned the church—the local congregation or the
regional Classical board. At the end of the day on January 5, only brute force
could decide. Two years later, in 1888, the Dutch Supreme Court found
otherwise and gave the property to the church hierarchy.[139]

The break-in, referred to by Kuyper's critics as the panel-sawing, was
the culmination of a larger dispute. Two days before the break-in, Abraham
Kuyper, along with seventy-four other members of the Amsterdam consistory, had been suspended from office by the Classical board for altering
article 41 of the Church Order of the Netherlands Reformed Church. They
changed the article so that in the event of a dispute over church property,
it would be placed in the hands of those who remained faithful to God's
Word. Kuyper had foreseen that it might come to this.

Church property, however, was only the tip of the iceberg. The change
in article 41 had been provoked by other events, events much graver to
Kuyper's mind. Three years prior, the synod of the Netherlands Reformed

Church had allowed that those who wanted to become full confessing members no longer needed to subscribe to the Reformed confessions or explicitly confess faith in Jesus Christ—traditionally a touchstone of Christianity—to fulfill their vows.[140] When orthodox congregations like Kuyper's refused to admit such men and women into membership, they ran afoul of the synod. So the synod provided another option for the refused members. They could apply for confessing membership at a different congregation. That only presented another set of difficulties because the members still had to present a certificate of good behavior from their original congregation, a certificate that Kuyper refused to give. Realizing that these disputes portended a larger clash, the Amsterdam congregation cleared an exit route for itself by amending article 41, thus giving the congregation a measure of autonomy from the synod. All the parties involved told the story a little differently. Kuyper's opponents said the panel-sawing and amending article 41 was an illegal power grab, while Kuyper's supporters faulted the Classical board for overreaching its own mandate and interfering in local matters. Kuyper believed that the underlying issue was the church's confession of Christ and that issues of polity and property ought to be subservient to that.

The panel-sawing brought Kuyper notoriety, though not the kind he would have wished, not only because of the political cartoons it engendered, but because of the events it set in motion. It also ultimately led to the formation of a new breakaway church by Kuyper's group, the NetherGerman Reformed Churches (Nederduitsche Gereformeerde Kerken), which Kuyper dubbed the Doleantie, or the Aggrieved. As complex as the circumstances surrounding the birth of this new church were, so also was the theological vision of the church by which Kuyper justified this break with the Netherlands Reformed Church. Why did Kuyper break into the church and then break with the church? What kind of church, theologically speaking, did he want?

Before Kuyper could break with the church, however, he had to believe in it. That is where this study begins.

The Emergence of a Free-Church Ecclesiology, 1863–1867

IF HE WAS anything like other recently graduated seminarians, Abraham Kuyper may have felt that he had little to learn from his first parish, certain as he would have been that he already knew nearly everything. The feeling could have been only exaggerated by the disparity between a Leiden Ph.D. and the country parishioners of Beesd. Vincent van Gogh imagined a scene resembling Kuyper's parishioners in the austere gathering portrayed in the *Potato Eaters*—conservative dress, gaunt determined faces, simple Dutch fare. Kuyper probably wished for a position at one of the state universities where he could carry on his historical research among his academic peers, but Beesd turned out to be a crucial intellectual turning point for Kuyper nonetheless. In the Gelderland village, a complex of concerns emerged that provoked a reconsideration of his views on church and society. In particular, Kuyper embraced two fundamental principles: the separation of church and state and the importance of objective institutional church forms. His commitment to these two principles set the context for his primary ethical question, the responsibility of the church with regard to the state and society.

Coming out of his university studies, Kuyper's ecclesiology was inchoate. Later he would recall Charlotte Yonge's *The Heir of Redclyffe*, a novel arising out of the Oxford movement, which he read before he arrived at his first pastorate in Beesd at the suggestion of his fiancée Jo Schaay. Upon reading it, he later said, "At that moment the predilection for prescribed ritual, the high estimation of the Sacrament, the appreciation for the Liturgy became rooted in me for all time."[1] Yet his first sermons at Beesd cast doubt on this memory. These sermons disavowed the church's forms like liturgy and sacrament but, in contrast, upheld subjective inner piety. Further, the distance between church and state proved to be rather small in his early work and words at Beesd. Four years later, however, something had changed. By the end of his years there he showed no more doubt about the benefits of church forms or disestablishment.

Among Dutch historians there is a debate over just what caused this change of mind. George Puchinger, following Kuyper's own autobiographical remarks, emphasized the pietist conventicles who withdrew themselves from Kuyper's ministrations—and one pietist in particular, Pietje Baltus. Puchinger said that Kuyper was converted to their simple Calvinist faith. More recently, Jasper Vree questioned Puchinger's account and argued that the modernist theologians who preached a religion of humanism transcending the archaic church sparked Kuyper's reconsideration.[2] But neither group, modernist or pious conventicles, should be discounted, though the role of the pietists was not the idealized one that Kuyper remembered or Puchinger claimed. These two groups—the modernist party, well represented among the intellectual elites, and the pietistic conventicle communities, not as urbane as the modernists but equally dogged—could not have been more different in most respects, yet they presented the same challenge to the young Kuyper: why go to church at all?

This was a question of both the church's nature and its role in society, and these two groups represented two extremes that Kuyper wanted to avoid. The dominance of the state in the modern era, Napoleon's grand centralized state, meant an ever-shrinking sphere for the church. Amid these pressures, Kuyper defended the church's unique nature and function against modernists who predicted its eventual disappearance. Yet Kuyper did not believe, as the conventiclers did, that a narrowly defined role for the church meant Christian withdrawal from society. Kuyper defended the relevance of Christianity for all areas of life. At the same time, his ongoing historical studies also show a new appreciation for a more distanced relationship between church and state as well as an appreciation for the church's objective forms.

This chapter examines the development of Kuyper's ecclesiology as a young pastor at Beesd and the difficulties he had reconciling the various principles important to him. Finally, Kuyper left Beesd in 1867 for the much larger and more prestigious Utrecht congregation. His inaugural sermon at Utrecht, "The Incarnation," was a preliminary attempt to make sense of the ecclesiological principles cultivated at Beesd: the church as the continuation of Christ's inner spiritual life and his outer ecclesial body; and the church's role in society.

Walk in the Light

The reason that Abraham Kuyper's earliest understanding of the church cannot be properly described as a free-church ecclesiology is simply that it was not very churchly.[3] Kuyper's sermons from his first two years shepherding the flock at Beesd (1863–1864) suggest a church grounded in pious subjective experience and a rejection of anything external or objective. On August 9, 1863, the recently promoted doctor gave his inaugural sermon at Beesd, titled "A Walk in the Light: The Foundation of All Communion in the Church of Christ." This sermon, a meditation on 1 John 1:7, stressed the importance of holiness of life and love, walking in the light, as the bond of the church community. "There is no other communion in the church of Christ than that which is grounded in holiness."[4] Selfishness especially must be overcome. This was explicitly in contrast to external forms as the basis of the unity of the church:

> All that the church of Christ has been able to do in the course of the centuries, she has wrought it through no power of doctrinal systems or forms, no, the Church has never been able or shall be able to do anything except through being the image-bearer of Christ, in Him making the spirit of the only-born of the Father eternally live, in him to fulfill the most ardent prayer of the Son of Man [i.e., that all may be one], through joining person to person in warm love as brothers.[5]

Years later Kuyper recollected the way the Ethical school of thought had influenced him during these early years, and his first sermons fit the pattern of this party in the Netherlands that emphasized personal holiness over dogmatic formulas.[6]

The Sunday following Kuyper's inaugural sermon, he began a series of sermons on the Heidelberg Catechism, presumably more out of convention than devotion. The first Sunday of February 1864, Kuyper came to Sunday 21 of the Heidelberg Catechism on the topic of the church. There could hardly be a more disputed topic, he observed. The problem that he addressed was directly connected to the subject of his inaugural sermon. The church was supposed to be a pure, holy church, yet that was manifestly not the case with the Netherlands Reformed Church (Nederlandse Hervormde Kerk, or NHK, also referred to as the *volkskerk* or national church). What, then, was the relationship between the NHK and the pure

Kingdom of Heaven that Jesus spoke of? What was to be done about the church, whose membership was once a matter of life and death but had become a matter of social prestige and had thus "thrown its doors open to millions, who bore an evil heart and a sinful life and nothing of the Spirit of Christ in them"?[7]

Kuyper began with a historical introduction to the problem. In response to the corruption of the medieval Roman Catholic Church, the Reformation pursued purity of life, but it also distinguished between the visible and the invisible church, which helped explain the obvious dissonance between what was experienced in the church on earth and the pure church of the elect known only to God:

> But unfortunately, as soon as our reformed church was unfaithful to her principles and forgot too quickly the invisible church and purity of walk, she became again the champion of a [false] doctrine and banned those who deviated. She even burned them.[8]

Kuyper bemoaned the seemingly never-ending process wherein a church became corrupt and a small group then seceded to form a pure church. The Afscheiding churches, the orthodox secession group that left the Netherlands Reformed Church in 1834, were a case in point. At this early stage, Kuyper abhorred the idea of secession.

To explain the difference between the church of true Christians and the mixed, earthly manifestation of the church and to justify why he remained in an impure institution, Kuyper distinguished between church (*kerk*) and church-association (*kerkgenootschap*). The "church," of which the apostles and the catechism spoke and of which only the elect were members, was the Kingdom of Heaven, and entrance depended solely on purity of heart. Its touchstones were "conversion and regeneration." A "church-association," on the other hand, was a voluntary organization established by people, not God. Strictly speaking the NHK could claim to be an association but not the church, yet even as an association it had a high purpose: out of that "seed...the church of Jesus grows."[9] To reconcile this insistence on inner purity with participation in external forms, Kuyper looked to Jesus, who always went to the feasts, as his example. So "honor the forms, but know that they are only forms to which your heart alone can give life."[10] The outward husk was a necessary part of the seed, but its life was within.

The tension in Kuyper's position—the necessity of remaining in the Netherlands Reformed church in spite of its dry husk—was highlighted in an 1864 sermon on the doctrine of regeneration in which he touched on the significance of baptism. Kuyper argued again that religious forms are of passing significance. Each age has the right to trans*form* its forms into relevant symbols. "No form is sacred, but rather what the form contains."[11] Participation in the Christian community and its symbol, baptism, was preparatory for regeneration, although the sacrament was only a passing form. True communion with the church was, again, via inner communion with Christ in the heart. The church was the community beyond which there was no salvation, though certainly not in its fixed institutional form.

Kuyper's initial position at Beesd was this. He wanted to remain in the Netherlands Reformed Church. He acknowledged that a good deal of chaff was mixed in with the wheat, but he rejected breaking with the church as the Afscheiding had done. Yet he would not settle for the church's current state. He insisted on purity of spirit as the source of the church's life, and the outward institutional forms, while necessary, were only of transitory significance and able to be changed as the needs of the times demanded. In the coming years, his zeal for purity of spirit would remain constant, but his estimate of the church's forms would change, the first indication of which appeared in his ongoing historical studies.

Recovering the Past

Although Abraham Kuyper is remembered for many things, his original vocation and training as a historian is often forgotten. Yet the power of history over Kuyper's mind was almost irresistible. Besides his pastoral responsibilities at Beesd, Kuyper continued his historical research and compiled an edition of sixteenth-century Polish Reformer John a Lasco's *opera*, which remains a standard scholarly source. During the summer of 1865, Kuyper also wrote several articles on the sixteenth-century Dutch exile church in London where a Lasco ministered for a time.[12] Though these articles were intended to be contributions to church history, Kuyper's editorial remarks scattered throughout reveal a new understanding of the church. In these articles, for the first time,[13] Kuyper embraced church forms such as liturgical formulas and doctrinal statements.

In his article on "The Worship of the Reformed Church and the Composition of Its Church-Book," Kuyper opined that the contemporary NHK lacked a real liturgy. Perhaps a bit overwhelmed by his own pastoral responsibilities, Kuyper appreciated the more balanced liturgy of the London church in which all the weight was not on the sermon. Further, sacraments, marriage, and burial services "were all administered according to fixed liturgical order by an excellent system of formulas, which belong to the most excellent things that the Reformation could in this respect set over against Rome."[14] In a 1574 meeting of the Dutch Reformed churches at Dordrecht, the worship service was officially regulated, but through corruptions, arbitrary changes, and paranoid fear of Romanizing tendencies, the liturgy declined "until the synod of 1817 abandoned the formulas through an incorrect idea of their origin and its lack of liturgical sense, and so promoted the liturgical anarchy to which [the *NHK*] is currently prey."[15] The rest of the article described the church book used by the early Reformed Church, which included the Bible, a psalter, the Heidelberg Catechism, the Belgic Confession, a formula for examining those wishing to come to Lord's Supper, and finally "the weightiest part of the volume," a set of liturgical formulas including baptismal and Eucharistic formulas.

It might seem strange that historical studies would have such a strong impact on Abraham Kuyper. However, he was a quintessential Victorian, and he and many of his contemporaries shared the common Victorian historicist mentality: to know something's history is to know it truly.[16] Kuyper was a historian by training, and throughout his career he entered various debates over church history. His assumption in these debates was that history was on the side of truth. It was a powerful, almost invincible, ally. The realization manifested in Kuyper's studies, that the contemporary Dutch church was out of sync with the Dutch church of history, would have been a blow to the status quo.

Mystics, Modernists, and the Church

Confrontation with modernists and the conventicles steeled Kuyper's decision for fixed church forms. Allard Pierson was one modernist who especially troubled Kuyper (see Figure 6.2b). In 1863 Pierson argued, much as Kuyper himself once believed, that for a time the church had been an important institution as the mother of humanity, but now its role was played out. The church specifically, not religion, was becoming obsolete. Pierson still advocated a general religion of humanity, a "humanism" in which the development of humanity occurred in society not in the church. Pierson allowed the church to remain for the time as a sort of institution or association for religion beside other institutions in society. In 1865, however, Pierson took a radical step. He decided that to remain true to his modernist principles, it was only right and consistent that he give up his ministerial credentials and leave the church. In October 1865 his apologia, *Dr. Pierson to His Last Congregation,* appeared. He argued for a noble humanism that would raise humanity above the divisions of Christendom. Pierson flatly rejected any further role for the church in humanity's upward progress. He argued that the church by its very nature is always exclusive and divisive, and therefore it could not further the goal of the solidarity of humanity. The church had to be abandoned once and for all, so he did like C. Busken-Huet, another prominent modernist, had already done and left the church.[17]

Pierson forced Kuyper to think more deeply about the nature and mission of the church. Kuyper responded immediately to Pierson's challenge in a series of three sermons on the church in November and December 1865. On the cover page of the first sermon, titled "Humanism and Christendom," Kuyper wrote in the bottom corner "cf. Pierson and Candidus."[18] To whom he referred as Candidus is unclear, but this comment made for an ironic connection between Pierson's humanism and the youth of Voltaire's novella. Kuyper, like Voltaire, saw through the optimistic naiveté of the modern mind. Humanity needed the church exactly because all was not as it should be.

Kuyper's first anti-Pierson sermon, "Humanism and Christendom"— like American J. Gresham Machen's *Christianity and Liberalism*— summarized two opposed views, two irreconcilable ways to understand human history. Humanity either reached perfection through natural development—the view of humanism—or attained to its highest end only by a supernatural act, regeneration. This introduced a theme that Kuyper returned to many times over in his career, notably in his 1892 speech, "The Blurring of the Boundaries," in which Kuyper explained the cosmic implications of regeneration.[19] Late in 1865, however, his concern was the church. The Kingdom of Heaven was the part of the world that had been renewed by God. This kingdom was invisible, however, since only God knew the heart. Hence, Jesus founded the church to give the kingdom visible manifestation. "Her renown [the church's] is that she contains the Kingdom of God within her." The supernatural regeneration by which only humanity would reach perfection came through the church alone. "The children of God are won over and born in her [i.e., the church's] womb and live in her midst.... To say that the church's role is played out is to assert that every person has been reborn, recreated; only then would the boundary of the church be lifted up because they would coincide with the boundaries of the world itself."[20] This was manifestly a still future reality.

Kuyper and Pierson agreed on at least one point: modernists, by their own principles, did not belong in the church. In a critique of the *volkskerk*'s broad policies, Kuyper concluded that the church must remain a pure church. There were indeed those who participated only superficially in the rites of the church. The only right course was that both members and teachers who did not truly belong to the church must be cut off from it. The slogan of the church must be "small but pure"!

Besides the modernists, these sermons on the church also addressed a second wayward group, one probably closer to home for Kuyper than Pierson. Since the early nineteenth century, these pious conventicles had dotted the Dutch landscape as part of the reaction to Enlightenment rationalism, and they were part of the spiritual revival occurring in various parts of Europe. "In this reaction," historian George Harinck explains, "a shift of the place of religion from the outer order to the inner was made."[21] Some of these groups joined the Afscheiding, but some remained nominally within the NHK. They kept their membership in the national church, but the conventicle, which had no formal pastoral oversight, was their spiritual home.

The importance of Kuyper's encounter with the Calvinistic-pietists in Beesd, and one named Pietje Baltus in particular, has grown to legendary proportions. In later autobiographical accounts in *Confidentially* (1873) and in an obituary for Baltus in *The Standard* from 1914, Kuyper remembered how this pious believer opened his eyes for the first time to the true meaning of the Reformed faith. But while Kuyper praised the conventiclers' Calvinist conviction in *Confidentially*, the same year in a separate publication he criticized their spirituality. "The conventicle," he said, "is in many ways the seed-bed of sickly mysticism."[22] The much later obituary likewise suggested, besides Reformed orthodoxy, a mystical piety combined with a deficient ecclesiology:

> She [Pietje Baltus] *attended no church* and did not even want to receive such a half-baked preacher into her home. She insisted on a *full* confession of the faith for which our martyrs had died....[I] suddenly grasped *the power of the absolute* in this woman.[23]

Of the two sides of Kuyper's opinion about the conventiclers, one more favorable and one less so, Kuyper's sermons from Beesd evidence the more critical one.

In his next sermon, Kuyper reprimanded those who thought religion was strictly a matter between God and their own hearts and who therefore preferred to worship in their closets. "Public common worship of your Creator is also laid upon you by him as a duty," and of all institutions, the church alone had the responsibility of conducting the worship of God.[24] Of course, worship was not therefore compulsory. It should be the sincere desire of one's heart, but the responsibility of public worship ensured the church's continued existence.

In the third sermon, "The Common Life of Humanity: The Goal of Jesus' Church and the Means to Her Development," Kuyper addressed Pierson's central claim that the church was divisive and therefore could not lead humanity to its goal, the solidarity of all people. In response, Kuyper challenged Pierson; unity was exactly the goal of church. Families, friendship circles, and—in direct opposition to Pierson—the state could never unite humanity:

> Now I ask you, what else shall join to reach that goal, what other than Jesus' Church whose only ambition is a spiritual movement, to establish the same spiritual principle in every heart and to create order in that chaos of passion and selfishness that divides person from person.[25]

To accomplish this goal, the church must not separate itself from the rest of the world but must work within the world to win it for Christ.

Uncertain Aims: Church and Society

At this time, Kuyper's social vision for the church was filled with competing and sometimes contradictory aims. Many of these aims continued through his life, and the challenge for his ecclesiology and social ethics was to bring them into some kind of harmony. But there was little of that at this early stage.

Although he believed in the separation of church and state, Kuyper did not plan to follow the pattern of Jefferson's strict "wall of separation." In his *Commentatio,* Kuyper had advised that the church should own its own property and pay its own ministers rather than have the state administer these, as had been the custom in the Dutch church.[26] Beyond that, however, he envisioned church and state as mutually supportive institutions. Following his inaugural sermon at Beesd, Kuyper gave customary addresses to the several noteworthies in the pews. To the mayor, Kuyper acknowledged that the separation between church and state was the distinctive feature of modern society, but "although the separation of church and state is the motto of our time, following the old custom I accept the leadership of the spiritual concerns of this congregation appealing to your sympathetic cooperation to promote the flowering of this congregation."[27] In exchange, Kuyper pledged the church to the work of promoting good citizenship, such as the honoring of law, to show that "citizenship in heaven, far from blowing out the spirit of citizenship here below, is exactly that which cultivates and sanctifies it."[28] In 1857, a new education law attempted to put the separation of church and state into practice in the public primary schools by establishing a form of religious neutrality. Public schools could teach only the most generic principles of Christian ethics and Bible history. In accord with this law, and perhaps interpreting it more broadly than was intended so to give the most room possible for Christian beliefs, Kuyper urged the schoolmaster to "sow the first seeds of love for God and Christ"[29]—a position on which Kuyper later reversed himself. Although the separation of church and state may have been the cry of the age, it certainly was not yet fully Kuyper's motto.[30] This is not to say that the seeds of discontent with the church's close relationship with society were not already sown. On another occasion, Kuyper lamented that church membership had become a mark of social standing rather than something to risk one's life for. After three centuries of scorn and persecution, Constantine had brought that dubious honor to the church, and it still weighed down the national church of Kuyper's day.[31]

Kuyper's historical work also showed his appreciation for the separation of church and state, especially for the sake of the church. A second article dealt with the Dutch Reformed church's early existence as an exile church in London, and here Kuyper found historical warrant for a wider separation between church and state. Much of the history of the Dutch church, he explained, was characterized by a hostile disposition between church and state. But examining the historical origin would reveal the pure source of the Dutch church:

Following Calvin's principles, the Church wanted to work completely out of its own principles and only permitted the ratifying of her decisions by the States out of respect. On their side, the States [i.e., the States General, the Dutch parliament] set over against this, as sharply as possible, the principle of their unlimited sovereignty even over the congregations in their provinces.[32]

The London church provided a model as well as the necessary precedent for Kuyper's vision for the Netherlands Reformed Church, "a free Church in a free State."[33] Thus, Kuyper broached the free church by name.

Although he believed in the separation of church and state, the church could not retreat or refrain from its social responsibility. Pierson's critique of the church, by its nature, was also a critique of Christian activity in society. As other institutions such as state and public schools came into their own, the church had declined in its social relevance. But Kuyper argued that the Kingdom of God, humanity's highest goal, was completely bound up with the church.[34] This was also a criticism of those who withdrew into pious enclaves, which could not be reconciled with Christianity's universal scope.

Kuyper's concern for Christian social engagement was a long-standing one, beginning at least with his university thesis on Pope Nicolas I, whom Kuyper praised for his attention to the downtrodden. Kuyper himself came from a frugal pastor's family, and anxiety over solvency touched him in various ways from an early age. His historiographical ambitions were also limited more by a shortage of income than by any shortage of ambition or intellect. At Beesd, besides his pastoral responsibilities and his historical research, he oversaw diaconal care and participated in the administration of a small savings bank established by the Society for the General Welfare (Nut).[35]

Therefore, Kuyper's response to Pierson also naturally included his developing concern for the public significance of religion, though it was now complicated by a growing appreciation for the separation of the church from the state. Kuyper's task was once again to guard against the extreme of the modernists as well as the opposite tendency to withdraw from society. First of all, as the mother of regeneration, the church had a legitimate place in the world alongside the "temples" of science and art. "It is not destined to be absorbed by the world, to continue to hover over the world as a guardian angel."[36] Christianity was not satisfied simply with a prayer house in every village: "it lays hand on your whole life."[37] Here Kuyper faced a dilemma. Pierson also believed in the universal religious nature of human society, so much so that (for him) the church and Christianity simply melted into society. Kuyper believed in the universal significance of Christianity, but he also believed in the unique role of the church.

He struggled to reconcile this with the separation of church and state. One way he did so was by distinguishing between the limited but necessary scope of church life (*kerkleven*), now using "church" (*kerk*) in a different manner than before, as the concrete institution (not the invisible gathering of elect) and the comprehensive scope of congregational life (*gemeenteleven*). The church was the place of the preaching of the Word, nurturing of the young, and public worship, but Christendom did not remain within the walls of the church. It penetrated family, school, state, and all societal life, though that did not imply any confusion between the church and the state:

> [The church] asks for freedom for herself, and she allows that also for the state. Her ministers must not rule the ministers of the King, but in the hearts of the King's ministers, Jesus' church must become the all-dominating power which subjects everything to Jesus' spirit. She does not want a Christendom above faith-division [contra Pierson], but she demands men even at the rudder of the state, who themselves possess a powerful conviction and just for that reason can honor the right of conviction in others.[38]

Christendom's influence would be through the hearts of individuals, that is, the members of the congregation, not through the church as an institution.

Elsewhere, Kuyper summarized the three erroneous responses to Christianity's social role: those who cut religion off from the rest of life; those who regarded religion as the enemy of human nature; and those who tried to reconcile religion and life by making religion as earthly as possible. The first group was perhaps the mystics like Pietje Baltus, the middle group, the French Revolutionaries, and the last undoubtedly the Protestant modernists. But the Sermon on the Mount did not teach a heavenly ethics that had no bearing on earthly life. True, the Kingdom of God was an interior spiritual reality, but Jesus taught the Kingdom *and its righteousness,* and true righteousness always occurred in relation to others.

Besides his culture warrior face, and in spite of all his criticism of the conventiclers, Kuyper kept his own sectarian mask. He showed this with slogans like "small but pure!" and with his criticism of the national church's undiscerning broadness. But he could go even further than this. There were times, he said, when Christendom must withdraw from a corrupt society rather than be corrupted itself. Otherwise, pure enjoyments like trade or agriculture, but especially art, could also be corrupt and corrupting, and they had in fact become so in his century, Kuyper judged. The impurity of the *volkskerk* was partly due to its uncritical accommodation of modern culture that "directs itself to the material and denies the spirit."[39] So "I . . . regard our days as a time that is better passed praying in the inner room than dawdling in the society, which is why I avoid many enjoyments, which otherwise can be pure, as dangerous and pernicious."[40] Kuyper clearly had some explaining to do.

Incarnation: The Free Church in Theory

Kuyper's developing appreciation for the externals of the church and his commitment to heartfelt spirituality demanded an ecclesiology that harmonized these two aspects. This ecclesiology would also have to reconcile the separation of church and state with the church's role in Christianity's universal social implications. Kuyper attempted such reconciliation in his 1867 sermon "The Incarnation: The Life Principle of the Church." Although this sermon (of November 10, 1867) was the beginning of his Utrecht ministry, ecclesiologically it attempted to integrate the concerns developed earlier at Beesd. To be sure, Utrecht was a formative period for Kuyper, but at the writing of this sermon those pivotal events were still before him. To this point, Kuyper's ecclesiological reflections had been occasional and inchoate. He had not yet attempted to make systematic sense of the issues that concerned him most, and, as advocates and detractors alike have recognized, Kuyper had an uncommonly great need for systemization.

The stakes were high in 1867. Modernists like L. W. E. Rauwenhoff and F. W. B. van Bell continued to question the church's legitimacy. As followers of German theologian Richard Rothe, they believed that the church would eventually dissolve into society. The antisupernaturalist Rauwenhoff viewed the church as a religious society, not as a supernatural institution, and he went even further than Rothe with his conclusions. Whereas Rothe believed that the dissolution of the church (the religious form of the human organism) was still far in the future, Rauwenhoff, illustrating the progressivism of the nineteenth century, believed that that future was now.

The argument that the church would eventually dissolve involved a combination of ecclesiology and social ethics. With the application of religious principles to social questions, the traditional functions of the church—education, raising the young, care for the poor, promoting civil virtues—had been transferred elsewhere in society. "If one asks from which remedy one may expect the most for social reform, the ecclesiastical or the purely societal, it cannot be doubtful how the answer would fall." A. van Toorenenbergen, a representative of the Groningen school and a moderate, responded by defending the church's civilizing and educating tasks, typical emphases of the Groningen movement. Toorenenbergen also picked up one of Rothe's themes: church forms must always be renewed in new situations, though the inner essence remains the same. Although they sharply differed in their understanding of the function of the church, Toorenenbergen and Rauwenhoff shared a commitment to accommodate the church to the demands of modern society, and society was clearly expected to take the lead in that dance.[41]

Kuyper responded to these challenges with an ecclesiology based on the doctrine of the incarnation. The church was the ongoing life of the incarnate Christ, a theme popularized by Friedrich Schleiermacher and echoed in the Mercersburg theology, and he dealt with the church from two aspects of the incarnation—the internal and the external. Humanity forms an organic unity, and through the incarnation the Word becomes part of that organism. The church, according to its internal aspect, "is not just a gathering of Jesus' followers, no she is in the fullest sense the body of Christ, the rich organism in which not only his spirit, but Christ himself lives on."[42] The new organism has a new life principle, divine life.

Like the incarnation, the church also had an external bodily form. Again, Kuyper addressed himself to both the "shallow" modernists and also those "pious circles that reveal themselves to be indifferent" to the church.[43] Just as the Son of God took on an external historic form, so also the divine life of the church must be manifested in tangible forms. Kuyper retained his debt to Schleiermacher through the insistence that spiritual life comes only through prior membership in the community. He also echoed Schleiermacher's insistence that the inner life must come to external historical expression, but he now departed from Schleiermacher by asserting that the external form of the community must have a definite form. (Kuyper allowed that the form, though definite, was not immutable.) For Schleiermacher the form was not definite or particular; every ecclesial form was included.[44] This turned out to be decisive for Kuyper's jousts in the church and the ecclesiology he developed in support, wherein spiritual life depended on very specific forms like the Trinitarian baptismal formula. The main external forms that Kuyper had in mind were doctrine, liturgy, and church government. Of course, fixed forms must be joined with freedom of conscience. Participation is for those who know what it means and want to participate in the church, and the lax policies of the national church violated this principle.

Finally, Kuyper made an important move that previewed his later social ethics. He addressed the implications of Christian involvement in society, though not through the external, institutional church but as an implication of membership in the divine *organism* of the body of Christ. He urged that for the organic church, there was no area of life estranged to Christians, and he explained the implications of this for those Christians involved in government institutions in his address to the government representatives in the audience. "Not more married, not more hand in hand, but still joined through similar striving the church and state each seek to perform their own calling."[45] The institutions of church and state would each work in its "own sphere" (sounding what eventually would be a characteristically Kuyperian note), thus solving the "thorniest question" of the age.[46]

"The Incarnation" set a trajectory for Kuyper's career. It enumerated several basic commitments that arose at Beesd and that Kuyper tried to harmonize in various ways and in various circumstances in the future: the internal spiritual "form" of the church, participation in which was sincere and therefore voluntary; the external forms of the church such as the sacraments; and the social responsibility of the church. One step in particular affected the course of Kuyper's thought and his participation in the church and Dutch public life. He attributed the church's social responsibility not to the external form of the church, as had been common from the Middle Ages through the Reformation, but to the internal church, or the "organism," as Kuyper called it. Just as Kuyper's position on article 23 had given a powerful democratic impulse to the institutional church by urging the congregation to retain the right to vote for church officials, Kuyper also added a powerful democratizing impetus to Christian public engagement by assigning this responsibility also to the organism.

Conclusion

Most free-church theologies are thought to deemphasize institutional forms for freedom of conscience. Kuyper had long appreciated the importance of freedom of conscience and active, participatory spirituality. What marked the emergence of Kuyper's free-church ecclesiology at Beesd was, in contrast, his new appreciation for the external forms of the church. As Troeltsch observed, the free church is a voluntary association, yet "theologically the community which thus comes into being may still continue to be considered as an objective, ecclesiastical institution."[47] In dispute with mystics like Allard Pierson and Pietje Baltus, Kuyper, the pastor, had to explain to his parishioners why they should go to church. That required an argument for the objective ecclesiastical institution that Troeltsch mentioned.

Kuyper's first attempt at a comprehensive ecclesiological program married the external and the internal forms of the church by analogy with Christ's incarnation. Defining the church this way also offered a convenient explanation of what aspects of the church had broad public relevance (namely, the church considered according to its internal, organic form) and what was not (the church's institutional existence). The incarnational model did not last, however. Critics said that it sounded more like Hegelian philosophy than theology, and as Kuyper moved on from Beesd to the larger Utrecht and Amsterdam parishes, he would have to go back to the ecclesiological drawing board.

3

The French Revolution as an Ecclesiological Crisis: Abraham Kuyper's Sacramental Ecclesiology

EDMUND BURKE, GROEN VAN Prinsterer, and Alexis d'Tocqueville cultivated in Abraham Kuyper an early and deep distaste for the French Revolution, so much so that whatever Kuyper may have stood for there was hardly any mistaking what he was against. After all, his was the Anti-Revolutionary Party. In church matters, however, not everyone was persuaded of Kuyper's anti-Revolutionary credentials. "I call *your* attempts *revolutionary*," Jacob Cramer wrote to Kuyper, and later when Kuyper did break with the national church he had to defend himself against charges of "conspiracy and revolution."[1] In fact, Kuyper ran hot and cold when it came to the Revolution. He opposed the secular humanism it symbolized, the revolutionary principle whereby "God's omnipotence was replaced by the doctrine of human sovereignty."[2] Yet he promoted principles like democracy and separation of church and state, which many associated with the French Revolution and which challenged traditional structures in government and in the church. He decried the "clericalism" of the established church, and at least once he accepted being included with "radicals on the left" for his social views, which he described as "Christian liberalism."[3] Cramer, it seems, was not wholly wrong.

"European (or indeed world) politics between 1789 and 1917 were," Eric Hobsbawn writes, "largely the struggle for and against the principles of 1789."[4] Besides political crises, Mark Noll observes that wars also cause theological crises. For example, the crisis of the American Civil War, Noll says, was one of scriptural interpretation: Americans could not agree on what the Bible said about slavery, and they had no means, short of war, to decide.[5] The French Revolution was likewise a theological crisis, but an ecclesiological one. It upset the social and political situation of European churches, forcing a demoted status on them in the form of disestablishment; bringing competition through religious pluralism that the churches had not experienced before; installing a powerful new master, the nation-state, whose allegiances were uncertain; and introducing the unpredictability of the newly self-conscious democratic laity. These challenges belonged to the churches at large and to Kuyper in particular, and he spoke for all of European Christianity when he said, "The *problem of the church* is none other than the problem of Christianity itself."[6]

After leaving Beesd with a new commitment to the institutional church, during the subsequent period of the late 1860s and 1870s, using a sacramental ecclesiology Kuyper tried to adjust the church to the pressures brought on by the French Revolution. Kuyper introduced this sacramental ecclesiology with a new formula—the church as organism and institution—wherein he described an institution with a sacramental role as a divinely instituted means of grace. The organism was the inner essence, and the institution was the outer form, which was no less important but was natural and necessary for the life of the organism. The organism encompassed aspects such as the members' active commitment and freedom of conscience, while the institution referred to the traditional, outward elements of Reformed Protestantism, such as doctrinal authority and sacraments. The inner and the outer aspects of the church were both essential elements of the church, and they existed in a necessary and complementary relationship. However, Kuyper's understanding of the inner and outer aspects of the church also included tension. While Kuyper's vision of the church was sacramental, the church was also a free church, exemplified in his commitment to freedom of conscience, democratic church polity, and the separation of church and state, which framed the church very nearly as a voluntary association. Bringing together the concept of the church as an objective means of grace and the idea that it was a voluntary group was a difficult undertaking.

This ecclesiology coincided with a particular approach to the church's social role. Although Kuyper considered the possibility of breaking with the national church, that was not his intention in the 1870s. His goal was to reform the church, and that decision was more than an ecclesiological one. It was one of weighty social consequence. Kuyper's high esteem for the objective and institutional features of the church went along with a high view of the church as a national institution. He did not want to rupture the historic connection between the Reformed church and the Dutch nation. The problem was how to simultaneously maintain the church's prominent social role and the separation of church and state and to reform the church's expected status among the Dutch people. This particular social position, Kuyper believed, produced a spiritual lethargy. He solved this problem by assigning the church a custodial role over the nation and offering a nuanced understanding of religious tolerance. This concept of tolerance permitted a good deal of religious variety in the nation while preserving the confessional integrity of the church.

During this period, Kuyper worked out his ecclesiological and social thought in various occasional pieces, especially sermons and newspaper articles. It was not a concatenated system and therefore did not address every question that might occur to later readers. He addressed the masses and concerned himself with large-scale religious and social issues and not the minutia of the theologians. Yet a picture does emerge of an ecclesiology that cohered in its framework, if not in every detail.

Social and Intellectual Pressures

Of the challenges facing the church in the nineteenth century, religious pluralism—within and without—was the most aggressive. Pluralism did not necessarily lead to skeptical relativism, Hugh McLeod explains; it could sometimes lead to more fervent ideological commitments,[7] and that was the case with Abraham Kuyper. At Beesd, Utrecht, and Amsterdam, Kuyper learned to negotiate the party system in ecclesiastical politics and even showed a natural affinity for it. Modernism in the church continued to upset Kuyper, perhaps because he saw there a shadow of his old self. Kuyper famously deconstructed modernism in a speech titled "Modernism: A Fata Mogana in the Christian Domain (1871)." Though modernism kept up Christian appearances, it was an unreal reflection, an optical illusion, of true Christianity. Modernists such as Allard Pierson and C. Busken-Huet saw through the illusion and abandoned it (also Christianity itself), thus proving Kuyper's point.

Pierson shared with Kuyper not the same conclusions but the same method of rigorously consistent reasoning as well as intolerance for ambiguity and equivocation.[8] Indeed, "The only place the evil does not hide is with the modernists," said Kuyper.[9] That is, his quarrel with the modernists was out in the open. It was different, however, with the more theologically moderate yet socially conservative groups like the Reveil and the Ethical party. The Reveil party, the patrician adherents of an earlier era of revivals, and the Ethical party, which sought to lend intellectual respectability to experiential Christianity, were composed of broadly orthodox Protestants, if not strict Reformed confessionalists like Kuyper. These groups took a more cautious and conciliatory posture toward modernism and generally tolerated a broader diversity of doctrinal and liturgical positions than Kuyper, who wanted strict adherence to Reformed doctrine, liturgy, and polity. Kuyper's thinking overlapped considerably with their views, but they parted ways over the church—not simply over the minutia of Reformed polity but particularly over how to deal with the overarching question of religious pluralism in the church. For Kuyper, ecclesiology was not a matter of indifference, wherein diversity could be tolerated. "One must not confuse ecclesiastical matters with one's faith," said J. Cramer.[10] To which Kuyper responded:

> I am often told, "we agree in our beliefs; we just differ on the church" thereby suggesting that my general beliefs and my views on the church are not related. . . . My whole soul rises against that notion. . . . And, provided that people open their hearts sufficiently, I believe that in many cases I can point to a deviation in the very first phase of their spiritual life which leads to a divergent concept on the "locus de ecclesia."[11]

Kuyper dubbed moderates like Cramer *irenicals*, though not for anything he found praiseworthy but simply for fleeing the good fight.

Democracy could either be good or bad in Kuyper's view, according to which form it took and where he found it. Kuyper was a populist leader, yet he also had reservations about just how much rein could be given to the people. The parties in the church each formed around their representative spokesmen (and men they were). Kuyper's mentor, Groen van Prinsterer, spoke for the Reveil; J. H. Gunning and Daniel Chantepie de la Saussaye for the Ethicals; and Kuyper for the Reformed confessionalists. Kuyper's rigorous schedule of pastoral visitation and catechesis, his editorship of the newspaper the *Herald*—subtitled *"for a free church and a free school in a free* Netherlands"—and his political posturing all designated him as a rising *volk* leader. Yet Kuyper was a different kind of leader from Groen or Gunning, who moved in establishment circles—Groen as secretary to William I and Gunning later as a university theologian at Leiden. Abraham Kuyper, son of a common pastor, was what Max Weber would have called a charismatic leader.[12]

As one of the great populist leaders of the Netherlands, Kuyper worked to broaden the right to vote. Initially, Kuyper advocated one vote per household, and later he supported universal male suffrage. In fact, the church was a testing ground for voting rights, as Kuyper helped broaden the enfranchisement in the church even before he entered politics.[13] He also empowered the people by bringing theology out of the academies and putting it on coffee tables through his newspaper articles. The repeal of the newspaper tax in 1869 made mass media possible for the first time, and Kuyper used it ably to enhance the laity's knowledge of Reformed theology. Many of his tomes, such as *The Holy Spirit* and *Common Grace*, first appeared as serial pieces in the newspapers, but the first studies to hit the presses were those from the 1870s, including many in which ecclesiology figured centrally.

Democracy could be taken too far, though, shown, for example, by the revival movements. At times, Kuyper chastised Methodism, Darbyism, the Dutch Reveil party, and Alexander Vinet and the French *Réveil*—all for circumventing the church. Democratization, he worried, threatened the proper exercise of religious authority. He worried that if biblical interpretation was taken from the church and given to individuals, "even the first principles of religion are unscrewed and a Babylonian confusion ensues."[14] One challenge for his ecclesiology was to reconcile the active involvement of the people with proper formal ecclesiastical structures.

Related to the problem of democratization was the threat of idealism, so-called by Kuyper, which, according to him, came in two forms: the Kantian highbrow form; and the populist "one-sided spiritualism" of modern revivalism.[15] Kuyper was a champion of the inward spiritual life and the need for conversion, and his ecclesiology had a strong idealist tint, seen in his conceptions of the church as incarnation and organism. Still, he insisted that "exactly the existence of the unconscious life in each individual demands that the church, as mother of believers, would offer…conscious form that can bring the yet embryonic life to clear consciousness."[16] Whereas renewal movements of the nineteenth century frequently opposed inner, personal renewal to external church rituals, Kuyper argued that true personal renewal always occurred in the context of the church. Consequently, his spiritual reforms went hand in hand with ecclesiastical reforms, exhibited in his writings by a dual concern for the "fixed church forms" and internal "embryonic life."

The liberal constitution of 1848, which established the separation of church and state and the freedom of assembly, furthered the proliferation of different religious groups in the Netherlands. It opened new possibilities for the tolerance of marginal groups like Catholics or Lutherans (which was helpful for men such as J. R. Thorbecke, the Lutheran author of the liberal constitution). Implementing this new arrangement, however, was not straightforward or immediate. As a pastor at Utrecht, Kuyper was paid out of state coffers.[17] In the separation between church and state, there was also the need to determine who got what in the settlement, with respect to welfare funds or church property, for instance. In the late 1860s, a series of government decisions made it possible for the congregations to take control of their own property, which Kuyper urged them to do as a final step in the separation of church and state. But he went further: he also questioned the legitimacy of the synodical hierarchy, because, he said, it had originally been the establishment of the state. These moves toward emancipating the church from the state and from the state-established synod angered many who were loath to give up the privileges and influence of establishment.[18] That kind of posturing by Kuyper was what provoked Cramer to say to him, "I call *your* attempts *revolutionary*."[19]

Conservatism dealt with these various challenges of modern life, especially pluralism, by trying to preserve the status quo so far as possible. Confessional theologians in the nineteenth century, like Charles Hodge in America or F. J. Stahl in Germany, tended to be supporters of conservative society.[20] The conservatives Kuyper met at Utrecht, after moving there from Beesd in 1867, were both theological and social conservatives. Like Kuyper, they opposed movements like theological modernism but were not willing to take the drastic steps he prescribed. When, for example, the synod in its oversight capacity sent around questionnaires inquiring into the faith and life of the church leadership, the Utrecht consistory refused to answer. They believed the synod only feigned to care about faith and morals because it clearly intended to do nothing to enforce them. However, Kuyper wanted an even harder line against the synod. Because it was, he said, an illegitimate creation of the state, the autonomy of the local congregations was part and parcel of the separation of church and state, and authority and control of both spiritual and material concerns ought to rest entirely with the local congregations.[21] Although some like Gunning were sympathetic to these ends, they resisted Kuyper's call to immediate action.[22] Kuyper also proposed stricter membership regulations and more careful examination of those coming for baptism, a measure that would sever the nation's assumed tie to the church. Meanwhile, the Utrecht consistory continued in its broad approach, permitting parents who though baptized were not full members to have their children baptized.[23] Kuyper's emerging social views, especially his ideas to allow Catholic schools along-side Protestant ones and to take religious education out of the public schools, also proved too radical for his colleagues at Utrecht and made his move to Amsterdam in 1870 inevitable. The Utrecht consistory did not want to even discuss such matters.[24] When Kuyper said, "under the motto 'safe and sound,' [conservatism] causes life to whither," he meant the safe and sound approach of the Utrecht church.[25]

Kuyper's parting sermon from Utrecht, "Conservatism and Orthodoxy," was a tirade against "false conservatism," which, he explained, was differ-ent from orthodoxy. Amid the growing religious diversity of the nineteenth century, Stephen Sykes notes, there was a peculiar uncertainty about the identity of Christianity.[26] Kuyper recognized conservatism at Utrecht as one solution to this problem, though he conceived of it as specifically a problem for the church, not Christianity. These conservatives identified the true Christian church with the church of the past and tried to preserve it by either returning to the past (repristination) or holding obstinately to what had been attained thus far, but such approaches killed inner reli-gious life, according to Kuyper.

Kuyper, however, did believe in a kind of true Christian conservatism. Christ implanted the principle of life, and "one can aim at preserving either that which has so far emerged from that principle or the principle itself. Conservatism does the former; genuine orthodoxy must do the latter."[27] This was not pure idealism, though, for real life created forms. Only, one had to be careful of false conservatism, which became too attached to past or present forms. This was a critique of conservatism's insensitivity to the historical consciousness that Roger Haight calls the "defining shift" in modern ecclesiology.[28] Naturally, such a critique required that Kuyper provide the proper interpretation of the church's form and essence.

Organism and Institution: Model for a Sacramental Free Church

Kuyper's first attempt (1867) at an integrated ecclesiology had taken the incarnation as its model, a theme popularized by Johann Adam Möhler of the Roman Catholic Tübingen School. Kuyper valued the incarnational model as a way to reconcile the internal spiritual aspect of the church with the outward forms, a point he wished to make against the "pious cir-cles" who are "indifferent to the external church" and the "spokesmen of divinity" who laid a "one-sided stress" on the "personal revelation of each Christian for themselves."[29] In response to these groups, he explained:

> The incarnation of God, which is only begun in the incarnation of the Word, is completed through the dwelling of the Christ among us, through the coming of the Holy Ghost....The Church is not just a collection of Jesus' followers, no, it is in the full sense the body of Christ, the rich organism in which not only his spirit but Christ himself lives on.[30]

Minister A. W. Bronsveld, however, thought this sounded more philosophical than biblical: "what else is it but Christian-tinted Hegelianism?"[31]

Perhaps aware of Bronsveld's critique (and tacitly in agreement), Kuyper broached a new model in 1870: the church as organism and institution, for which he found biblical support in Paul's description of the church as "rooted and grounded."[32] This model described the church's inner and outer aspects as organism and institution and set them in sacramental relationship. Avery Dulles defines the sacramental model of the church as that model wherein the visible social expression sustains the spiritual reality.[33] Kuyper's ecclesiology resembled this formulation when Kuyper said that the institution was not an artificial shell of the organism but was the tangible expression of the organism. Accordingly, Kuyper explained, "Real life creates itself a form. A life without a firmly defined form cannot exist in this finite world."[34] He also made the point by comparing the church as institution and organism to a river: "the free church! *Free*, because the flow of the Christian life must be able to surge but nonetheless she should remain *the church*, because the current dies away in the flat fields if you demolish its banks."[35] Life surged from the inner organism, but it could not exist without the outward forms any more than a river could exist without its banks.

As rooted in Christ, the church was a spiritual organism. "'*Rooted*,' that is the metaphor of the free life that does not come through the human skill, but immediately from the hand of the Creator, bearing power in its own core and the law of its life in its own germ."[36] The Roman Catholic Church erred by forcibly imposing the institutional church on this freely growing organism. It must be allowed to grow according to the new inner life principle given by God when, through election, he created this new human organism from the old one corrupted by sin.

The organism, however, was incomplete without expressive life forms, and the life form of the Christian organism was the institutional church. Kuyper opposed the modernists' "hyper-spiritualism that evaporates everything" and the "petrifaction" of the conservatives, but rather "we should not abandon the church either as organism or as institution, but rather join both in a free church."[37] Grounded was the metaphor for the institutional church. Whereas the organism grew, the institutional church was built. Yet the institution was not a human invention, was not simply a society of like-minded persons like the voluntary societies cropping up everywhere (many by Kuyper's own hand). The institution was a divine work, and it depended on the organism as the organism did on it. The institution nurtured the organism, and the organism gave birth to the institution. The institution created a "life sphere" that fed and protected the person from the world.

Some like J. Cramer thought that Kuyper stifled the spirit through his advocacy of strict confessional subscription. The church, Cramer said, should confess from the heart, not have an externally imposed confession. "The reformation of the church must proceed from inside out. First the church changed, and then the church's form."[38] In fact, Kuyper did not believe that the organism could be reformed by imposing institutional forms on it. The proper movement was not from outside in or, as Cramer believed, from inside out. Rather, the organism and institution existed in a constant reciprocal relationship; the movement occurred in both directions at once: inside out, and outside in, the institution nourishing the organism, the organism blossoming into an institution.

There was continuity and difference between Kuyper's earlier incarnational ecclesiology and this ecclesiology of organism–institution. The incarnational ecclesiology had pantheistic tendencies because it so closely equated the church with the incarnate Christ. The organism–institution model avoided this problem while retaining the essential nature of the outward forms so well articulated by the incarnational ecclesiology. Even after Kuyper had abandoned the incarnational model, he still compared the church to the incarnation on the matter of its external forms. "Exactly the existence of the unconscious life in each individual demands that the church, as mother of believers, would offer the conscious form that can bring the yet embryonic life to clear consciousness."[39] It was a basic principle of human existence that the spiritual depended on the outer form.

The body–spirit metaphor was one common way of relating the internal and external aspects of the church in the nineteenth century.[40] It is still the metaphor that most closely approximates how Kuyper related the organism to the institution and a metaphor hospitable to sacramental ecclesiology.[41] The body–spirit metaphor makes the important point that the person is both body and spirit. The body is not an appendage; it is the person. In an analogous way, the external forms of the church are the church, and the spirit of the church lives through them. Kuyper espoused a similar concept, when, for example, he compared the external forms of the church to the skin of a snake, which "does not change artificially but only as a result of the vitality of the life which manifests itself at every point on the surface."[42] R. W. Moberly, Regius Professor of Theology at Oxford, contrasted the concept of the church as spirit–body, with the idea that the institution was a "practical necessity" and "an unfortunate condescension, diplomatically necessary, instead of being the inevitable condition, to inwardness."[43] In his later theology, when Kuyper was moving toward a break with the national church, he adopted the "practical necessity" view, but this earlier sacramental ecclesiology presented the institution as "an institution of God" that "not only manifests the organism, but it is one of the God-given means, to feed and grow that organism."[44]

Although the body–spirit metaphor best describes how Kuyper related the organism and institution, he used another common metaphor to explain the history and development of the institution: it was a building built by human hands[45] and consequently could be built incorrectly. The building metaphor, better than the spirit–body one, countenanced the possibility that the church could be constructed incorrectly through human error.[46] Kuyper's criticism of the false conservatism that stifled the living organism with out-of-date forms reflected this concern.

Sacramental Ecclesiology

Although Kuyper rarely used the binary formula of organism–institution again through the 1870s (NB Jasper Vree says he never did[47]), the principles of this model governed Kuyper's ecclesiology during this period. This ecclesiology was sacramental because of two characteristics that, according to Avery Dulles, characterize a sacramental model.[48] First, as a visible sign of an invisible reality, Kuyper's sacramental church embodied and transmitted grace. Kuyper's ecclesiology fit Augustine's classic definition of a sacrament: the organic church was the invisible reality of the Mystical Body of Christ, of which the institutional church was the visible sign, or "form." In the sacramental model, Dulles says, "the sign itself produces or intensifies that of which it is a sign." This encompasses what Kuyper meant when he said that the church was an instrument or means of grace. Second, the sacramental church, like the sacraments themselves, is a communal reality and is likewise one of the defining elements of Kuyper's ecclesiology in both its inner and outer aspects.[49]

In the 1870s, as Kuyper also wrote his anti-Revolutionary political philosophy, he relied on Edmund Burke (introduced to Kuyper by political liberal and theological modernist C. W. Opzoomer) for a portrait of the French Revolution.[50] Burke, though a political liberal, was nonetheless concerned about a type of individualism that dissolved the social order into a mass of individuals and severed ties between generations.[51] Kuyper feared this kind of individualism, where "each person must make religion into a matter between God and his own heart," where corporate and set prayers were disparaged, where preachers constructed their own theologies, but especially where the sacraments were slighted.[52] "The spirit of separation, of self-sufficiency, of licentiousness that the word *individualism* indicated and that lead people to do what was good in their own eyes was nothing but the application of the principle of the French Revolution in the field of religion."[53] One antidote to this revolutionary individualism was a recovery of the doctrine of the church as the Mystical Body of Christ.

In briefest terms, the Mystical Body was the "fullness of eternal power...an eternally filled reservoir in which the Fountain of life has poured out her divine waters."[54] Part of its mystery was its invisible reality, which did not completely coincide with the visible church. The Mystical Body of Christ was not the continuance of the incarnate Christ but rather Christ and church related as head and body, with love as the power that flowed through the members. This organic church did not originate by members coming together but was born from an organic kernel (*kiem*) from which members likewise grew. The members could be said to have been ever present in the kernel, as the elect had their names written in the Book of Life from eternity.[55]

The church was not a gathering of individuals but a Mystical Body, which had a twofold mystical organic bond established by God—first with Christ the head, and then between the members—virtually identical to Kuyper's organic church. Organicity denoted members' living interdependence as opposed to a mechanical metaphor that portrayed them as parts of machine. The organic bond also tied the church to the past and present generations, and though it was invisible it was manifest in external forms like the confessions handed down from one generation to the next.[56]

The extent to which the church question had a hold on Kuyper's mind is illustrated by his series of articles on the doctrine of election (1873). He considered this a contribution to ecclesiology, since election was the *cor ecclesia* in two senses: election was the cardinal doctrine of the Reformed church from which its religious genius and its benefits for society flowed; and it was the origin of the invisible, organic church. Kuyper's formulation of election supported his corporatist concept of the organism. God did not elect individuals and then gather individuals to form the church. The reverse was true. Election began with Christ, then God elected the church in Christ, and, finally, he elected the individual as a member of the church:

> One should not first of all conceive of election as a counsel to the salvation of individual persons...but as the election of the Christ, in Him [the election] of the church, and only in the church election of the individuals who are her living members.[57]

In the Old Testament, for example, the election of the people of Israel preceded the election of particular people in Israel. These two elections differed, however, in their meaning for salvation. Election to the church corporate was not the same as election to salvation. It was preparatory to the election of individuals, which was, strictly speaking, election to salvation.

Kuyper's articles on election exemplified the loose ends left by his occasional writings. There was a tension between his corporatist doctrine of the Mystical Body and his concept of election. While the election of the church did precede the election of individuals, and in that sense corporate election was prior, this corporate election was not salvific. Yet membership in the corporate Mystical Body was salvific. Kuyper did not explain how, on one hand, in the matter of election only the election of individuals was election for salvation yet, on the other hand, those elect individuals never existed as individuals but only as members of the Mystical Body.

The church as institution, the outer form of the church, also had a divine foundation. "Like the invisible church flows from the fact of election [and the Mystical Body], so the externally appearing church flows from the 'power of the keys of the Kingdom.'"[58] There was a tendency, Kuyper thought, to view the ecclesiastical institution as an arbitrary human contrivance, but the institutional church had a divine foundation. The church in its visible forms, however, "was not invented or made by men, but entrusted to men by the Son of God in the name of his Father."[59] This raised questions of the relation between the church and the Kingdom, and Kuyper labored to distinguish his view from several other alternatives. Rome too simply equated the visible church with the Kingdom of God, yet the kingdom was not simply an ideal ("the Kingdom of God is within you"), as modernists claimed. Rather, the Kingdom was gradually becoming public and observable in the church, specifically in the congregation (*gemeente*): "The congregation is the revelation of the Kingdom of Christ on earth."[60] Thus the external form of the church was a divine body, if an imperfectly expressed one.

The keys of the Kingdom gave to the church power over the "external life area." Kuyper felt that individualism was running unchecked in the national church: "Can it be contradicted that the believers in our fatherland are hopelessly divided and cast apart...each believer thinks that he can stand before God alone and have a monopoly on the truth."[61] The keys represented the church's authority to resolve disputes and bind believers together, an authority that rested with the congregation, "itself a standing revelation of Jesus' authority," and was exercised through the officers whom the congregation had selected.[62] Here again, Kuyper tried to find the middle way between two extremes roughly portrayed: clericalism, the notion that authority rested with a "faithful few"; and a tyrannical religious democracy, the "unspiritual ballot box." Finally, the exercise of authority in the church was truly the authority to bind things on earth and in heaven, for "only an authority whose origin hides in the eternal deep is truly divine or is, in short, authority."[63]

Kuyper's appreciation for Reformed Orthodoxy and especially for John Calvin grew during the early 1870s. Intellectually, he knew Calvin well, since his dissertation dealt with Calvin's ecclesiology, but there he had preferred John a Lasco's ecclesiology to Calvin's rigid insistence on the institution. However, Kuyper underwent a conversion, so to speak, to Calvin, the seeds of which were sown in Beesd and came to full flower in his sacramental ecclesiology. It was not Calvin generally that he came to appreciate but specifically his ecclesiology, which he had earlier repudiated. Kuyper blessed Calvin for founding a "fixed church form," and he "remembered what Calvin has so beautifully stated in the fourth book of his *Institutes* about God as our Father and 'the church as our Mother.'"[64] There were those who said Europe's church question was only a matter of organization, a "thorny problem of canon law," but to Kuyper it struck deeper, it struck "at the heart of the Christian faith and therefore concerned the honor of God and the salvation of souls."[65] Besides the divine nature and origin of the church,

Kuyper had come to appreciate the church's mission in the world as nothing less than God's mission of rescuing and redeeming the world, not just from workaday hardships or social ills but also from the power of evil.

The church as institution fulfilled this mission as a means of grace. The confession of the Mystical Body, he said, had to do with not only the inner form but also the visible form of the church, because only through this church did one come into contact with the Mystical Body.[66] The error of individualism was to think that communion with God was strictly between the individual and God, without the corporate body intervening; it was also the error of supposing that the work of grace was a purely hidden work of the Spirit:

> If the communion of our soul in the Mystical Body of the Lord is to be healthy, then we need a church that 1. brings us the truth in a manner suited to our earthly nature; 2. administers the sacrament to us; 3. exercises discipline over us; 4. extends to us the communion of saints; 5 adopts our families and my children after our death for spiritual nourishment; and 6. in and through this all opens to us a quiet, always ongoing communion with the benefits of salvation that are laid up for us in the high-priestly heart of the Mediator.[67]

Kuyper described these forms of the church, especially preaching and the sacraments, as part of God's "preparing grace."[68] His logic was Pauline. Regeneration, whereby God restored fallen human nature, came by faith; faith came by hearing the Word; and hearing the Word came from preaching. Kuyper stressed this point against various groups like the Reveil and the Ethical parties, which emphasized immediate connection between God and the person and the inner work of conversion to the diminishment of external rituals. He complained, "conversion is one and all, and birth in God's covenant is forgotten, and the value of baptism is overlooked and all the preparatory grace which precedes conversion counted for nothing."[69] Elsewhere, he went even further in his claims about baptism: "Through baptism a mystical bond between the one baptized and the body of Christ is created, through which the terrain before personal regeneration is smoothed....Therefore there is no regeneration except from the church."[70] True to Calvin, Kuyper believed one could not have God as a father without the church as a mother.

Friedrich Schleiermacher said that Catholicism makes individuals' relationship to Christ depend on their relationship to the church;

Protestantism makes their relationship to the church depend on their relationship to Christ.[71] By Schleiermacher's lights (once among the bright-
est for Kuyper but now considerably dimmer), Kuyper (not to mention
Calvin) had set his face toward Rome.

The Free Church: A Church Attuned to Modern Times

Christians' relationship to the church was dependent on their relationship
to Christ, according to Kuyper. Traditionally, in established, state churches
membership was given with citizenship. In the Dutch national church,
membership in the church was not simply a coincidence of membership
in the nation, though the national church may have wished for that. Hence,
William I, when he established the Netherlands Reformed Church in 1816,
had even tried to merge Catholic, Calvinist, and Lutheran churches into a
single unit to bring all Dutch people under the same church.[72] Kuyper's
free church, in contrast, severed ties with nation and state. Rather than
making church membership a reflex of state or national membership,
Kuyper wanted a membership based on voluntary commitment. Three
qualities in particular made Kuyper's church into a free church: the separation of church and state; freedom of conscience; and the autonomy of
the congregation.[73]

Kuyper departed from Calvin and his Reformation forbears on one critical point, a deviation that imprinted his ecclesiology with a distinctively
modern tint. The church had to be absolutely separated from the state.
The Reformation was right to break up Rome's *worldchurch*, wherein a single institution had been foisted on all Christians, but the Reformation had
not gone far enough. It had stopped short at the settlement of *cuius regio,
eius religio*, the state or societal church. "The Spirit of Christ yielded to
an institution that wanted to twist the spiritual lines of humanity according to her geographical boundaries."[74] In practical terms, separation of
church and state meant giving churches control over their own property[75];
it meant that the state should stop subsidizing the salaries of the ministers
(an ongoing reality even after the 1848 constitutional separation of church
and state)[76]; and it meant that the state should relinquish its role in social
welfare. Most importantly though, it meant abolishing article 36 of the
Belgic Confession, which charged the magistrates

> that they protect the sacred ministry, and thus may remove and pre-
> vent all idolatry and false worship; that the kingdom of antichrist

may be thus destroyed, and the kingdom of Christ promoted. They must, therefore, countenance the preaching of the word of the gospel everywhere, that God may be honored and worshiped by everyone, as he commands in his Word.[77]

Abolishing article 36 as Kuyper proposed was the logical step in securing the doctrinal freedom of the church,[78] but it went against tradition and conservative sentiment. As a pastor at Beesd, though Kuyper believed in the separation of church and state, he still asked for cooperation between the two.[79] Now he saw much less room for cooperation.

For the national church, however, the most potentially disturbing aspect of Kuyper's idea of separation was his congregationalism. William I had made the Netherlands Reformed Church an administrative unit through the synod, and Kuyper therefore viewed the synod as an illegitimate institution and an ongoing intrusion of the state. Freedom, thoroughgoing separation from the state, meant freedom from the synod's control and giving autonomy in spiritual and administrative matters to the local, city-wide congregations. Kuyper called on several sources in support of his city congregation church. According to Calvin, the congregation was the basic unit of the church, and therefore "each local Congregation should be recognized as a Church."[80] Calvin had permitted synods or councils only in certain circumstances. "A united church (*eenheidkerk*) is a Romish idea... A confederacy of free churches is the idea that flows from the deepest life-idea of the Reformed church."[81] So the various higher church courts above the congregation (i.e., the classical board, the provincial board, and the synod) were all voluntary gatherings. They might advise local congregations on various matters, but they wielded no binding power.

Besides Calvin, Kuyper's congregationalism was inspired by his localism in politics and his idealistic vision of America. Kuyper feared the massiveness of the nation-state, which he believed destroyed the intervening structures of civil society like family and church: "Think of Italy; think of Germany; think of the panSlavicism." (Italy was finally unified in 1870 with the annexing of Rome. In 1871 Kaiser Wilhelm and Otto von Bismarck declared a German Empire.) A choice was set before the Dutch church: "Following that double movement, the national church must split itself into smaller free churches or drive towards an all encompassing mass. America or Rome!"[82] This comparison of the synodical hierarchy to the Roman Catholic hierarchy also tempted Kuyper to accuse the Dutch church of "clericalism."[83]

One way Kuyper tried to deal with the contemporary pluralism in the Netherlands Reformed Church was to propose a parish system within the congregation. Recognizing that within large congregations like his at Amsterdam there was a great deal of difference between various ministers and among the laity, he allowed that the citywide congregation might be further broken down into parishes. Each parish, then, might choose a minister that suited its theological tastes.[84]

The flip side of the separation of church and state was the freedom of conscience, and Kuyper viewed it as at once a theological principle, a practical necessity, and the inevitable conclusion for the church in the modern day. The church was the construction not of the state but of freely consenting believers.[85] Theologically, freedom of conscience was based on the freedom of the Spirit to work where it would.[86]

Kuyper believed that the Netherlands Reformed Church stood to benefit greatly from a shift from a state sponsored church to one arising from the voluntary participation of the members. Kuyper compared the Amsterdam congregation of the Nederlandse Hervormde Kerk (NHK) with the Christian Reformed Church (CGK), the secession church of 1834. The Amsterdam congregation of the NHK counted almost one hundred forty thousand members, while the whole CGK church totaled about one hundred thousand, which was forty thousand less than Kuyper's own Amsterdam congregation. He estimated that since 1834 (the year of the secession of the CGK from the NHK) his Amsterdam congregation had received almost eight million Guilders in state subsidy, yet the entire CGK had not gotten a cent. What did the NHK have to show for it? The Amsterdam congregation had fourteen buildings and twenty-seven pastors. The CGK, on the other hand, had two hundred buildings and two hundred and twenty pastors—with nothing but the free will gifts of its members! Kuyper went on for half a dozen pages with example after example of the deadening effects of state subsidy.[87]

Yet even if these arguments were unconvincing, Kuyper still foresaw that the days of the national church "are numbered...The movement of spirits is more powerful than our wishes....The [contemporary] mind (*denkwet*) demands a future in which either every church-community ceases or every spiritual circle finds a church according to the needs of the heart."[88] Either the national church would break up into free churches, or mysticism would win the day.

Tensions in the Free Church

Kuyper worked to bring the church's sacramental nature and well-defined external forms into harmony with the free-church qualities that he espoused with equal vigor, but this created tensions in his theology, only some of which he managed well. The occasional nature of his theology meant that he often dealt with these topics in separate treatises or sermons, and any disparity between them fully appeared only in retrospect. The tensions of his theology appeared in topics such as the role of doctrinal confessions, democratic church polity, and his experience with American revivalism, which Kuyper dealt with on an ad hoc basis.

The loose ends in Kuyper's ecclesiology were due only in part to their occasional nature, though. They also arose from the inherent difficulty of his position. From a theological perspective the church was a divine, sacramental reality, but sociologically it was a voluntary, and therefore human, organization. Dietrich Bonhoeffer highlighted that difficulty in his criticism of Ernst Troeltsch and Max Weber. The dilemma of a sociological description of the church, Bonhoeffer says, is that though it is true enough that the church is an empirical entity, it is also established by God, and therefore pure sociology could never account for the church's metaphysical reality.[89] In fact, Troeltsch's definition of the free church did countenance that tension. The free church, he says, was "outwardly" a voluntary association, yet "theologically" it was still an objective ecclesiastical institution.[90] The succinctness of this definition, however, passed too easily over the problem Bonhoeffer alerted us to. The precariousness of Kuyper's ecclesiology was located in the danger of sliding to one side (the institutionalism potentially arising from the sacramental nature of the church) or the other (a radical atomization and desacralization of the church arising from its voluntary nature). In other words, the difficulty of ecclesiological description arose equally from Kuyper's theological understanding of the church and from his social-political understanding, the two of which were distinct but not separate.

In very brief compass, Kuyper directly addressed the problem of ecclesiastical forms and freedom of conscience at least once, though his solution was unsatisfying. The forms, Kuyper said, should be chosen freely by believers, not imposed by an ecclesiastical bureaucracy. Once the false unity of the synod was broken, he assured,

> then the Church of Christ shall be free...to choose a definite form
> and confession and way of life, and yet the right of freedom would

remain for every man and woman not to participate in any form that did not satisfy the needs of the heart.[91]

The inadequacy of this response lay in its stunning optimism, if not naiveté, that the mass of laity could come to a satisfactory (i.e., Reformed) consensus on matters of doctrine and liturgy, when the relatively small synod of the trained and ordained could not. All that was needed, Kuyper promised, was the free preaching of the Word.[92] Incidentally, the naiveté was not Kuyper's alone. It was fueled by his reading of Alexis de Tocqueville's *Democracy in America*, a picture of boundless freedom and fervent religiosity that Kuyper took to be pure Calvinism.[93]

Elsewhere, Kuyper was more realistic about the problems of democratization for Reformed confessionalism. Jaroslav Pelikan explains that the demand for each person to decide their religious convictions for themselves, the "radical individualization of confession," created a "discomfort" with creedal statements in the nineteenth century.[94] Kuyper's ministerial colleague, J. J. van Toorenenbergen, offered one solution. He distinguished between the main points of the confessional statements and the subordinate points; he rejected the notion of an unchangeable confession; he distinguished between the letter of the confessions and the substance; and he argued that adherence to doctrinal standards meant adherence to their substance, not the letter, in one's heart.[95] Kuyper accepted this in part. The confession lived in the heart of the church as an organism, where it had no printed letter, but, he continued, "every expression of life of the church, and thus also her confession, bears a double character. She has a confession as organism, but also a confession *as institute*."[96] The institute had to have an agreed upon confession in definite public form.

Kuyper's conception of the church's doctrinal statements was akin to his constitutionalism in politics. The confessions stood as the church's authoritative interpretation of the Bible. Interpretation of Scripture was too weighty a matter to be left up to individuals, even individual theologians. That was the danger of individualism. When the ethical theologian J. H. Gunning concluded that parts of the Bible must be mythological, Kuyper said that this was an authority problem and therefore an ecclesiological problem. Specifically, the problem Gunning posed was not the demise of religious authority—"No one works outside of Authority"—but its democratization—"One lives out of his own caprice (*wilkeur*) or the arbitrary authority of one who forces himself on us." Kuyper warned that if biblical interpretation was taken from the church and given to individuals,

"even the first principles of religion are unscrewed and a Babylonian confusion ensues."[97] He believed in a close reading and a strict interpretation
of the confessions. They could be amended, but, failing that, ministers
had to subscribe wholeheartedly to every jot and tittle.

This appreciation for the authority of doctrinal statements did not,
however, diminish Kuyper's appreciation of democracy in church government. His first involvement in ecclesiastical politics, his 1867 tract, "What
Should We Do?" dealt precisely with the problem of ecclesiastical authority and the personal commitment of the laity. The issue was the democratization of church polity, a matter related to larger social trends. Since
its establishment by King William I, the Netherlands Reformed Church
essentially reflected the class structure of Dutch society, with the king at
the top and members of the upper strata in most positions of ecclesiastical
power. With the restructuring of the church in the wake of disestablishment came the opportunity for more democratic representation in church
bureaucracies. In 1867, per article 23 of the new church order, congregations had to decide whether they would retain for themselves the power
to choose church officers or leave it to the long-standing consistories that
heretofore had made these decisions.[98] Was the church a democracy? If
so, how could it also be a divine establishment?

Kuyper was caught between his resentment toward the patrician class
that dominated the church ("almost Jesus' whole entourage is from the petit
bourgeoisie [i.e., the lower middle class]," he protested[99]) and his loathing for
the principles of the French Revolution that grounded democracy in radical
human autonomy. There is "no other judgment possible but that the recep-
tion of article 23 must be ascribed to the after-effects of the non-churchly but
rather social influence of the modern concept of the state."[100] Kuyper had
to explain how democracy could be Christian and how it could be unlike
the French notion of popular sovereignty. Indeed, he believed that all true
democracy was Christian and true Christianity was democratic: "God's
Word shall only again be fully honored if people no longer separate the
divinely-joined ideas of Church and Democracy."[101] He distinguished, therefore, between popular sovereignty (*volkssouvereiniteit*) and Christian democracy. The difference was the basis from which sovereignty was derived: was
the sovereignty of the people derived from innate human autonomy or from
the Holy Spirit investing the people with authority? Kuyper argued that the
Holy Spirit dwells in the heart of every believer, and "therefore the *vox populi*
knows more and more to attune to the *vox Dei*."[102] So the church members were free to choose their own church officers based on their spiritual

qualifications. Kuyper believed this was the true ecclesiology of Calvin and a Lasco, but the 1816 arrangement had subverted it.

Democratic church polity was, besides theological conviction, a shrewd calculation in ecclesiastical politics. Inspired by his confrontation with Calvinistic pietists like Pietje Baltus, and in spite of other differences with them, Kuyper recognized that theologically he still had far more in common with the laity than with most of the ecclesiastical hierarchy. Kuyper's calculations turned out to be correct, and after democratic procedures were implemented, pulpits began to fill with orthodox preachers. More importantly for the Netherlands at large, democracy in the church paved the way for democracy in political society (not vice versa). Through church elections and their trappings—issue-based associations, platform-oriented parties, electoral colleges, and various other mechanisms—the Dutch people learned democracy and first gained a voice in society.[103]

In 1875, Hannah Whitehall and Robert Pearsall Smith, a pair of American evangelists who brought their message of new life to the old world, tested Kuyper's ecclesiology. The Smiths taught personal holiness and did not emphasize doctrine or denominational differences, the things that consumed Kuyper's mind in the early 1870s. Kuyper attended their meetings in Brighton, England, with a small band of pilgrims. "Brighton," Kuyper wrote, "was a Bethel for me," and he and his fellow pilgrims set about establishing local groups (apparently ignoring his own warnings against conventicles) and a periodical, *The Way to Godliness,* to further the Smiths' message in their native country.[104] Gunning objected, calling Kuyper back to corporate Calvinism. Gunning said that the Smiths' doctrine of a second conversion obscured the promises and obligations of baptism, but Kuyper interpreted things differently. Seventeenth-century Reformed scholastic Petrus van Mastricht had spoken of a subsequent sealing by the Holy Spirit that brings a deeper knowledge of the spiritual life. The Smiths' teachings echoed this older Reformed view. Still, Kuyper conceded, the revival movement suffered from "insufficient forms."[105] Although Kuyper did not specify which forms or how they were insufficient, it is not surprising that he should have disagreements with the Smiths, who came from a Quaker background, where neither the institutional church nor the sacraments ranked very highly.

The Smiths' doctrine was not accepted without critique. Kuyper and those working to bring spiritual revival from Brighton to the Netherlands corrected their doctrine of sanctification according to Reformed standards, affirming that sanctification was not a human achievement but a divine work.[106] Kuyper's series of articles on the "Mystical Body of Christ," which he wrote just weeks after returning from Brighton, might be taken as a correction to the Smiths' theology (though Kuyper did not mention them by name). In these articles, Kuyper stressed the corporate and churchly nature of Christianity—in obvious contrast to the Smiths' parachurch work—in both its hidden Mystical Body and the external forms. There was no life, he said, outside of the Mystical Body; members could not live disconnected from it. Further, the Mystical Body had to do with the external life of the church, not only the internal. "The confession of the Mystical Body of Christ is the foundation on which the external church rests.... [yet] only through the church do you come into contact with the Mystical Body of Christ and remain so." This union occurred preeminently in the Lord's Supper. There, according to the Reformed fathers, "the soul is taken up to heaven, to the place where Christ is to be fed with the power of his life."[107] This stress on participation in the church and sacraments countered the individualistic and moralistic elements of the Smiths' teaching.

Caretaker of the Nation: The Social Ethics of the Free Church

The dilemma of Kuyper's social ethics was what to do with the Dutch nation. In his earlier doctoral dissertation on a Lasco and Calvin, Kuyper was "not so much concerned with a revitalization of the church in general [i.e., across the world], but of the 'patria ecclesia' (the National Church: 'de Vaderlandse Kerk')," and in a Lasco, rather than Calvin, Kuyper found a model for a *Dutch* church.[108] Yet now Kuyper located the source of the spiritual laxity in the nature of the national church (*landskerk*). One belonged to this church by birth or custom; it was the church in its "most diluted form."[109] Should it be or not be the church of the Dutch nation?

Kuyper's free church was a mixture of the characteristics typical of the church and the sect, and that made the church's social role all the more difficult to explain. Separation of church and state and freedom of conscience typified the sect and coincided with its withdrawal from society, since that was necessary to preserve religious purity. The church, on the other hand, presumed a comprehensive approach to society and was able to do so because of its divine constitution, which did not depend on the purity of its human members. And yet Kuyper wanted a church of sincere believers and one with God-given ordinances. His criticisms of the taken-for-granted relationship between the Dutch church and the Dutch people (i.e., the nation, the *volk*) pushed in the direction of sectarianism. Yet Kuyper resisted breaking with the Netherlands Reformed Church—the logical sectarian move—and hoped instead to transform it wholly into the free church he envisioned. "Deep in the soul convinced of the blessing [of a free church]...I may not only wish it for myself but I must desire it for others also."[110] Such a church would remain the dominant Dutch religious institution. It would probably still contain more than half of the Dutch population and retain ties to influential social institutions like the university theology departments. The social challenge of Kuyper's ecclesiology was to mesh his sect-like emphasis on commitment with the comprehensive social role he imagined for the church. To do so, Kuyper's church would be the caretaker of the nation.[111]

Like his ecclesiological writings, Kuyper's social ethics were also occasional in nature during the 1870s and 1880s. He put forth various principles, but they were nowhere gathered into a single system like the later *Lectures on Calvinism*. The 1874 lecture "Calvinism: Source and Stronghold of Our Constitutional Liberties" is one of the clearest statements, though it differed from the *Lectures* in a distinctive way. In the *Lectures on Calvinism* Kuyper attributed the public, social role of religion to an idealistic Calvinist worldview; in "Source and Stronghold" he attributed it to the nation-nurturing and society-forming Calvinist church. Kuyper's main concern was the suffocating power of the modern centralized state. The church functioned as a mediating structure, securing freedom and sheltering the nation from overwhelming state power. As he had written a year earlier in *Confidentially*, whereas "the state according to its nature makes one stoop under the spirit of servitude," the church offers "space for the freedom of the spirit."[112]

The paradox of Kuyper's conception of the church's social role appeared in his notion of the Dutch nation as a Reformed nation. Kuyper distinguished between the Dutch nation (*volk*), a mythic group with a common history, language, values and even religion, and the state. "So for us not only the church, but the nation as a nation is Reformed,"[113] and he urged the Dutch Protestants to "be what you are by birth, by baptism, and by confession. Be Reformed."[114] Yet Kuyper consistently opposed the national church (*volkskerk*) settlement.

This seeming paradox was explained by the organic connection Kuyper posited between the Reformed church and the Dutch nation. After the separation of church and state, in place of institutional connection, an organic connection was commonly assumed between church and nation.[115] The Netherlands Reformed Church would be truly a Dutch church according to

J. Cramer, "when [the church] has grown together and continues to grow together with the life of the Dutch *volk*, when her existence not only coincides with the emergence of the Dutch *volk*, but also her life holds the same pace with our *volk*-life."[116] Kuyper was not explicit here, but it was clear that he did not agree with Cramer's approach to the national church. Instead, he spoke of a Reformed kernel or core of the nation, from which the rest of the nation also grew and prospered.[117] He could speak of Reformed particulars as having broad significance for forming the people,[118] and by analogy he described his Free University, an academic secession of sorts from the state universities, as nonetheless not only for the glory of God (a typical excuse for societal retreat) but also for the good of the nation.[119] It seems that the institutional church had to do directly with this kernel of the nation and only indirectly with the whole nation, which allowed him to speak of the Reformed character of the nation in a broad sense and the Reformed character of the church in a very narrow one. The obvious political payoff was that Kuyper's confessional Reformed group was portrayed as the most truly Dutch portion of the nation, while not denying that the nation as a whole was broadly Reformed and the better for it, and ecclesiastically it allowed Kuyper to shirk charges of Reformed sectarianism.[120]

The evidence for the Reformed church's role as caretaker came from history. Kuyper looked across the border at Bismark's Germany and decided that Lutheranism had done little for the cause of freedom.[121] Supported by authorities like American historian George Bancroft and Tocqueville, Kuyper believed the church's role as caretaker of the nation was a distinctive strength of the Calvinist church:[122]

> The Lutheran church, at least so far, has not done what the church of Calvin did: penetrate with its spirit the whole of the life of a people [*volkskeven*] in all its expressions, to such a degree that a new nationality was born. The Reformed church has established two nations: the republic of the United Netherlands and the United States of North America.[123]

He also believed it to be the duty of the church. Quite obviously conflating historical reality with his own ideals, Kuyper said of Cromwell's England:

> Theocracy remained, but in a different form. No longer was there a church in the state nor a state bound to the church. The church

of Christ was the point of departure. She was to make sure that the principles of justice and truth held sway in the hearts of the citizens, but the citizens in their everyday life found free organization in the state to be indispensable. Once the ideal of freedom had established itself in the bosom of the church, it inevitably sought civil rights in the domain of the state.[124]

True Christian theocracy ruled by the power of the freely preached Word over free consciences. Under the separation of church and state (originally Calvin's genius, Kuyper said), the church retained an indirect influence in government by its influence over the consciences of the people of government, if not over the institution of state.[125]

Tolerance

If Kuyper's writings on the church and social ethics were occasional, his views on religious tolerance were diffuse, yet a distinct pattern emerged as a direct consequence of his free-church ecclesiology. Troeltsch and, more recently, John Bolt agree that religious tolerance distinguished Kuyper's neo-Calvinism from traditional Calvinism, but neither venture a claim about the nature of this tolerance.[126] Given the previous outline of Kuyper's ecclesiology, a picture of the concept of tolerance at work in Kuyper's ecclesiology is now possible.

Although the Netherlands Reformed Church, like Kuyper, did not have an explicit or agreed upon statement on tolerance, there was a de facto policy operating in the church through the nineteenth century. The national church practiced a generous toleration of doctrinal views within its halls, indeed generous enough to potentially embrace the whole nation. But defending its primacy in Dutch society, the Netherlands Reformed Church worked to curtail freedom for other groups, as happened, for example, in the case of the Afscheiding churches in the 1830s (see chapter 1) or when the Roman Catholic Church finally received freedom to worship publicly and to install a bishop in the 1850s and Dutch Protestants erupted in protest. Even the Lutheran Johan Thorbecke, author of the constitutional separation of church and state, did not give up the ideal of a unified Christian society, only the ideal of one unified under the auspices of the Netherlands Reformed Church. The national church thus pursued a policy of a uniform society under the aegis of a tolerant church.[127]

Kuyper's view was exactly the opposite. The church should be narrowly confessional. Its Reformed confessions and Reformed liturgical formulas should be strictly interpreted and consistently applied. Where the synod removed explicit reference to the Reformed confessions and even Jesus Christ from the ministerial vows and permitted a variety of baptismal liturgies that did not include the Trinitarian formula, Kuyper remonstrated—insisting on complete conformity to the confessions and the Trinitarian liturgy. Dutch civil society, however, should permit a broad range of religious groups. In later years, such an approach led to Kuyper's scandalous (so said some) collaboration with Catholics in parliament.

Kuyper argued that, in fact, it was the present synodical system that was coercive, "a system of spiritual subjugation."[128] It presumed upon its members, took for granted their participation and consent, and forced religious communion on many who had deep religious differences. In his free church, sociologically a voluntary association, Kuyper expected that the ministers would subscribe to the Reformed confessions (the outward forms) by free (inner) choice.

Conclusion

In effect, the national church of Kuyper's day tried to continue, so far as possible, the church-type social settlement bequeathed to it from the middle ages and the Reformation era, but growing religious diversity and the separation of church and state made that a difficult endeavor. In market terms, the national church envisioned itself as a kind of public utility (to borrow the conclusion of Grace Davie and Peter Berger[129]), covering the whole nation and asking little by way of approval or active participation. Kuyper, in contrast, wanted the church to be a corporation, every member buying in and everyone having a stake in its success. The question was whether Kuyper could convince Dutch Protestants to buy shares in a utility, the free use of which they already enjoyed. It would be a hard sell.

4

A Believers' Church: Abraham Kuyper's Ecclesiology for Reformation

IN 1876, A new Dutch law provided the freedom to start new universities in the Netherlands. In 1880, Abraham Kuyper exercised this new right by founding the Free University of Amsterdam, an institution tied to his efforts to reform the Netherlands Reformed Church. Although it had greater aspirations, in the beginning the Free University was primarily a divinity school. The Netherlands Reformed Church, however, refused to accept into ministry anyone who had not studied at the state universities. In 1882 and again in 1885, then, the NHK upheld this decision, which meant that modernist candidates educated at state universities might enter the ministry of the church while orthodox Calvinist pupils from the Free University could not. This was a fact that, no doubt, rankled Kuyper. Historian Johannes Stellingwerff says, "Without the urgency of church reform no Free University would have existed."[1]

In 1886, Kuyper launched his new church, and together the new university and the new church were harbingers of the new age, the age that Charles Taylor calls the "Age of Mobilization"[2] (Figure 4.1). The distinctive features of Kuyper's university and church were their separation from other historic Dutch institutions and their reliance on the goodwill of their supporters and the ability of leaders like Kuyper to rally the faithful and organize them into an efficient movement. Kuyper's sacramental ecclesiology, however, was poorly fitted to that task. It taught a high view of the institutional church as a God-given institution and a means of grace, not one reliant on Kuyper's organizational skills and the will of the people. Kuyper needed an ecclesiology that provided for the more agile church that modern society demanded. The ecclesiology he developed would be a model for a believers' church.

Figure 4.1 Kuyper (in clerical collar) and Family, 1886, the year of Kuyper's secession from the Netherlands Reformed Church and the year that son Frederik Kuyper left to visit America. Collection Historisch Documentatiecentrum voor het Nederlands Protestantisme (1800-heden) VU University Amsterdam.

Besides the problem of getting his graduates ordained in the national church, Kuyper also suffered setbacks in his appeal for strict subscription to the Reformed confessions. In the church's membership vows, the synod replaced a confession of fidelity to Jesus Christ and the Reformed confessions with a declaration of loyalty to the Netherlands Reformed Church "so that even mention of the gospel of Jesus Christ was wholly removed."[3] Further, congregations were allowed to inquire not into a potential member's personal religious beliefs but only into their behavior when judging their qualifications for membership. In protesting these changes, Kuyper's Amsterdam consistory refused to accept several young, modernist members seeking full membership by way of public confession; it even refused to give them the certificates of good behavior necessary to transfer to another congregation unless they confessed Jesus Christ as Lord. The students took their case to the higher classical and provincial church boards. When the provincial board ordered the Amsterdam consistory to issue the requested certificates, the consistory appealed to the synod. Finally, in November 1885, the synod sided with the students and the provincial board.[4]

Kuyper and the Amsterdam consistory saw a conflict coming, and in anticipation they tried to secure their position by amending article 41 of the church order to place control of the church property in local consistorial hands. If it came to a break with the synod, the symbolic value of the New Church in Amsterdam would have demonstrated the legitimacy of Kuyper's party. For their actions, eighty members of the Amsterdam consistory were suspended by the classical board.[5] Disputes over church property were thereby tied to disputes over membership requirements, though Kuyper thought his opponents confused the issues. He argued that "by mixing the question of Faith with the question of administration [of property], you have pushed the more noble motive to the background."[6] While his opponents accused Kuyper of robbery, the actions of the classical board seemed to prove Kuyper right, that the real issue was the certificate question and not church property. For after the classical board suspended the eighty members of the Amsterdam consistory on January 4 for violating church property rules, it immediately moved to issue membership certificates to the modernists in question.[7] But that was not the only action the classical board took.

To enforce disciplinary measures against the Amsterdam consistory, the president of the classical board, A. J. Westhoff, went to the New Church in Amsterdam and locked the doors. Then he changed the locks, reinforced the door with steel plates, and, just in case, posted a guard. Nonetheless, he underestimated Kuyper. When Kuyper and jurist F. L. Rutgers arrived at the church on January 6, they got into the church with the help of a carpenter and a crowbar. Getting into the church, however, was perhaps the least of their worries at that point. By then Kuyper's ouster from the national church and the formation of a new church were all but inevitable.

Kuyper was prepared for that, too. Through his theological reflections on ecclesiology he had already been laying the foundation for a new church. In 1883, he offered a set of ecclesiological principles for reforming the church in his *Tract on the Reformation of the* Churches,[8] and not just for reforming the church but leaving it and forming a new one. Here and elsewhere, Kuyper explained how and why one might break with a corrupt church, an argument that pivoted on the precise relation between the church as organism and as institution, which Kuyper now retooled.

Kuyper's earlier sacramental ecclesiology had placed a high value on the institutional church and made it difficult to explain how anyone could leave the church. To leave the Netherlands Reformed Church, Kuyper needed to delegitimize it, and that required deemphasizing the church's institutional presence. This chapter begins by examining the two changes Kuyper made to his ecclesiology, particularly in his understanding of the organism and institution. These placed greater importance on the organism and the believers themselves, making the institution more plastic. With these adjustments, Kuyper transformed his sacramental church into a believers' church, a church defined primarily by the subjective participation of believers rather than objective structures.[9] Yet he consistently maintained the irreducibly social and corporate nature of the church; it was a believers' church, constituted by the plural, not a believer's church, that is, a collection of singular individuals.

Kuyper developed this ecclesiology as part of the larger ecclesiological program that this chapter next examines. Kuyper's believers' church debuted in his instructions for breaking with the old church and building a new one. Surprisingly, the believers' church model later provided the basis for Kuyper's arguments for union between his breakaway church, the Doleantie, and the Christian Reformed Church, the secession church of the 1834 Afscheiding. The believers' church was not without its challenges, however, which were most obvious in Kuyper's inability to forge a plausible theology of ecclesiastical office and the increasingly obvious need for a new account of the church's social role.

Organism and Institute Revisited and Revised

In response to the crisis over membership and Christian confession, Kuyper and his orthodox constituency gathered in 1883 to make plans. The gathering, called the Broederkring ("circle of brothers"), required that all members subscribe completely to the threefold Reformed confessions (Belgic Confession, Heidelberg Catechism, and Canons of Dort), a move meant to exclude not only modernists but also theological moderates like the Reveil followers. Members of the Broederkring pledged to uphold the Reformed confessions against the new regulations from the synod, to maintain the preeminence of Jesus Christ in the face of church structures that would not, and to break with them if necessary.[10] Conflict was unavoidable if these membership vows were taken seriously.

Out of these meetings of the Broederkring came Kuyper's *Tract on the Reformation of the Churches*, but it was not really a tract at all. Kuyper published it in celebration of the four hundredth anniversary of Martin Luther's birthday (1883) with no confusion about who he thought Luther's successor to be. It included sixty-five chapters totaling over two hundred pages, and Kuyper regarded it as a definitive statement of his ecclesiology.[11] When the *Tract* first appeared, Kuyper refused to answer critical reviews, because "such a work as the *Tract of the Reformation* is not dashed off but the result of ten years of wrestling and thinking"—as if to say that he would consider the criticisms of real challengers but not those of dilettantes and dabblers.[12]

Kuyper viewed the *Tract* as a unique venture because of its topic and treatment. It was divided according not to any traditional arrangement of ecclesiological themes (e.g., unity, holiness, catholicity, and apostolicity) but to the stages of the church's life: (1) first principles of ecclesiology; (2) the formation of the church; (3) the deformation of the church; and (4) the reformation of the church. Besides an ecclesiology, it was a theory of church history and development arranged around the theme of reformation. This was all the more necessary, said Kuyper, because—oddly—no Reformed theologian had ever explained just what reformation was.[13]

The *Tract* turned on Kuyper's distinction between the church as organism and the church as institution, though he introduced two new features of the organism and institution that had not characterized his earlier formulations. By means of these, he was able explain the unity and diversity of the church in such a way that opened the possibility of reforming the church. The first novel concept was the visible organism. Typically, in the nineteenth century, the church as an organic body was a common metaphor for the ideal fellowship of Christian believers. It described the corporate and social nature of the church and so distinguished the church from a collection of parts like a machine or a gathering of individuals who came together only after their separate spiritual experiences. Organic metaphors focused on the inner essence of the church to explain continuity and change, which was much more difficult to do with the church's external forms. Friedrich Schleiermacher, for example, described the church as organism and associated this organism with the invisible, spiritual fellowship of believers, in contrast to ecclesiologies that stressed the church as an institution.[14] Kuyper's original contribution to the ubiquitous organicist ecclesiologies of his day had been to bring the institution and organism together as equally essential aspects of the church (i.e., in his sacramental ecclesiology). Now, in the

Tract, he introduced a middle term between the church as organism and church as institute: the *visible* organic church.

In the *Tract*, Kuyper explained that there are several ways to conceive of the church, the church in the mind of God, the church in glory, and the church hidden in Christ, for example. But these were all ideal perspectives on the church, he thought. Kuyper was concerned instead with the visible church on earth because only the church so considered ever became deformed and hence was ever in need of reformation. In his account of reformation, Kuyper premised that this visible church on Earth might exist in two forms: first, as an institution; and second, as a preinstitutional and extrainstitutional gathering of believers existing in organic connection.

Two scholars have examined the development of Kuyper's organism–institution ecclesiology. Jasper Vree says that after the sermon "Rooted and Grounded (1870)," Kuyper "let the distinction rest" until his *Encyclopedia* of 1893–1894.[15] While Kuyper may not have reflected explicitly on the relation of the organism to the institution until the 1890s, the organism and institution framework consistently structured his ecclesiology. There is no shortage of references to the church as organism and its organic qualities in the *Tract*, for instance, or to the church's institutional forms such as confessions, office, and sacraments. There is also debate over Kuyper's first reference to the visible organism. Vree says that Kuyper first distinguished the visible organic church from the invisible organism—the "extraCuperisticum," Vree calls it—in his *Encyclopedia*. Analogous to Calvinist belief that the Son of God was incarnate in Jesus Christ yet not bound to his incarnate body, the "extraCalvinisticum," Kuyper taught that the visible organic church existed as an institution but was not bound in its visible appearance to the institution. P. A. van Leeuwen dates the term *visible organic church* even earlier to a series of articles from 1887, just after Kuyper's actual break with the national church.[16] Vree and van Leeuwen, however, focus too narrowly on the precise term visible organic church. Although it may not have appeared until 1887, the concept of the visible organism was present earlier, at least as early as the *Tract*, where it enabled Kuyper to explain how believers could move from one institution to another or, if need be, form a new institution altogether.

The essence of the church, Kuyper said, is always the invisible, organic union of the elect. Yet this essence may further be considered both according to its ability (*potentia*) to form an institution or its actual functioning (*actu*) as an institution. Here Kuyper spoke not of an ideal, organic body but of a concrete gathering of believers with two possible modes of relation to the church institution, potential and act:

> A gathering possesses the essence of the church even though it may lack every office, because it continues to have *the ability* to establish office. According to this *ability*, or as some said in olden times, reckoned according to *potential*, nothing else is necessary for the essence of the church except the gathering of believers in Christ, because this gathering has in itself the ability to establish and use the office and the means of grace. On the other hand, according to its *operation*, or *act*, as men used to say, the office as well as the means of grace cannot be separated from the essence of the church. And whereas the essence almost always appears actively (*actu*) in the visible church, our fathers have correctly placed the essence of the church in 'the gathering of the believers.'[17]

The gathering of believers, apart from the formation office (office, Kuyper said, was the first manifestation of the institution), is a manifestation of the essence of the church, albeit according to its potential to form the institution not necessarily the actual operation of the institution. This visible gathering of the essence of the church is the same as the visible organism. The same premise operated in the concise list of the main points of his ecclesiology published a year later. He said, "Christ reveals the presence of his church already in this circle of persons (appearing in the *organic connection* that they claim to have from the *Corpus Christi*) and *not* first through the appearance of *office*."[18] In his 1892 dogmatic lectures on the *Locus de Ecclesia*, Kuyper clarified the difference between the visible organism and the institution as a difference between the appearance of the church (*apparatio*) and the institution (*institutio*) of the church. Following Gisbert Voet, the appearance, not the institution, was the first visible form of the organism of the church.[19]

Indispensible to this gathering of believers was the will to form a church. The essence of the church lay in the living members of the organism, not in the means of grace, although the means of grace certainly nourish the organism. The essence was present in a given village or city, when the elect members of the body of Christ were there, yet this essence came to conscious expression only when believers gathered with the intent of bringing this communion to fuller expression in the formation of the institution. This formulation also enabled Kuyper to distinguish the church from other religious societies. Other voluntary religious associations were not the church, although members of the body of Christ (the essence) may be present "because the mind and will is lacking to manifest ecclesiastical formation."[20] Therefore, church institution depended on the commitment of believers, and Kuyper denied any possibility that it could be propped up by external supports.

This new concept of the visible organic church coincided with a new understanding of the relationship of the organism and institution: the institution was a necessary but contingent part of the church. The point of Kuyper's earlier sacramental ecclesiology against the modernists, who often rejected all external forms of the church, and against ethical theologians like D. Chantepie de la Saussaye or J. H. Gunning, who accepted the institution as only a historically contingent form, had been that the institution, in well-defined forms, was an essential aspect of the church.[21] The church is organism and institution. The organism lived through the institution as the soul lived through the body.[22] The organism without the institution was like a river without banks: "the flow of the Christian life must be able to surge but nonetheless she should remain *the church*, because the current dies away in the flat fields if you demolish its banks."[23] With the advent of the visible organism, however, the church could exist in some form, even a visible form, without the institution, and therefore salvation was not necessarily tied to the institution.

The institution was necessary but not essential to the church. In technical terms, the institution belonged not to the being or essence of the church (*wezen* or *esse*) but to the well-being of the church (*welwezen* or *bene esse*). Hence, "the development and possession of office belongs to the well-being (*bene esse*) [of the visible church], confessing and the gathering of persons to the being (*esse*) of the visible church."[24] It followed that the organism, not the institution, was the true church: "the Church consisted not in office, nor in an independent institute, the believers themselves were the church."[25] In the more precise formulation of his *Locus de Ecclesia* Kuyper explained that the institution was a necessary but "contingent" part of the church since the organism always led to the formation of an institution, though the institution was not of the essence of the church.[26]

One of the most common and successful metaphors for explaining continuity and difference in the development of Christianity is the metaphor of the body and spirit.[27] Kuyper's sacramental ecclesiology resembled this spirit–body paradigm. The church was like a person who is both inner spirit and an outer body. The institution, like the body, was part of the church's life, even if the spirit was the deeper, animating force. Kuyper's later believers' church ecclesiology, however, no longer fit this paradigm. Here the institution was comparable to the clothes that one put on the body, not to the body itself. Certainly clothes were necessary for life, but they were not an essential part of the person. Clothes belong rather to the person's well-being, and they can be changed when they wear out. Likewise, the institution was part of the church's well-being, not its being. One could not say the church is the institution any more than one could say the clothes are the person. Only the organism is the church. When the church's institutional "clothing" failed to serve its intended purpose, when it constricted or retarded movement, these garments could be exchanged for new ones.

The difference between Kuyper's earlier and later positions was similar to the differences between R. C. Moberly and J. B. Lightfoot, two nineteenth-century Anglican theologians who also wrestled with the modern church problem. Moberly argued that the outward form of the church was an essential part of the church and a necessary mediator between the inner spiritual life of the church and God. In Lightfoot's view the inward, spiritual reality was essentially necessary for the outward, but the outward was only conventionally necessary for the inward. Moberly charged Lightfoot with downgrading the importance of the outward forms, denying that they were part of the essence of the gospel and affirming that the soul had immediate communion with God. Moberly used the spirit–body metaphor to argue, on the contrary, that the church, like a human, is a spirit in and through the body, whereas Lightfoot's view resembled the body–clothing model.[28] Clothing is necessary for the body, but it is not the body. Analogously, the institution is necessary for the church, but it is not the church. The shift from Kuyper's earlier sacramental ecclesiology to his later position was comparable to a shift from Moberly's position to Lightfoot's.

This new understanding of the organism and institution allowed Kuyper to avoid two wrong positions, as he understood them: the mystics and the synodical party (i.e., those who remained under the synod of the Netherlands Reformed Church). By acknowledging the necessity of the institution, Kuyper maintained his polemic against those who wished to abolish all churchly ceremony[29] while describing the institution as contingent helped him justify breaking with the Netherlands Reformed Church by providing a measure of institutional flexibility. In retrospect, Kuyper said that the key difference between himself and those who remained in the Netherlands Reformed Church was his notion that the visible church could appear apart from institutional form.[30] Whatever that said about the theology of the Netherlands Reformed Church, it said a lot about the significance of the doctrine of the visible organism as part of Kuyper's justification for breaking with the Netherlands Reformed Church.

One of the main consequences of Kuyper's organism–institution ecclesiology was that the traditional ecclesiological notes of unity and catholicity were ascribed to the invisible organic church, which delegitimated any single institution as the one true church, but in particular challenged the national church as well as the Roman Catholic Church. "The spiritual and the organic unity of all God's children through the whole of the land is always undamaged and inviolable lying in the *Corpus Christi*, but the attempt to express this spiritual unity also *institutionally* in the visible church is always faulty."[31] Such a point excluded the Roman Catholic notion that a single institution could ever comprehend the complete unity of the Christian church in all its multiformity through history. Against the national church's attempt to comprehend the whole nation in a single church institution, Kuyper argued that since Pentecost, the church was not limited to a single nation but had become a world church. The universality of the New Testament Church could not be comprehended by looking at any one particular church institution but only by considering the organism behind all churches.[32]

A Time to Refrain from Embracing: A Theology for Leaving the Church

The *Tract* provided a theology for the Reformation of the Church, explaining how and under what circumstances the church could be reformed. This theology depended upon Kuyper's new notions of the gathering of believers as the visible organism distinct from the church as institution and his view of the institution as a contingent entity, not an essential part of the church. These principles provided for the possibility of the deformation of the institution as well as for the spontaneous formation of a new institution by believers.

The church, Kuyper explained, could be viewed from several perspectives. There was the church considered ideally in the mind of God, the church as hidden in Christ, the church realized on Earth, and the church in its final glory. The subject of the *Tract* was the Reformation of the church, and since only the church considered according to its existence on earth could be ever deformed, the main subject of the *Tract* was the church in its earthly existence.[33]

Kuyper's basic point was simple: the institution comes from the organism and not the other way around. This amended his earlier claim that there was a reciprocal relationship between the organism and institution.[34] Now the direction of influence went one way, from organism to institution. When believers gathered such that the organism of the church became visible, then they could form the institution of the church with its offices, means of grace, and forms of discipline.

The role of the human and the divine was a difficult matter because Kuyper wanted to maintain both. He was unequivocal that God alone established the organic church through election, but in the formation of the institutional church God and humanity both had a role. To ask whether Kuyper's understanding of institution was voluntary may prejudice the answer. That was Dietrich Bonhoeffer's caution to Ernst Troeltsch.[35] The institution might be a product of both human and divine will. Kuyper explained this conjoint work of the human and divine through a concept of instrumentalism whereby God "bound himself" to the visible means of the church and wherein human agents were "instruments" of divine work, instruments but not inanimate tools.[36] God gave instructions for forming the church in his Word, and he implanted in believers the impulse to form a church. Therefore, Kuyper said that the church "was formed principally by God himself and only instrumentally by believers."[37] This instrumental ecclesiology allowed Kuyper to distinguish the institutional church from other gatherings of believers, which organized themselves according to their own interests and their own power.

This instrumentalist concept empowered believers to form their own churches, and it emphasized freedom of conscience and the autonomy of believers over institutions. Kuyper insisted that the essence of the church was not in the institution or the means of grace but the believers themselves. Consequently, the power to form a visible church lay with the members of the body of Christ.[38] On the question of unity between different congregations in the same locale, freedom of conscience reigned. Congregations may join only if they have the same confession.[39] Similarly, common conviction held the members of the congregation together: "the church remains the gathering which has, in her spiritual root, a bond in Christ, but in her visible manifestation, she has no other bond than one of mutual agreement."[40] In this instrumentalist, account divine power worked through the believers themselves as God's instruments but not through the institution. Later in his *Lectures on Calvinism*, Kuyper carried this principle to its logical end, arguing that true religion (i.e., the religion of Calvin) is immediate between humanity and God and is not mediated in any sense by the institutional church.[41]

The concept of the church as a visible, preinstitutional, and extrainstitutional gathering of believers, which Kuyper would later call the visible organic church, was a basic principle of this account of the formation of the institution. The establishment of office was the first manifestation of the institutional church. Office could be established either "from without," when officers from other churches helped in the formation of a church, or "from within," when believers, apart from other institutions, freely gathered and of their own accord instituted office.[42] Such a gathering of believers already possessed the essence of the church, even before any office operated, as long as there was the intention to establish office and the institution.[43] The gathering of believers in which the essence of the church was present apart from institutional structures made it possible for believers who had left one institution to form their own church according to the dictates of conscience.

Kuyper also spoke of the organic church as the church considered according to its potential, and the institutional church as the church considered according to its act. When believers gathered together as the organism, there was the potential to form an institution, yet the institution did not exist necessarily by virtue of the gathering of believers; the institution depended on their willingness to form an institution. This explained how the organism could be visible yet apart from a church institution It also enabled Kuyper to distinguish the institutional church from other types of religious associations, since such associations were not churches, "not because no living members of Christ are included in these groups, nor because men do not attempt to exercise the fellowship of the saints in these groups, but because the mind and the will is lacking to manifest ecclesiastical formation when that becomes possible."[44] Every gathering of believers did not constitute a church institution, and in fact, it may constitute something else, a Christian political party or school, for example. Later this became a pillar in his Calvinistic social theory (see chapter 7), but here it was crucial for the reformation of the church because it gave believers the power to form an institution according to what they considered to be right and without the permission of a higher ecclesiastical body.

When believers did gather to form an institution, it was always, first of all, a local congregation. God providentially divided humanity by regional differences like towns and lands and ethnic idiosyncrasies like language, and the church reflected these local identities. On the basis of this divine providence, the local or city congregation formed the primary unit of the church. The congregation contained the essence of the church the way a cell contained the "outline" of the whole body yet without being the whole body.[45] Of course, an individual congregation did not contain the full organic church (i.e., the complete Mystical Body of Christ), but because it contained a part of the organism the local congregation had a legitimate claim to be *a* church without claiming to be *the* catholic church. Therefore, local congregations did not have to be part of a larger church body, like the Netherlands Reformed Church, to be fully a church.

In addition to God's providence, which divided people according to cities and towns, Scripture also provided the norm for Kuyper's congregational polity, though not as a rule book or textbook of ecclesiology. It was not what the apostles said but what they did that was normative, and now the church could not build except as that apostolic foundation would bear:

> Indeed, the potter can make out of the lump of clay a bowl or a jug or a vase according to his free choice just as it pleases him; but when the form, e.g. of the bowl, is once chosen and when the form of the bowl is impressed on the clay, then all further preparation of the bowl is bound to a fixed basic form.[46]

That scriptural example was the city congregation, congregations in places like Corinth, Ephesus, and Jerusalem, which were fully churches in their own right, not just parts of the church. "One will never find in the writings of the apostles even a trace of the idea that the apostles considered the merging of local congregations into a national unity a condition for the retention and essence of the church."[47] The biblical example and providence pointed away from the national church toward a more locally autonomous form of church.

That did not, however, lead to an antiecumenical theology. The underlying organic unity of the church also formed the basis for connectionalism between congregations. On the basis of shared membership in the larger organic church, local congregations could, even should, form bonds or federations with other local churches. Membership in these federations was strictly free and, again, voluntary—just as membership in any church was.

"Broader bonds of churches can never be anything else than temporal or extremely loose and elastic."[48] So just as voluntary action was the basis for forming interchurch bonds, it was also the basis for dissolving them. Ideally, churches of the same confessional basis should join, and there should not be two separate churches under the same confession in one city. Under the NHK synod, Kuyper had been frustrated in being forced ("coerced," he said) by a synod with which he had little agreement and in being bound in ecclesiastical union with modernists with whom he shared almost nothing. A voluntary federation in place of the synod would prevent just such a situation.

That the church institution could be formed and reformed implied that it could likewise be deformed. Deformation differed from other possible imperfections in the church because it assumed that the form of the church had been corrupted. The institution had once achieved a higher state but had since declined. Various kinds of churches such as mission churches or persecuted churches might lack the elements of a well-formed church yet without having somehow become deformed. They were, rather, "imperfectly formed," by which Kuyper meant that these churches were not yet perfectly formed, though they were not deformed in any sense that implied culpability.[49] Even the church of the apostles was not perfectly formed, though of course it was not deformed.

Deform was different; it implied decay and willful corruption. Imperfect formation "was never considered deformation, either in the first or the sixteenth century, because deformation, disfigurement, corruption, degeneration always supposes that the form or nature was first good but since then has suffered and decayed."[50] Deformation was specifically a move from a higher to a lower state. This perspective underlay Kuyper's accusation of his chief ecclesiastical rivals, the *irenicals*.

To these opponents such as J. Cramer and J. H. Gunning, Kuyper's exclusivity had been more troubling than his actual theological convictions. To them, Kuyper was a party man, while Cramer's and Gunning's allegiance was to the whole church, not a specific faction.[51] They worked to hold the NHK together, and Kuyper seemed to be tearing it apart. Kuyper, for his part, termed them irenicals, a reproach for their peace-at-all costs posture. According to Kuyper's definition of the deformation of the church, far worse than imperfection, error, or sin in the church—all which were to be expected—was the toleration of imperfection, error, or sin:

The church in her visible manifestation comes under the obligation of reformation only when deviation sinks *beneath this normal standard*, not only by bringing the unholy into herself, but by tolerating it through *remaining silent* and *failing to punish it*; or worse yet, through giving power and mastery over truth and holiness to lies and sacrilege.[52]

Whereas the irenicals accused Kuyper of lacking self-control, of rashness and crazed excitement,[53] he charged them with silence and inaction. Abraham Kuyper could find something acceptable in virtually all of his rivals—liberals, socialists, or Catholics—but he never had any kind words for the indifference he perceived in the irenicals.[54] Consequently, when a break with the church finally did come, Kuyper explained that the dispute was "not as has been heard, between the Confessors [i.e., Kuyper's party] and the Deniers [i.e., modernist theologians] of the Lord Jesus Christ, but *between the Confessors themselves*, and we have not sought that conflict, but you, *Irenicals*, have wanted it."[55] The account of deformation as the tolerance of error supported this accusation.

Just as the formation of the church begins with the inner organism and moves outward, so also deformation begins in the organism and moves outward to the institution. Deformation begins when faith loses its animation:

> The church becomes less receptive, less intimate, less spiritual, and presently others see that the inner fellowship of the Holy Spirit, and by this the inner life of love with the Bridegroom, begins to fade from the heart of the bride. Then really the deformation of the church has already happened, even though it is not yet manifest.[56]

Worldliness is one of the main sources behind the deadening of the organism's faith. The church feels pressure from the world, begins to be ashamed of its Christian way of life, and finally excuses itself rather than condemning the world. Eventually, deformation spreads from the members of the body to the officers, and then from the officers into the forms of the church, doctrine, and worship. Indeed, the institution could not exist without the healthy spiritual life of the organism, even though it may do many good deeds. "A church without any sincere members, consisting only of members each of whom is adorned with civil virtues, but is far away from faith in the Lord Jesus, would not only not form a good church, but would form no church at all."[57]

The nature and degree of deformation in the organism determined the kind of deformation suffered by the institution. Without the vitality of the organism, the institution was merely a sham church, or worse, a false church.[58] A sham church might exist by shear institutional inertia—a distinct possibility where the church lived by state support rather than free offerings:

> Such sham churches one finds, for example, in our East Indies colonies where governmental authority and state money keeps the churches standing. One finds them in North Brabant where they, artificially cultivated, can never shoot out roots, but by means of state salaries remain hanging like a withered flower on a nearby supporting stick.[59]

Worse still was the false church, which actually served the antichrist.

The Roman Catholic Church was a particularly difficult case to explain on this point. This was true for several reasons: first, because the Protestant churches had come out of the Roman Catholic Church, and no living organism could come out of a dead one; next, because Kuyper, following the pattern of the Synod of Dort, accepted the validity of Roman Catholic baptism; and finally, we may surmise, because Kuyper did not want to alienate Roman Catholics completely since he needed their support in various political matters. Kuyper decided that the Roman Catholic Church was only "partly false." "There was very positively an antichristian power in her church organism," but it had not yet consumed the entire organism.[60]

When the church had become deformed, there were several possible courses of reformation, depending on the nature and extent of the deformation. The least invasive form of reformation was spiritual revival or awakening, which was necessary when the spiritual life of the church grew faint though it retained the pure outward forms. If, however, corruption penetrated the institution as well as the spiritual life, a more drastic reformation was called for, the "medicinal" course. The aim of this type of reformation was to repair church structures and renew spiritual life through normal processes of ecclesiastical discipline or juridical processes.[61] In very extreme cases, when "the extermination of deviance and the restoration of the honor of God's Word was permanently impossible by the pastors of the church," still more drastic measures were required.[62] This surgical method was reformation in the strictest sense, the type of reformation pursued by Luther and Calvin. In every case, whether deformation affected the organism or both the organism and the institution, reformation had to begin with spiritual awakening, since "what is from the outside to the inside produces only an appearance of life; what endures is not worked in any other way than out of the Spirit."[63]

The looming question, however, was whether Kuyper and his group would or should leave the Netherlands Reformed Church, so he gave the most attention to the third and most severe type of reformation, which entailed a break with the existing structures. This kind of reformation presupposed either a sham church or a false church, and it might take several forms, again depending on the nature and extent of the deformation. The less severe form of reformation, which was temporary and aimed to reform church structures without actually forming a new church, Kuyper called *doleantie* or *grieving churches,* the colloquial name that his secession churches adopted for themselves.[64] Then there was reformation that was permanent and that did result in the formation of a new congregation beside the old.[65] This was separation, not *doleantie,* because *doleantie* was not a thoroughgoing institutional break. The difference between separation and *doleantie* was like the difference between a divorce and a temporary separation between husband and wife. In the case of *doleantie,* the goal was to restore the old church; in the case of separation that had become impossible.

The autonomy and continuity of the organism and institution of the city congregation was decisive for determining what kind of reformation was necessary. The congregation could be reformed by reformulating its organizational structure (i.e., the institution)[66] or by breaking its connections with other churches.[67] In both of these cases, the continuity of the congregation, the local gathering of believers was preserved. In neither case did believers face the question of whether their own church was a false church, since reform concerned only the outer organization or the connection with churches besides one's own, none of which were essential to the church. But in the most egregious circumstances, a break within the congregation could occur, leading to two distinct congregations with two distinct institutions.[68] In such a case, the question was not only whether the well-being of the church had been lost, the *bene esse* of which the institution was part, but also whether the *esse* or being of the church had been lost.[69] Kuyper, it seemed, had thought of every possibility, no doubt to persuade his readers that they had a multitude of options.

Finally, various types of false reformation had to be identified and avoided. Kuyper deemed the type of revivalism purveyed by Robert Pearsall Smith and Dwight Moody a false kind of reformation because it "dodged the ecclesiastical channels," it "adulterated doctrine," by which Kuyper surely thought of Smith's holiness theology, and it "sought power in over-stimulating gimmicks."[70] The last charge resembled John Williamson Nevin's critique of the anxious bench, for Nevin had experienced the ephemeral benefits of American revivalism and judged it wanting.[71] Like Nevin, Kuyper was initially smitten with revivalism. He returned from his trip to hear revivalist Smith in Brighton, England (1875), enthusiastic about promoting Smith's teaching and methods as a way to rejuvenate the national church. After several months, however, Kuyper suffered a serious personal breakdown, likely brought on by the stress of the perfectionistic quest to which Smith's teachings had inspired Kuyper.[72] Thereafter, Kuyper knew firsthand how detrimentally overstimulating false revivalism could be.

Reformation also differed from ecclesiastical "revolution." In fact, there were two types of revolution: good and bad. The illicit kind of revolution was that where human authority supplanted divine. It was the revolution in France.[73] Yet Kuyper later asked, "Is revolution always a sin?" Not when William of Orange revolted against Spain. Whether revolution was right or wrong, therefore, depended on one's "measuring stick." Fidelity to the king compels one to revolution against an unfaithful governor. "Revolution!? O very certainly! Revolution in the church of Christ against every authority renouncing Christ, reviling his majesty, and departing from his Word!"[74]

Narrating the Reformation

History and tradition are typically associated with churchly communities that stress the external and objective features of Christianity, since history and tradition are themselves things open to public view. Though they can be internalized, one encounters them as part of the exterior of religious life. Therefore, a strong emphasis on history and tradition often means an equally strong emphasis on the institutional structures that do the handing down. Abraham Kuyper, who broke with the institutional carriers of tradition but who valued history and tradition nonetheless, was in a precarious situation, having to explain how his breakaway church could be the legitimate successor of the sixteenth-century "Great Reformation" and heir of the Dutch church tradition. This was as much a historiographical problem as a theological one.

As well as providing a theology of church reformation, the *Tract* also defended reformation by placing Kuyper and his sympathizers within a much larger history. The formation–deformation–reformation framework was the superstructure that provided the shape and integrity of Kuyper's ecclesiology in the *Tract*, while beneath it and running all through it was a narrative substructure. Through this narrative substructure Kuyper showed that the church could be reformed, indeed had been reformed even by the most drastic measures, yet retained continuity with the broader historic Christian church, in spite of any ruptures in the institution.

The nineteenth century was a century of significant advances in historical science. Roger Haight argues that a historical consciousness was one of the most important features of ecclesiology of the period, Protestant and Catholic.[75] In Kuyper's *Tract* one finds no explicit theory of historical development, yet it is the theme of the entire volume. The idea of the church as organism and institute included the inherent mutability of both institution and organism, but historic continuity, like unity and catholicity, belonged solely to the church as organism. The process of formation–deformation–reformation then provided a clear logic for historical development and for a coherent narrative of church history. Kuyper's model was one of *dynamic development*, and a rough comparison with other models offered in the nineteenth century highlights the particularity of this one.

Schleiermacher's concepts of theology and of the church produced a model of radical historical contingency. Dogmatics was a matter of reflection on historical religious experience, and the church was "a social phenomenon caught up in historical flux .... Theological studies in their entirety and as such are historical by reason of the historical career—the church as process—which is their datum."[76] The subject and the object of study were both historically contingent.

Far less sophisticated, but no less influential, was the historical model of Barton Stone and Alexander Campbell, also shared by Pentecostals. Stone, Campbell, and the Pentecostals sought very simply (at least in theory) to restore the apostolic church of the first century, which had been lost in the intervening eighteen hundred years.[77] If Schleiermacher offered radical historical contingency, the restorationism of the Stone–Campbell movement proposed radical biblical absolutism.

John Henry Newman offered yet another historical model, a developmental one. According to Newman, the church's definition of doctrine developed as an organic process, like the growth of a plant. History affected the church's understanding of doctrine, but history was not all-determinative as it was for Schleiermacher because the object of reflection, divine revelation, was constant. Further, the Roman Catholic Church was the infallible interpreter of revelation.[78] This all but assured that there would not be any retrogression in the church's development of doctrine, even if contingent historical circumstances affected its course. This was a model of constant development.

Kuyper's model was, like Newman's, a model of development, but a model of constant development dependent on an infallible interpreter would not do for a Protestant theologian, obviously. Kuyper's model portrayed the history of the church as a dynamic development. As an organism it grew, and as an institution it was built up. Jesus Christ, ruling the church through his Word in Scripture, was the eternal and infallible king of the church. The church, whose job it was to interpret the Word of the King, was not infallible—hence the periodic need for reformation. The distinction between Christ as Lord of the church and the officers as stewards corresponded to the transition in the Spirit's work in the church at Pentecost. Whereas before Pentecost the Spirit inspired the apostles and prophets in the production of an infallible Scripture, afterward the Spirit illumined the church to interpret Scripture. The church's understanding of the Word, contained preeminently in its confessions, was not a static set of concepts. The historical context forced the church to reevaluate and reapply old doctrines. For example, God occasionally sent heretics along to spur the church on in its understanding of the Word. There was a general progress in the church's understanding of doctrine, though the rate of progress was not constant but dynamic. It varied, moving in fits and spurts and even sometimes backward.

Kuyper was more than a logician. As a movement leader, he wanted to persuade the peoples' minds, but he also wanted to capture their imaginations and their hearts. Historical narrative was one of his most consistent and effective tools for capturing these. His accounts of Dutch resistance to Spanish oppression in the seventeenth century, for example, wove together past and present Calvinist pursuits of political liberty. John Bolt explores this mytho-poetic political imagination, by which Kuyper "effectively captured the political *imagination* of the Dutch *Gereformeerde volk* with powerful rhetoric, well-chosen biblical images, and national mythology, and in this way moved them to action."[79] Arie Molendijk adds that Kuyper's rhetoric helped form a group consciousness by distinguishing his Calvinist "us" from "them." A strong historical narrative for the church was also urgent for capturing the peoples' ecclesiastical imagination. Kuyper's opponents understood this as well: the "call upon history was advanced as an argument against the *Doleantie*."[80] Kuyper's historical narrative attempted the nearly impossible: to show that a break with the Netherlands Reformed Church was not an asterisk in Dutch Protestant history but indeed the main storyline.

The historical narrative Kuyper presented in the *Tract* and other polemical pieces surrounding the break with the NHK had a beginning, middle, and end or an introduction, crisis, and resolution. Kuyper traced the beginning of the story back through the sixteenth-century Reformation, through Christ and his apostles, right back to Adam. Since Old Testament times the history of the church had been a constant movement between decline and reform. Some reformations were of the spiritual awakening type that did not break with the church, such as when Moses destroyed the calf, or the ministries of the Judges or John the Baptist. Other reformations did split the church, such as the separation between Seth and Cain or the separation that came through Noah's flood. After biblical times, "the great councils which began in 325 with the Council of Nicea were all reformatory councils," and since then groups like the Waldensians and Hussites had carried out smaller reformations.[81]

The sixteenth century witnessed a variety of different kinds of reformations. The locus of continuity and discontinuity in Kuyper's model of dynamic development was the local congregation, in its dual aspects as organism and institution. In the example of the Dutch and Swiss churches during the sixteenth-century reformation, Kuyper claimed that no new church had been formed because the local congregations had remained intact. The outer, organizational form had been renewed and the ecclesiastical bonds with other churches had been broken, but new congregations had not been formed. In places like Italy or France, Protestants had in fact left their Roman Catholic congregations and formed Protestant ones and new churches had arisen, but not in the Netherlands. This set a critical precedent in the seventeenth century at the time of the Synod of Dort, when a group of *doleantie* churches was erected in protest to the Arminians, yet without leaving the church federation. Finally, the 1834 secession that resulted in the Christian Reformed Church (CGK) had been the most recent reformation in the Dutch church.[82]

The present crisis began in 1816, when King William I, with good Napoleonic precedent, created the Netherlands Reformed Church, the "national church," by bringing the church under power of the government. The king also transformed the Dutch church from one based on the autonomy of the local congregations to a top-down hierarchy. He did so before even asking the opinion of the churches.[83] This was illegal, said

Kuyper. The church order that had stood since the Synod of Dort (1619) was not followed, not even legally abolished. Yet this was not the first time that the church had been so constructed. "It was this second Hierarchy (presently in Synodical form) that like the first Hierarchy three centuries earlier, then in her Papal form, established human authority in the church and dared to shove the authority of the Lord to the side."[84]

Foisting a synodical hierarchy on the church was the "original sin" from which others proceeded.[85] Besides treason it also led to oppression, "the characteristic of all hierarchies."[86] Christian freedom found expression in the church in the office of believers, but the synodical hierarchy disempowered this office. Instead, the synod was a yoke on believers. Kuyper urged his people to embrace liberation and the casting off of the yoke of oppression. That could be achieved through reformation of the church alone, for freedom was the characteristic of all reformation, as oppression was of hierarchy.[87]

Kuyper's historical constructions also plied the class consciousness and the Protestant prejudices of his populist base. Out of good but ignorant intentions King William I, in establishing the Netherlands Reformed Church, "merely copied what he had seen among the Episcopalians and national churches." He thereby established a system of lordships in the church, which were originally a Roman Catholic invention: a classical government in place of a bishop; a provincial government in place of an archbishop; and the synod instead of the pope. There was the thing if not the name. Inevitably, then, the church began to resemble the worldly social hierarchy. The higher classes received "distinguished pews," and the poor were literally pushed to the back of the church or crowded out. The nobility of church office was lost in a lust for respectability, and lawful ecclesiastical courts "lapsed into mindless bureaucratic patchwork."[88]

The resolution came when in 1886 Kuyper's churches restored the true church of Dutch history. They took their official name from the church of the seventeenth-century Dutch golden age, the Nether German Reformed Churches (Nederduitse Gereformeerde Kerken, or NGK).[89] They adopted the threefold Reformed confessional statements of the sixteenth and seventeenth centuries and reintroduced the church polity of the 1619 Synod of Dort. They took as their precedent events from the time of the Dort synod, when the Calvinist churches had formed temporary *doleantie* churches, "but through gradual church renewal this evil [of separation] was averted at the Dordt synod in 1619."[90] Kuyper called his breakaway churches the Doleantie, invoking this history and introducing this movement as the returning heir of the historic Dutch church.

A Time to Embrace: A Theology and Narrative for Church Union

The most surprising thing about Kuyper's church reform movement and all his rationale for breaking with the church was not that he left the Netherlands Reformed Church. Anyone could see that coming. Rather, it was surprising that the same principles that supported leaving also supported his movement for church union and a theology of ecumenism. The separation between Kuyper's Doleantie and the Netherlands Reformed Church was bitter, and the worst fighting was between Kuyper and those who were relatively theologically conservative, his nearest theological kin in the NHK. Therefore, Minister A. W. Bronsveld, for one, did not believe there was much real opportunity for reconciliation, when in 1887 (only a year after Kuyper's departure from the Netherlands Reformed Church) delegates from Kuyper's churches met unofficially with members of the Christian Reformed Church to discuss ecclesiastical union.[91] The Christian Reformed Church was the confessional Reformed church that had broken with the Netherlands Reformed Church fifty years earlier in 1834. Theologically, the CGK had a lot in common with Kuyper's Doleantie churches. Both groups had left the Netherlands Reformed Church because they believed it held too loosely to the Reformed touchstones, confessions, liturgy, and polity. The problem was, as Bronsveld indicated, it would be hard for anyone to get along with someone like Kuyper, who had worked so hard to get away.

The review of Kuyper's *Tract on the Reformation of the Churches* by Herman Bavinck, a young theologian at the CGK seminary, exemplified some of the differences between the CGK and Kuyper's Doleantie churches. Bavinck was well disposed toward Kuyper and one of the strongest supporters of union between the two churches, but he also had criticisms of Kuyper reflective of CGK sentiment. At root of many of the ecclesiological differences between Kuyper's Doleantie churches and Bavinck's CGK was the place of the local congregation. Bavinck said Kuyper emphasized the local congregation to the detriment of interchurch bonds: he "does not do justice to the unity and solidarity of all churches."[92] Calvin had stressed the unity and peace of the church and pursued the unity of all churches more than Kuyper acknowledged. The local church does not come into being through its connections to other churches, Bavinck argued; nonetheless "it is only one cell in the organism of the congregation of Christ," and it is not good and perfect without the others.

On the basis of his understanding of the congregation, Bavinck also took issue with Kuyper's history of the sixteenth-century reformation in the Netherlands and Calvin's Swiss reformation, and, further, the differences between their accounts of the sixteenth century corresponded with the different self-understandings of their respective churches. Kuyper, who wanted to preserve the continuity and unity of his Amsterdam congregation so far as possible in view of a looming break with the NHK, emphasized the continuity of Calvin's church and the Dutch churches at the local level.[93] Bavinck, however, as a member of a secession church, viewed Calvin as having formed a "new [read "secession"] church." Calvin had not only broken with a corrupt church bond but had also reformed the whole organization of the church, doctrine, and life, and, whatever continuity of the organism remained, for Bavinck that meant that a new church had been formed.[94]

In 1890, four years after Kuyper's break with the Netherlands Reformed Church, Kuyper published a small book explaining the ecclesiological basis for union between his Doleantie churches and Bavinck's CGK. In this book, entitled *Separation and Doleantie*, Kuyper returned to two types of church reformation he had introduced in the *Tract*, now in more detail, with an eye to defending the legitimacy of both actions and explaining how these two churches, arising out of these two different histories, could be united. The booklet covered a variety of topics from the formation of the institution to the nature of secession and *doleantie* to social and civil consequences and the way to union. Throughout the treatise, the arguments are grounded on the same principles to which Kuyper had appealed in the *Tract*, especially the unity of the whole church in its organic nature; the visible, local appearance of the organic church as the base from which the institution is built; and the twin themes of freedom of conscience and voluntarism.

Locating the unity of the church in the organism rather than the institute had enabled Kuyper to explain how he could leave the Netherlands Reformed Church without violating the unity of the church. Simply, the unity of the church did not depend on external forms. That also meant, conversely, that organic unity already existed even between churches where institutional unity did not. Christians in different institutions ought to strive for external unity where possible.[95] Significant mitigating factors, like language or geographical barriers, may legitimately preclude institutional union, but otherwise Reformed churches were obligated to join together into federations on the basis of their common confession, government, and history.[96] Moreover, Kuyper felt "organically one in the body of Christ" with the CGK.[97]

Each church's self-understanding depended on its respective argument for the legitimacy of its break with the Netherlands Reformed Church. Therefore, Kuyper had to apply his principles in a way that satisfied the self-understanding of the CGK and the Doleantie churches. He accomplished this through a subtle distinction between union and *reunion*. In the *Tract,* Kuyper had depicted the CGK as a fellow *doleantie* church—an attempt to create common ground—but Bavinck and the CGK rejected this. They had unequivocally separated from the NHK.[98] Now Kuyper acknowledged the CGK as a separated church. In that case, he said, there could be no reunion between these two churches, only union. Reunion was the proper course for a doleantie church returning to the restored, original church. But the union between the CGK and the Doleantie churches was not that. Although each group traced its history to the Netherlands Reformed Church, they had no shared history to which they could appeal. Therefore, union was the appropriate course. "Indeed *reunion* can only pertain to what was once one; and since these two sets of instituted churches were never one as such and never could be because the one set only came to exist later, nothing but *reunion* could ever take place."[99]

Finally, Kuyper's arguments for union turned on the principle of ecclesiastical voluntarism. Although an obligation existed for congregations to exhibit their unity in external federations, it did not trump the freedom of conscience. (Otherwise Kuyper's arguments for union would have voided his earlier arguments for breaking with the NHK.) In fact, two levels of voluntarism played off each other in Kuyper's ecclesiology. The first level was the freedom of the individual conscience, by which believers gathered and formed an institution.[100] The second level of voluntarism pertained to the congregation. The congregation ought to join in voluntary federations with other congregations. The CGK, for instance, could not be forced to reunite" with the Doleantie churches, though they represented in some sense a continuation of the church that the CGK had left; instead, the goal was "one free synodical gathering."[101]

The Paradox of Office

Kuyper's theology of office aided his polemics for breaking with the Netherlands Reformed Church and for joining with the Christian Reformed Church. Kuyper justified these actions by empowering believers to act in accordance with their consciences, by virtue of the priesthood of all believers. He had long wished to make the church more democratic, to give all members equal say in church affairs, and to disempower the synodical hierarchy whose officials reflected the vestiges of the old Dutch social hierarchy. However, he also saw the dangers of pure democracy, and special office was a check on that. Kuyper was a democrat conscious of the excesses to which democracy might lead. These principles produced a paradoxical church polity: "spiritually the church is strictly monarchical, being a kingdom under the absolute kingship of Christ; in her visible form decidedly democratic, but bound to an aristocratic form in her operation."[102] In the end, democracy and freedom of conscience trumped the rights of the church's special office.

Kuyper empowered believers by invoking the Protestant concept of the priesthood of believers, which he found support for in the Belgic Confession (chapter 28) and in those places where Scripture "adorns the people of the Lord with the honorable title of kings and priests."[103] This office flowed from the bond the Holy Spirit formed between believers and Christ, and it was the foundation of the visible, institutional church. The most important function of this general office was surely the election of special officers.[104] Ideally, in a sinless world, Christ would work directly through all believers, but because of sin Christ's work rested on a small group of officers: ministers, elders, and deacons.[105] Believers could form a new church where there was none:

> In a church on a solitary island, where a plague drags all the office bearers to the grave, the believers themselves, by virtue of their office, would have to take the place of these office bearers and execute the official work of the church. Further, they would have to choose new office bearers.[106]

Believers could also reform an existing institution when necessary: "when the special office decays and degenerates, the office of believers powerfully revives it again."[107] Not only could believers reform the church, but also when the church had become corrupt they were obligated to join a true church or form a new one.[108] According to the *Tract,* the office of believers was *"first of all"* for this purpose.[109] This official capacity of believers pertained specifically to believers' responsibilities with regard to the church institution and besides electing officers also included some

decisions regarding discipline and ecclesiastical union with other congregations. But even where no institution had ever existed, believers
spontaneously gathering still had a right and responsibility to form an
institution.[110] These distinctions empowered believers to form or reform a
church institution in any situation.

Although special office was elected by the general office of believers, it
did not rule by consent of the governed. Special office ruled by the Spirit of
Christ. Christ's messianic office was divided fourfold into ministers, teachers, elders, and deacons. The Holy Spirit bound these officers so closely
to Christ that when ministers preached or administered the sacraments,
Christ himself preached and baptized.[111] The general office of believers and
the special office were both under Christ, but they differed in function.
The task of special office was to rule and administer the church.[112] With
regard to doctrine, ultimate legislative authority belonged to Christ and
his Word, and special office had judicial authority to minister the Word
and interpret it, a task supremely exercised in the writing of the church's
confessions. Special office was also commissioned with the actual establishing of a church order and the execution of justice in ecclesiastical discipline, though the general office had a responsibility of oversight in these
matters.[113]

The paradox of this polity was that Kuyper's ideal of office contradicted
the experience of individual believers that he described and even advocated. General office was not subordinate to special office, but both stood
directly under Christ. Ideally, therefore, special office kept the general
office in check, and vice versa. So,

> if the congregation attempts to bring pressure to bear upon the
> officebearers which is outside of the Word of God or against it,
> then the authority of such a congregation is of no worth and does
> not concern the officebearer. And in like manner, if an officebearer
> attempts to exercise authority over the believers outside of or over
> against the Word of God, then this authority falls away completely,
> is no longer authority, but becomes pure arrogance.[114]

This raised the question: in practice, who was in a position to adjudicate between the congregation (general office) and the officebearers (special office)? Kuyper seemed to give with one hand and take away with the
other. Believers needed the church to interpret Scripture, and "a child of
God is deprived of his church which he needs if he no longer firmly relies

on and trusts in the word of his church as interpreting the will of the Lord."[115] Yet,

> never may a believer acquiesce in something simply because the ministers of the church say so. This is Romish, not Reformed. In a Reformed church each believer must have spiritual judgment and must permit this judgment to operate...out of spiritual obedience."[116]

It was not clear whether believers should submit to special office. In theory, special office had binding doctrinal authority,[117] but believers did not experience it as binding. Their submission to special office was purely voluntary.[118] Believers could leave any time they deemed special office to have deviated from Scripture. Indeed, they had the responsibility to do so! A church hierarchy, "a spiritual aristocracy," restrained the excesses of unbridled democracy, but in practice believers owed no reverence or submission to office except what they deemed right. Conscience was, in fact, the final court of appeal.

Lurking here was a change that Kuyper was reticent to recognize. Previously in *Confidentially* (1873), Kuyper had responded to the problem of authority by arguing that the responsibility of the church was to define doctrine amid the pressures of democratization that threatened to make individuals authorities to themselves:

> No one in their individual spiritual life has the right to hold as decided for themselves anything that significantly deviates from the doctrinal form of the Congregation, unless the Congregation in her legal organ has put its stamp on it.[119]

Now, although office retained a doctrinal function, it was a different doctrinal function. The new task of office was to represent rather than decide the beliefs of believers. As Miroslav Volf describes how modern people see the church, "Church membership is important for them not so much for determining their faith as for supporting it."[120] Volf's two poles marked the distance between Kuyper's sacramental church and the believer's church.

An Emerging Dilemma for Kuyper's Social Ethics

In the *Tract*, several principles emerged that would require a reconsideration of the church's social position and responsibilities. These principles

were not necessarily new, but they emerged more clearly than before, like
the lines and colors of a photograph becoming more definite through the
developing process. The shift toward the believer's church undoubtedly
hurried this process along. The overall effect was to distance the church,
both as an organism and as an institute, from public entities like the state
and the Dutch people and thus to push the church toward an ever more
private stance and therefore away from a church in the Troeltschian sense
and toward denominational status.

A broad social anthropology underlay Kuyper's concept of the church as
an organism. Not only the church but also all humanity was an organism.
As an organism humanity, like the church, was a social body, not a collection of individual parts, even though the organism had been corrupted
by sin.[121] Every organism had a life "principle," the internal power of life
that motivated and directed the organism, and sin, more than its forensic
element of guilt, was the false principle that corrupted the human organism.[122] When God redeemed humanity, he destroyed the power of sin and
recreated a new human organism, the church, with a new life principle.
The *Tract* began with the thesis that all of humanity now belonged to one
of these two organisms, the old or the new.[123] This contrasted with the
national church's incorrect assumption that nation constituted a distinct
organic unit and the national church's attempt to impose upon the nation
a single ecclesiastical institution.[124]

This notion of the church as a distinct organism conflicted, however,
with other elements in Kuyper's thinking. He occasionally referred to the
nation as an organic whole. In *Confidentially* (1873), he had portrayed the
Dutch nation as a whole as Reformed, and even later he still spoke of his
Reformed people as the "kernel and pit of the nation," as if the rest of the
nation grew up from this organic center.[125] Yet this could not be reconciled
with his assertion that the church was one organism and the rest of fallen
humanity another. Did this not divide the Dutch people into two organisms, the redeemed and the unredeemed? Jeroen Koch says that Kuyper
vacillated between describing the nation as Reformed and describing
his group of sympathizers as Reformed.[126] How could the church be the
redeemed organism of humanity and the nation as a whole be Reformed
Calvinist as well? This portended a decision. Kuyper would have to choose
between the Dutch people and his Reformed subgroup.

Kuyper's beliefs about church and state also emerged more clearly and
likewise proved the need for a new account of the church's social position.
Kuyper had long advocated a more thorough separation of church and

state than was actually practiced in the Netherlands, and he argued that separation of church and state and the religious freedom that it brought was originally the insight of Calvinism, not the French Revolution. In fact, Calvin had taught the separation of church and state, but he had also taught that the two institutions, though separate, ought to cooperate.[127] In the *Tract*, it became apparent that Kuyper disagreed with this latter belief of Calvin. The cooperation between the church and the state was impossible because the state was not competent to decide with which church to cooperate. This, naturally, was a result of the religious pluralism that Kuyper experienced but of which Calvin knew nothing.

Kuyper took his leave from Calvin most forthrightly on the matter of the state punishment of heretics. At one time, Kuyper had excused Calvin's participation in the trial and execution of the heretic Michel Servetus as the action of one caught in a system not of his choosing and, moreover, no different from the actions of many of his contemporaries.[128] In the *Tract*, Kuyper showed less leniency and unequivocally broke with Calvin and also with Theodore Beza, Gisbert Voet, Johan a Marck, Francis Turretin, Friedrich Spanheim, and others on this matter.[129] The problem with the supposition that the state ought to aid the church in enforcing right belief was that "this proposition supposes that the magistrate is in a position to judge the difference between truth and heresy, an office of grace which, as appears from the history of eighteen centuries, has *not* been granted by the Holy Spirit, but *withheld.*"[130]

Kuyper interpreted the history of the Christian Reformed Church according to these principles. When the CGK seceded from the Netherlands Reformed Church in 1834, Kuyper said, it misjudged this point to its own detriment. The CGK had expected the government to decide in its favor, since although it broke institutionally with the NHK it was manifestly the true spiritual inheritor of the old church of the Dutch Republic. But lacking the competence to judge in spiritual matters, Kuyper explained, the civil government could decide only based on legal and institutional points, and as a result, the seceding Christian Reformed Churches lost their civil disputes with the Netherlands Reformed Church.[131]

Yet Kuyper did not believe that the government rested on a purely earthly foundation or was concerned solely with worldly cares. In politics, Kuyper was a constitutional monarchist, and he believed that the king was God's steward on earth. In the cosmic order, the king ruled the state as Christ ruled the church.[132] Therefore, though Kuyper argued for an "absolute" separation of church and state, he also argued that the magistrate had the responsibility to uphold both tables of the law (the Mosaic Law's injunction to love neighbor and God).[33] Thus church and state were separate, but religion and politics were not. How this could be achieved without the state interfering in the church's business or apart from Protestantism's old territorial church system was the question that Kuyper's public theology had to solve.

Conclusion

Kuyper's new ecclesiology definitively subordinated the church institution to the organism, with its qualities of voluntary participation and freedom of conscience. This was not a straightforward or indisputable application of Reformed ecclesiology. Calvin gradually diminished the priesthood of believers until he omitted it entirely from the *Institutes* after 1543, a result of Bucer's warnings about the Anabaptists using this doctrine to reject office completely, suggests Eddy van der Borght.[34] Kuyper took the opposite turn. The office of believers was not prominent in his ecclesiology until he drew close to what seemed to be an inevitable break with the national church. Through his theology of the organism, newly empowered to act visibly and concretely, believers received new power in the church.

In practice, Kuyper's church institution was a manifestation of the consensus of believers, guided, he said, by the Word and Spirit. As such, it was a distinctly modern form of religious association, a denomination. It was a voluntary, religious gathering. It was distinct from public entities like nation and state, and it presumed to be no more than one free Christian community in a society that tolerated a variety of other Christian communities. Kuyper came to call this the pluriformity of the Christian church: there was a plurality of institutional forms yet an underlying unity of the Christian organism.[35]

A denomination assumes two things: voluntary participation and a plurality of churches. There cannot be only one denomination; there must be at least two. Perhaps the most disturbing thing about Kuyper's free church, in upsetting both national church supporters and the social landscape, was that his break with the Netherlands Reformed Church transformed it also from a church (in the Troeltschian sense) into a denomination.[36] As a voluntary form of religious association, a denomination implies a choice between alternatives, and the alternatives now were Kuyper's Doleantie or the NHK. The Netherlands Reformed Church had never been, in any meaningful sense, *an alternative*. Generally, under the old compromise,

Roman Catholics or members of smaller Protestant sects did not experience their ecclesiastical participation as a choice but simply as the course of life.[37] (The apathy this engendered among members of the national church was what revival movements like the Dutch Reveil and the Ethical theologians protested, though these groups had no desire to solve the problem by such drastic measures as Kuyper took.) The Roman Catholic Church and the Protestant sects did not, by and large, try to convert NHK members to their group, but Kuyper did. His ecclesiological polemics took place in the public eye, in the newspapers, in public gatherings. His reformation of the church was a grassroots movement that required his grassroots organizing skills.[38] Even if Protestants remained in the Netherlands Reformed Church in spite of Kuyper's politicking, they did so deliberately much more so than before, and the sheer quantity of polemics against Kuyper indicates that his opponents also deemed it important that Dutch Protestants make the right choice between Kuyper and the NHK. Moreover, with the Doleantie the national church lost its numerical dominance, falling to less than 50% of the population. Taken together, these things made the NHK a denomination.

5

The Ins and Outs of Baptism: The Development of Kuyper's Theology of Baptism

ONE OF THE most dismaying problems for contemporary Reformed theologians is not that they disagree on whether infants should be baptized—they generally agree on that—but that they cannot agree why.[1] Abraham Kuyper exemplified this conundrum. Along with the transformation from a sacramental church to a believers' church, Kuyper's theology of baptism and covenant also underwent a transformation. Infant baptism was an old Reformed tradition that Kuyper believed in, but it was a practice that conflicted, at least prima facie, with Kuyper's insistence on active personal spirituality. Part of his complaint against the *volkskerk* was its indiscriminate baptismal policies, and he conceded that the practice of infant baptism was in part to blame for the creation of the *volkskerk*.[2] Dietrich Bonhoeffer pinpointed the problem Kuyper faced: the practice of infant baptism could not be reconciled with a strictly voluntary communion.[3] If Kuyper wanted to maintain historic Reformed practice and a church that prized heartfelt spirituality, he would have to reconsider the meaning of baptism and the reasons for it.

This chapter traces the development of Kuyper's baptismal theology from one that coincided with his sacramental church to one that better supported the believers' church. In his sacramental church model, Kuyper viewed baptism as a preparing grace and an instrument of grace as well as part of an external covenant that effected an inner work of grace. But like the sacramental church model, this view of baptism made it far too difficult to break with the institutional church, since it was a means of grace. So as Kuyper developed his believers' church model (in the 1880s), he also developed a theology of baptism to accompany it. In this model, baptism followed and presumed the prior inner work of grace (hence it is called Kuyper's doctrine of *presumptive regeneration*), and he denied an external covenant as an invention of the *volkskerk*.

Two interrelated issues were at play here: the rationale for baptism (i.e., the question of who should be baptized and why); and the efficacy of baptism as a means of grace. Kuyper's understanding of baptism as a preparatory means of grace correlated with a high appreciation for the church as an institution of the so-called external covenant and with a broad policy of admission to the sacrament.[4] Kuyper's subsequent shift to the priority of the inner and therefore private work of the Spirit as a precondition for baptism (or more precisely, the *presumption* of such) corresponded with his rejection of the institutional church as a salvation-granting institution and stricter policies of admission to the sacrament.

Like his early ecclesiology, Kuyper's theology of baptism fluctuated as he searched for an adequate account of baptism while dealing with theological challenges and pastoral responsibilities. Therefore, this chapter begins by tracing some of his earliest thoughts on baptism. Here no consistent theology but rather a series of fits and starts is to be found. This study reveals a student, pastor, and theologian concerned to deal with practical and theoretical pressures. What persisted throughout Kuyper's career was not the answers formed here so much as the questions, especially of baptismal efficacy and of the basis for admittance to baptism as well as the significance and form of the baptismal liturgy. The question underlying all these concerns was the same one that oriented his ecclesiology in general: how to relate Christianity's inner and outer aspects.

The Ins and Outs of Baptism: Its Inner Working and Its Outer Meaning

Because the church's social position was part of Kuyper's ecclesiological concern it is important to understand that baptismal theology and practice have implications not only for the church's inner workings but also for its relation to society at large. Baptism has meaning as the sacrament of entrance into the church. Consequently, baptism deals with the constitution and makeup of the church. The theology of baptism turns on an explanation of who belongs within the church and why, which is inseparable from an account of who does not. This leads to the social aspect of baptism: how the church relates to the world outside it and how it is distinguished from the world. This is the sociological import of baptism, while the first aspect is the theological or ecclesial import of the sacrament. Generally, theologians strive for complementary accounts of these two aspects.

Modern society, however, forces the church's hand with regard to the sociological meaning of baptism. David Martin, Ernst Troeltsch, and Peter Berger explain why. Concerning the *church type*, the category where he places Reformed Christianity, Troeltsch says, "The Essence of the Church is its objective institutional character. The individual is born into it, and through infant baptism he comes under its miraculous influence."[5] Entrance in the Reformed church is not voluntary, at least for children it is given, automatic, and inherited. Further, as a consequence, the practice of infant baptism, in imitation of circumcision, ties baptism to the organic and solidary community of the family and to the extended family, the nation. In Troeltsch's terms, therefore, baptism is based on objective considerations, that is, on factors beyond the spiritual life of the child baptized. That was fine in premodern society, when churches really were objective social institutions, but they are no longer so. Churches in the modern West are not churches in Troeltsch's sense anymore; they are voluntary religious communions, that is, denominations. Most civil governments do not prop up churches and ensure or presume their givenness, and where states try it is most often to the detriment of the church. Church membership is also no longer a reflex of membership in national or civil society, which is not necessarily bad.[6] Instead, denominations depend wholly on the voluntary participation of their members. That is the sociological construction of Christian communities in the modern West, but the Reformed practice of infant baptism is antagonistic to it because it ignores the will of the person baptized.

Speaking of the Church of England, David Martin says, "As the Church slips anchor with the natural community and moves towards the open sea of voluntary associations it begins to reconsider the doctrine and practice of baptism."[7] This was what happened with Abraham Kuyper. By natural community, Martin means the nation, the *Anglo* in Anglicanism; in the Netherlands, the situation of the Dutch national church, the *volkskerk*, was comparable.

Disestablishment weakened the assumed membership in the church, and the gradually greater explicit commitment on the part of members was required. This automatically throws infant baptism into question because as a religious practice it requires absolutely nothing on the part of the person baptized whereas the larger social system requires everything of them. Yet the Dutch Reformed Church, like the Church of England, had a long theological and liturgical tradition of infant baptism that could not easily be swept away.[8] The socio-theological dilemma of infant baptism is the key to the development of Kuyper's theology of baptism. Kuyper wanted a free church, which was grounded in the subjective support of members more than in the objective and public support of nation or state, but he also wanted to preserve the historic Reformed practice of infant baptism and its inherently involuntary nature. His baptismal theology had to reconcile these competing forces.

Kuyper's theology of baptism developed as a function of two factors: the change in his views of the church—indeed, his changing theology of baptism was itself a changing ecclesiology—and the changes in the church's contextual, social standing as it became a voluntary church. In the national church, baptism for Kuyper had depended heavily on the objective institution, fitting the pattern of the ecclesiology he was developing to restoring a proper appreciation of ecclesiastical forms like sacraments in the church. But when he broke with the *volkskerk*, such a high theology of church institutions was counterproductive. His ecclesiology and his theology of baptism came to emphasize, even more than before, the subjective spirituality of the person baptized, and, consequently, Kuyper's mature theology of baptism was not quite believer's baptism. Kuyper's theology of baptism was an account not only for a church that located true religion in the heart but also for a whole society that increasingly did the same.

Some Comments on Secondary Literature

Theologians and historians disagree over the nature of Kuyper's theology of baptism, especially Kuyper's critics. American William Young says that Kuyper's later theology of presumptive regeneration neglected personal spirituality and suffers from hypercovenantism.[9] Young prefers the more pietistic spirituality of the Princeton theologians of the same century. But Kuyper's confessional Dutch opponents thought just the opposite. Traditionally, one of the main Reformed arguments for infant baptism had been that infants were members of the Covenant of Grace by birth. Many Dutch Calvinists believed that Kuyper obscured the covenant by putting his idea of "presumed regeneration" in place of the promises of the covenant.[10] In other words, Kuyper's Dutch critics thought that he did not do justice to the objectivity of the covenant, while his American critics thought he did not do justice to the subjectivity of the covenant.

The estimates of Dutch theologians, both pro and con, are generally trustworthier. Since Kuyper's mature theology of presumptive regeneration caused so much controversy, most commentators—understandably—deal primarily with that issue.[11] While there is some recognition of the development of Kuyper's thought, there is little consensus. E. Smilde's 1946 study, probably the most thorough one, examines Kuyper's mature theology of baptism in relation to covenant and regeneration. Smilde notes the change in Kuyper's views that took place in the 1880s but does not offer an explanation for it. His study, written two years after the 1944 split in Kuyper's church, mainly concerns counteraccusations that Kuyper had abandoned the covenant.[12] C. Graafland explains the development in Kuyper's theology of baptism in terms of the different intellectual influences on Kuyper's mind, from antimodernism to John Calvin to J. C. Appelius to G. Voet.[13] W. H. Velema and J. Kamphuis note that the change had something to do with Kuyper's ecclesiology and his switch in emphasis from the objective side of the church to the subjective side. Velema recognizes the same path of intellectual influence in Kuyper as Graafland does,[14] whereas Kamphuis suggests that Friedrich Schleiermacher was the source of Kuyper's emphasis on subjective measures and reads this as a polemic against the *volkskerk*.[15] Each of these studies offers a particular insight, though often only a portion of the larger picture. This chapter recreates the larger picture by setting the development of Kuyper's baptismal theology in its religious and ecclesiastical context, and hopefully thereby provides a more nuanced and integrated account.

Theological Experimentation and Pastoral Practice: Kuyper's Early Baptismal Theology

Baptism was one facet of certain larger questions about the church's relation to entities like nation and state, which the Dutch church faced in the nineteenth century. In the nineteenth century the boundaries of the national church were broad, after 1830 coinciding almost completely with the Protestant majority of the population. Membership in the church and society were virtually indistinguishable, illustrated by the fact that until 1811 baptism records were the only registration of newborn children in the Netherlands. Even those who were not members of the Netherlands Reformed Church could and did have their children baptized in the church. The Netherlands was a "baptized nation," says historian David Bos.[16] The government also exercised a certain amount of control over internal workings of the church, for example, through the governmental department for worship established in 1808 to bring greater uniformity to worship. But separation of church and state questioned the simple equation of church and nation that had defined the national church. In the 1850s, a new category of membership was added, the "birth member," which did away with the age limits for members who had not made public profession of faith. This meant that anyone born to members of the national church were members of the church for life, and this strengthened the church's connection to the whole of the Dutch people, even after the separation of church and state, since membership coincided not with individual decision but was given with membership in a broader organic community.[17] It seems that this close relation between the *volkskerk* and the *volk* still—as late as 1879—led to some confusion as to which sphere properly had authority over baptism. At that time Kuyper felt it necessary to remonstrate, "The government has absolutely nothing to do with the administration of Holy Baptism, and even the regulation that with Holy Baptism 'a letter of registry office' must first be shown to the one officiating is below the dignity of so sacred a sacrament."[18]

From the beginning, Kuyper's ecclesiology dealt with the church's broader social predicament as well as the problem of theological description, and his early baptismal theology followed the general contours of his ecclesiology, which were fluid. He changed his mind so often that his early baptismal theology seems highly experimental, as if he was trying out different solutions until he found one that fit. As a theology student and initially as a pastor in Beesd, Kuyper placed little importance on baptism, as he likewise did with the institutional forms of the church in general. Kuyper's first known theological writing, his 1859 student essay on Pope Nicolas I, altogether abandoned the church as a passing form, a common view among Dutch modernists influenced by Richard Rothe.[19] But only a year later, in his prize-winning essay on the ecclesiologies of Calvin and John a Lasco, he decided the church deserved more, not less, attention. Kuyper's new ecclesiology was indebted to Schleiermacher for its social plan: the church was not a gathering of individuals but an organism united by the Spirit. This spontaneous gathering issued in an institution, but doctrines and rituals were not the church's essence.

In this ecclesiological model, the sacraments were symbolic prompts to Christian solidarity. They did not objectively precede the gathering of believers but arose out of it and promoted the unity of the church and sincerity of heart, which were Kuyper's chief concerns:

> Therefore from the mind of the gospel, baptism and the Supper
> are actions of a *symbolic appointing*, which in the glorious memory
> of our Lord advance the unity of the institute of the church, at the
> same time also pricking and inspiring us, in order that we may
> embrace Christ with a whole heart and that we may foster the most
> tender love towards our brothers.[20]

Further, Christ never assigned any efficacy to the rituals of baptism
and the Lord's Supper, so Calvin had wrongly ascribed a "magical power"
and "excessive stability" to the sacraments. The Spirit, not baptism (or any
set of doctrines), formed the bond of unity of the church.[21] Although the
church had gained significance for Kuyper in 1860, the sacraments still
held a low priority since they were part of the institutional church, which
was only a by-product of the more important, organic church.

Kuyper began to appreciate the institutional church and its rituals
more when he had to stand in the pulpit and baptize children himself.
During these years in the late 1860s and throughout the 1870s, Kuyper
committed himself to a program of church reform that emphasized both
fixed outward forms, such as baptismal liturgy and doctrinal confessions,
and inner spiritual life. Just prior to taking his first parish in Beesd, in the
midst of a vocational crisis that resulted in his giving up his aspirations for
scholarly renown for the call of a country pastorate, Kuyper read Charlotte
Yonge's *Heir of Redclyffe*, a literary contribution to the high-church Oxford
Movement. According to Kuyper's 1873 autobiographical account in
Confidentially, upon reading the novel, "at that moment the predilection
for prescribed ritual, the high estimation of the Sacrament, the appreciation for the Liturgy became rooted in me for all time."[22] If Yonge's novel
did prick a high-church sentiment in Kuyper, it remained latent for several
years. He dismissed church forms while at Beesd until he had to defend
them against modernists like Allard Pierson and mystics like Pietje Baltus
(see chapter 2).[23]

His ongoing historical studies on the sixteenth-century Dutch
Reformed exile church in London also provoked a reconsideration of the
church as an institution. In 1865 Kuyper wrote two articles titled "The
First Church Gathering or The Establishment of Our Reformed Church,
and the Struggle for her Independent Existence" and "The Worship of the
Reformed Church and the Construction of Her Church Order." The subjects of these articles and the occasional editorial comments within them
reveal Kuyper's new appreciation for liturgy. After describing the liturgy

of the London church, he observed, "If the whole is a bit overloaded, still it gives exactly through that broad establishment and its fixed formulaic prayers exactly what we lack, a real liturgy."[24] These set formulas for prayers, baptism, and Lord's Supper were preferable to the liturgical "anarchy" of the Netherlands Reformed Church.[25] In addition to these studies, a favorable review of J. I. Doedes's study of the Heidelberg Catechism and his entry into disputes over church government indicated a threefold concern for the church's outward features—doctrine, worship, and polity. This was clearly apparent by the time Kuyper left Beesd in 1867.[26]

That year Kuyper moved from Beesd to the much larger Utrecht parish, a congregation known for its conservatism amid the growing diversity in the NHK. While in Utrecht, Kuyper engaged in various ecclesiastical controversies wherein he defended the importance of adhering to set forms like confessional statements. Certain actions by the synod seemed hypocritical to Kuyper and the Utrecht consistory. The synod investigated the doctrinal fidelity of church leadership yearly, but it refused to do anything about deviant beliefs or practices. Kuyper charged the synod with "lying."[27] He did not want a confessional straightjacket, but he did want a testable set of standards for doctrine and liturgy. "'Fixity but not unchangability of form for liturgy and confession both,' was then and still remains my motto."[28] But the attempt at definition per se struck at the character of the *volkskerk*, which aimed to be the church of the people, not one part of them.

Baptism became a nexus for Kuyper's concerns and a riddle for him since it involved objective forms and personal piety. A series of synodical decisions in the late 1860s made the Trinitarian baptismal formula optional. Instead of Father, Son, and Holy Spirit, one could now be baptized "into the name of the Father," "into the name of the congregation," "into faith, hope, and love," or "for the initiation into Christendom."[29] Against the synod's decision, Kuyper argued that the Trinitarian formula was not arbitrary but essential if baptism was to be Christian baptism:

But if in your heart, O church of the Lord, the band braided by God himself is not frayed, that which binds the most intimate parts of your hidden life to that power of the resurrection, to that vine of grace, to that condescending God who in the thrice holy name of "Father, Son, and Holy Spirit" stretches his wings over you, descends to you and comforts you, then rather let go of every person, even the most beloved and dear to you, than that you would ever permit the high glorious Name to be separated from your Christian baptism![30]

The church's indiscriminate policy of baptizing all and sundry also troubled Kuyper. Kuyper said it was "lying" if the liturgist used a formula in baptism that had nothing to do with the formula given in the New Testament or in church regulations or if he believed the formula was mere metaphysical nonsense. It was also "lying" if the person coming for baptism did so unwillingly or for the wrong reasons, for example, if the husband went along with the baptism of a child only to appease his wife, if the mother sought baptism of a child only out of superstition, or if the liturgist used the traditional baptismal formula but believed nothing of it. Greater discipline in administering the sacrament was necessary,[31] lest

> there was with such an act a complete absence of everything that makes such a solemnity into baptism—absence of form, absence of formula of baptismal confession of the church, absence of faith in the baptism both by the liturgist and by the parents, absence of both the objective character and of subjective appropriation. Yet the child will soon be enrolled in our church registers as baptized![32]

Kuyper's developing vision of a true Calvinist church demanded both solemnity and sincerity, two things that were inseparable but not easy to reconcile.

Kuyper left Utrecht frustrated with what he felt was confusion between conservatism and Christian orthodoxy. The two were not at all the same to Kuyper. The conservatives' attachment to tradition inhibited them from taking the more radical steps that Kuyper thought necessary to preserve spiritual life. The forms of the church were essential to its life, but they must grow and develop with the life of the church.[33] His solution was a *free church*, the true Calvinist model that avoided two errors: first, that of the Roman Catholic Church and the established churches that neglected the internal, organic, and instinctive life of the church for the mechanical and outward spirituality of the institutional church[34]; and second, the tendency to ignore the forms of life. Even some conservatives missed this point. It was not only modernists who threatened the institutional church, but "more than one supposes, [idealism] has determined the methodistic, darbyistic, and carelessly-evangelizing school of thought, in which one saw the enlivened life of faith appear on the scene during the Réveil."[35]

Ongoing controversies offered opportunities to explore what this meant for baptism, and much hung in the balance. When Kuyper became editor of the ecclesiastical news weekly the *Herald,* the baptism question was among the most frequent concerns he addressed. After all, he believed that with the decision to allow a variety of baptismal formulas, "the Modernists suddenly, unexpectedly, without any reason, laid the whole weight of the church fight on the baptism-question."[36] A healthy church depended on a right understanding of baptism, for too low a view of baptism, such as that of Zwingli, the Socinians, or the Rationalists, had "crumbled the foundation of the church."[37] But a comprehensive solution was not immediately forthcoming. Kuyper's occasional studies on baptism initially provided conflicting accounts.

At least once (in 1871), Kuyper toyed with the idea of believer's baptism as a remedy for the lax *volkskerk* spirituality. He argued that the sacrament followed the individual's faith, though the sacrament properly belonged to the church corporate. Sacraments were a particular kind of sign, a covenant sign, given to the church, the covenant community, not to individuals. The basis for the covenant signs was the intimate union between Christ and his church; the sacraments, wherein God and humanity acted together, externalized this union.[38] This communion between the church and Christ was even more intimate than that of the individual Christian and Christ:

> The church, not the individual, is now already completely in Christ and fully united with him. This applies to the individual only in so far as he is actually a living member of the Church; never if you take him by himself, never in his aloneness and isolation.[39]

Full communion with God depended on participation with the Mystical Body of Christ.

Nonetheless, participation in the sacraments was not an automatic benefit for members of the community; the sacraments did not produce faith in those who had none. Rather, the sacraments strengthened faith. "With the covenant signs of the church, *faith is first then the sign*"; that is, faith must precede participation in the sacramental signs.[40] Quoting Heidelberg Catechism question 65, Kuyper concluded that the sacramental sign could not be used as a means for the first working of faith, a conclusion, Kuyper said, "especially with regard to Holy Baptism." This clearly addressed the national church and the baptismal practices that

Kuyper believed were entirely too lax. Those practices ventured close to Rome's error, which taught that baptism could be both a means to bring one to faith and a converting ordinance.[41] There might be a few in the church, hypocrites and the like, with whom faith never "breaks through"; on the whole, though, the church was "the church of faith," and baptism should reflect that.[42]

Ongoing debates about the baptismal formula forced Kuyper to consider again the objective significance of the sacrament and its efficacy. The Utrecht consistory—and, after his move in 1870, the Amsterdam consistory—disappointed Kuyper by not adequately defending the traditional baptismal formula.[43] Kuyper's polemics turned to address not only the modernists but also the lukewarm conservatives. Doedes of Utrecht, one such conservative, argued that the traditional translation of Matthew 28:19 and the historic baptismal formula, "*in* the name of the Father, and of the Son, and of the Holy Spirit," were incorrect. Jesus did not baptize "in the name" but "*to* the name."[44] The consequence of such a position, Kuyper said, was a symbolic view of baptism, and he defended the "in" formula by arguing that the efficacy of the sacrament depended on it.[45] The difference between baptizing "to the name" and baptizing "in the name" was nothing less than the difference between Pelagius and Augustine, who represented two opposite concepts of religion: "we *bring* something to God, [or] . . . that salvation is just the opposite, something *received* from God."[46] When a person was baptized "in," that indicated what God had done in salvation. In baptism, the heathen are not merely brought into contact with the life sphere of grace and then left to their own devices to get in; they are brought out of their heathen life sphere into that life sphere of grace, which is "the 'Name' of God." But when instead one is baptized "'*To* (*Tot*) the Name' one would thus be brought up to that life-sphere, but not brought *into* it. Not being in the Kingdom, at most one hears: 'You are not far from the Kingdom of God!'"[47]

It could be argued that Kuyper's theology of baptism was at odds with itself. If faith was a prerequisite for baptism, were infants, the main people being baptized, also expected to demonstrate their faith? If, on the other hand, baptism brought one into the life sphere of grace from a previously ungracious state, what did faith add beyond that? The most that Kuyper said was that the "highest harmony has been made between the inner working of life and the external symbol," which did not really explain much at all.[48]

Sacraments for a Sacramental Church: Baptism as Preparing Grace

An answer to these questions emerged in Kuyper's further studies on election and regeneration. It was straightforward: the church and its means of grace (like baptism) were preparatory graces, without which no one came to faith and salvation. There were two types of election Kuyper said: particular and general. Only particular election was an election to salvation, but the general election of a people, whether Israel in the Old Testament or the church in the New Testament, was the necessary context for preparing those individuals elected to salvation. Faith was impossible apart from the community and the means of grace entrusted to it: "faith worked by the Holy Ghost without the Word is, therefore, unthinkable."[49] The same reasoning justified infant baptism; otherwise, "if there is no preparing grace, if election is not bound to the congregation...then [you must] cut off everyone from the church whose conversion you are not sure of [and] break off the custom of infant baptism."[50]

A similar logic applied to regeneration. Modernist theologians and certain theologians of Groningen University had replaced metaphysical accounts of salvation and the church with ethical ones. The Groningen theologians rejected the traditional Reformed theology of penal, substitutionary atonement for an exemplary, moral one, and conversion and regeneration were similarly interpreted as ethical transformation and progress. Hence, Kuyper believed that "even where they stress mortification [of sin] and self-denial, they do not escape this trap [of self-righteousness]. They cannot do this while they cut off the atonement that makes all soul-conversion [or conversion to salvation] possible."[51] In the Groningen scheme, regeneration was the process of ethical improvement that continued throughout life, and the church was the institution inculcating this process. This placed a high value on the church, so high that some claimed there was no salvation outside of it, though what they meant by salvation was the process of ethical transformation.[52] A. van Toorenenbergen, otherwise more conservative than most Groningen theologians, exemplified this ethical task of the church: "only the Church of Christ can prepare a person to make their life useful and fitting for life."[53] Otherwise, humanity would sink into materialism.

In contrast, Kuyper construed regeneration and the church's role in terms of a grander metaphysical contest. Regeneration remedied corrupt human nature, not just behavior, and the church was the context where this radical change took place. In this process, baptism was the ordinance given to the church by which a person was brought into the regenerated community and prepared for personal regeneration:

> Least of all is said here that the rebirth of the church excludes the personal regeneration, or takes the place of it or makes it superfluous, but rather that through baptism a mystical bond between the one baptized and the body of Christ exists, through which the terrain before personal regeneration is smoothed.[54]

The church and baptism were not the "origin" of regeneration—God was the author of regeneration; the church was the "means" and "instruments" to regeneration, and baptism was "the bath of regeneration."[55] This theology of baptism was part of Kuyper's sacramental ecclesiology. Although baptism was not the direct cause of regeneration, it brought one into contact with the regenerate community; that was absolutely necessary, for "there is no regeneration except from the church."[56]

Yet while baptism was not the cause of regeneration, it did have an important gracious effect. It was the necessary remedy for the guilt that plagued humanity as a result of Adam's sin. Baptism brought one into mystical union with the body of Christ, the church, and as part of the body of Christ the person received a new communal head and therewith new legal standing: Christ instead of Adam, innocence instead of guilt. The original guilt remedied by baptism was not the same as original sin. Original sin was a power, not a legal standing, and that remained. Kuyper explained his position by appeal to the Belgic Confession. According to Kuyper, the Reformers and the members of the Synod of Dort did not think, "Inherited sin is also through Baptism, wholly *not taken away*," which would have denied all baptismal grace. Rather, according to the words of the confession, "The inherited sin is also through baptism *not wholly* taken away," implying that, in fact, it was partially taken away. The corruption of inherited sin is not taken away in baptism, but inherited guilt is. "'Inherited sin is also through baptism not wholly taken away.' That is, as appears from the following articles, it is taken away in respect of the accountability of *inherited guilt*, but not taken away as the *root* of later sins."[57]

In his study of regeneration, Kuyper first broached a version of presumptive regeneration, though in an innocuous form.[58] In this first appearance, the idea had no explicit connection to baptism at all. Rather, the hard reality of child mortality raised the issue, a tragedy that Kuyper knew firsthand. Four of Kuyper's sisters had died young; in 1872 his wife, Jo, suffered a miscarriage; and later, in 1892, one of his sons, Levinus Willem Christiaan Kuyper, died at age nine.[59] Kuyper asked what comfort could be offered to believing parents in such grim circumstances. He turned to Dort for help. "In the articles, which the Dort Synod placed against the Remonstrants, they explained that believing parents, supported by the Covenant of Grace, must not be anxious over the eternal lot of their children who die young."[60] What did this imply for the regeneration of these children? It could not be the case that these children were not born in sin or that the way of salvation was different for them. The only possible conclusion was that if these children were saved, regeneration had taken place. If these children partook of Adam's sinful nature and if, by virtue of God's covenant, parents could take comfort in the salvation of their children, then it stood to reason that these children must have been regenerated. Two hundred years earlier, the Westminster Confession had made the same point.[61]

Kuyper solved the riddle of the work of grace in the sacrament, the inner meaning, by prioritizing the objective grace available in the church and the necessity of community membership for individual spiritual life. The grace of the sacrament was objective since it came from outside the person, and it was public insofar as baptism was not a hidden work but an external one that could be witnessed by all. The term *preparing grace* highlighted the priority of the church, yet it did not forget about faith; the goal of the sacraments was to make faith possible, not to obviate it. It was a theology suitable for a strong institutional church, and it harmonized with the obvious givenness of the national church. Here, in 1874, Kuyper drew especially on the eighteenth-century Dutch theologian Appelius, who was known for his stress on the ecclesial community and its covenantal foundations,[62] and this reliance on Appelius continued in the treatise on covenant theology that Kuyper wrote several years later.

Kuyper fortified his high-church baptismal theology in 1880 with a comprehensive study of covenant theology, *The Doctrine of the Covenants*. This series of articles concluded that the covenant drew a divine boundary line around the church, defining who belonged and who did not. As the ritual of entrance into the covenantal camp, baptism crowned this discussion, and, crucially, Kuyper located the warrant for administering the sacrament to infants in the objective ecclesial community rather than in religious experience.

One motivation for Kuyper's churchly, covenantal scheme came from the original impetus for the study. J. W. Felix, curator of the Free University of Amsterdam, had requested that Kuyper write these articles to prove his suitability for the chair of dogmatic theology. Kuyper had recently completed a series on particular grace,[63] but Felix and perhaps Philip Hoedemaker feared that Kuyper's free-church vision was a bit too modern and the series on particular grace potentially individualistic and sectarian, if not given sufficient covenantal counterweight.[64] So Felix asked Kuyper to demonstrate his Reformed credentials by writing on the doctrine of the covenant; on the assurance that Kuyper would do so, "so that calling as well as election would be made sure," he was assigned the position in dogmatics.[65]

In his covenant theology, Kuyper took up the question of who should be baptized and on what basis, but this time from a slightly different perspective than before. The question was not only who to baptize but also what the baptismal strategy implied for the church's relation to the world, two issues naturally related since the flip side of who to baptize was who not to. This made baptism a question of the church's public role as much as one about its inner workings. Kuyper took pains to distinguish his covenantal theology from sectarian, individualistic solutions for distinguishing between church and world. He took a broad approach to the question of who should be baptized, and, notably, his rationale for admission to the sacrament, like his account of baptismal efficacy, hinged on objective and public measures.

With regard to adults, church membership did not depend on election or regeneration but on covenant fidelity. Whereas sects like the seventeenth-century Dutch Labadists had pursued a church of the truly regenerated or the elect, Kuyper felt these mysteries were too deep to penetrate. Although he did not doubt that believers enjoyed every benefit of Perkins's golden chain, these things, from election to sanctification, were invisible and of little practical value in the visible church:

> Neither the middle nor the very first nor any link in the golden chain of salvation can bring us farther.... Therefore God has now bestowed his covenant on us so that distinguishing according to that Covenant we would escape the dangers which every other division brings with it, and yet avoid identification with the world.[66]

Judging according to covenantal measures meant judging according to tangible evidence, namely, a person's confession of faith and life. The group in view in election and the group determined by these visible measures did not perfectly coincide,[67] and that explained why the church could never be a church of the regenerate. The church was always a mixed body composed of elect and nonelect, and the sectarian pursuit of a pure church was consigned to futility because of this.

This left the question of children. On what basis could they be included and initiated by baptism when they could not yet live up to the covenantal conditions? They were included in the church for a different, but no less covenantal, reason: because the covenant consisted of generations. Children were baptized and included in the church not on account of their own faith but as members of the Covenant of Grace:[68]

> Salvation is certainly not bound to generations. The Lord has his own from every nation. But God the Lord has freely thus ordained that by far most of his elect would be born from particular nations and in those nations from particular families.... Consequently, the earthly Covenant of Grace consists not out of individual persons, but on the contrary of a group of families organically belonging together.[69]

Based on this covenantal rationale, the rule Appelius gave (and Kuyper followed) for baptism was broad: "Baptize all who enter the house of baptism."[70]

The so-called external covenant, another concept borrowed from Appelius, further explained the church's sacramental function and its proper boundaries. The covenant had two sides, said Kuyper, an external side and an internal side. The external form was the church, the covenant institution, while the internal side was a hidden reality within persons. In its external form, the covenant was the divine ladder between heaven and earth. It joined the institutional church to God's eternal decrees, establishing the church as God's ordained means to work out his decrees in history. The external covenant in the institutional church could not be simply equated with the whole number of covenant members on earth, since of course there were true covenant members in other church institutions such as the Roman Catholic Church. Nonetheless, "in working appearance the earthly Covenant of Grace is wholly bound up in the visible church."[71] This covenantal delineation of the church's boundaries reinforced Kuyper's account of the work of grace through the objective, institutional church and its means of grace. "[Spiritual] life does not bring one into the Covenant; the Covenant brings one into life."[72]

The external covenant also laid the church boundaries in a way that erred on the side of caution and graciousness. It was a supreme error to assume either that the external covenant coincided perfectly with the internal covenant or that the two covenants could be distinguished from one another. Rather, in actual practice, many members of the church, the external covenant, ought to be assumed to be members of the circle of the elect. Consequently, by virtue of their membership in the external covenant some would be treated "'as though they actually were' what they probably were not."[73]

The question remaining was how baptism could strengthen faith, as the Heidelberg Catechism said,[74] in infants too young to believe. Kuyper did not simply adapt Appelius here; he quoted him—for ten pages.[75] Infant baptism was not for the sake of the faith of the child, at least not yet (it might later be a means to his conversion), not even for the sake of the parents, be they unbelievers; it was for strengthening the faith of the church and, once the baptized child had been converted, for strengthening his or her faith.[76] Thus, the ground for baptism was objective (outside of the child being baptized) and public (based on common, shared concerns), and to some extent the efficacy of baptism was, too. While the insistence for a rigorous judgment according to covenantal fidelity would certainly pare down the national church's adult membership, Kuyper's arguments for infant baptism, based on membership in the covenant family and nation, showed a great deal of sympathy for the ethic of the national church.

On the basis of this covenant theology, Kuyper proposed several changes in liturgical practice, which were, if anything, a plan to make the *volkskerk* more consistent in its principles, not a gauntlet thrown down before it. It was common practice in the Netherlands Reformed Church, especially in larger churches like the Amsterdam congregation, to hold baptism services separately from the regular worship services. Kuyper had once advocated the practice of separate baptismal services,[77] but after his study of the covenant he railed against them because "it feeds the false idea, as if the children were baptized as individuals and not as members of the church."[78] So strong was the covenantal–ecclesial bond that it stretched beyond the nuclear family. Although the child's parent may not have been in good ecclesiastical standing, the child could still be baptized on the basis of other witnesses or the consistory: "even slave-children were baptized by our fathers."[79] Baptism, except in very special circumstances, may never be refused, even for those of Turkish or Jewish parentage. The only condition was that "a single member of the congregation has charge over them"—a broad church policy if ever there was one.[80]

In spite of his drum beating for church reform, Kuyper's covenant theology made clear that he was not thereby seeking a break with the church. The covenant established an organic link between the church and the nation through its familial workings. It would have been difficult from these arguments to predict or defend secession from the church. Two historical considerations suggest that a break would not have appeared inevitable when Kuyper drafted his first covenant theology. First, the controversies over certificates for ministers and subscription vows that so upset Kuyper had not yet happened in February 1882, when he finished his articles on covenant. Only later that year did the synod decide that ordinands need not confess Christ or his forgiveness, an action that roused Kuyper to definitive action. Second, Kuyper had recently founded the Free University of Amsterdam, but there was not yet any practical need for a church to accompany the university. Initially Kuyper expected that graduates of the Free University would serve in the Netherlands Reformed Church. He did not learn that they were not allowed, until the 1882 synod (a decision that was reconfirmed in 1885).[81] Therefore, two of the weightiest considerations propelling Kuyper into an ecclesiastical frenzy still had not occurred when he rested his case for infant baptism on the Covenant of Grace. In 1880 he might well have hoped that his own children and grandchildren would be baptized by the same church that baptized him.

Presumptive Regeneration: Private Church, Private Sacrament

In 1886, only a few years after Kuyper's treatise on covenant theology, he, five other officers of the Amsterdam congregation, and various others around the Netherlands broke with the *volkskerk* to form a secession church, the Nether German Reformed Churches (Nederduitsche Gereformeerde Kerken, a name that recalled the Dutch church of the seventeenth-century golden age), also known as the Doleantie or the Aggrieved. Events leading up to this break came to a climax in the "panel-sawing," when Kuyper and his crew broke into the New Church in Amsterdam. The outcome of the break-in was the free church that Kuyper had long sought—only not on the terms he had hoped, since he received far less support than he had wished. Sociologically speaking—and in hindsight—the free church was a denomination. It was a voluntary religious association set in a liberal society wherein the constitutional separation of church and state ensured religious pluralism. One of the key changes for Kuyper's church, therefore, was a social one. Kuyper's church now had a completely different social standing from the national church, and the twofold function of baptism, as a work of grace and a social marker, had to be revised to fit this new social situation. His new theology of baptism, based on the concept of presumptive regeneration, put the emphasis exactly where this believers' church did: on the subjective spiritual life of the individual believer.

Before the Doleantie broke with the national church, there was already a tension in Kuyper's theology of baptism. He finished his articles on covenant theology with his account of the members of the covenant in 1881, and immediately he began a new work on the practical application of covenant theology. There Kuyper invoked seventeenth-century pietist and Reformed scholastic Voet, alongside Appelius, in support of his theology of baptism.[82] Yet there was a discrepancy between Appelius and Voet. Whereas Appelius urged the baptism of infants on the basis of their membership in the community, Voet said infants should be baptized for their own sake. Kuyper did not even hint at a possible incongruity between these two accounts, though after the Doleantie he did and sided entirely with Voet. In 1895, pressed on this earlier contradiction, Kuyper pleaded:

> Do not forget that I was first brought over from modernist fold into the Ethical circle, and so came into Reformed circles only at a rather advanced age, and then I had to find my own way, little by little, without a teacher, in the middle of a very stressful and eventful life, in order to understand the writings of the Confession of our fathers.[83]

Beside the content of Kuyper's new theology of baptism, the way he promoted it also supported his free-church ecclesiology with its stress on popular support rather than presumed status. Kuyper debuted his new theology of baptism, fully committed to Voet's position, in 1890 in his commentary on the Heidelberg Catechism, *From the Voice of Dortrecht*.[84] To make sure the Reformed confessions were familiar to clergy and laypeople alike, Kuyper oversaw the printing of multiple cheap editions of the three forms of unity (the Heidelberg Catechism, Canons of Dort, and Belgic Confession), and largely due to these efforts the Reformed confessions became widely available to the laity for the first time in the nineteenth century.[85] The commentary on the Heidelberg Catechism ran in the newspaper, instead of an academic journal, to educate this broad, popular audience. Written on the morn of the Doleantie, it articulated Kuyper's mature theology for the young church.

This new theology of baptism prioritized the immediate work of grace by the Holy Spirit in the individual over the corporate and mediated grace of the church as the grounds for admitting people to the sacraments. The prerequisite for admitting anyone to the sacraments was faith, but this was a different faith than he meant before.[86] Whereas earlier Kuyper referred to the shared faith of the congregation, now he referred to the faith of the person being baptized. Grace could then work through the sacraments to strengthen faith.

This, however, raised further questions about the nature and origin of faith and the case of infants whose faith was yet uncertain. Previously, Kuyper had said this was a preparing grace: "through baptism a mystical bond between the one baptized and the body of Christ exists, through which the terrain before personal regeneration is smoothed."[87] That is, baptism preceded faith. Now, however, Kuyper argued that a kind of faith came through the immediate work of the Spirit in regeneration, and baptism followed the Spirit's implantation of faith in regeneration. The distinction between act and potential further explained the precise nature of faith that such a regenerated child might have. In regeneration, the Holy Spirit implanted the ability to believe or the potential of faith (*geloofsvermogen*).[88] Baptism as a means of grace was still means of grace but was no longer a means toward the first work of grace in a person's life. For that, the Spirit worked directly on the person, independent of church and means. The work of the church was to nurture that potential faith into actual faith.

Kuyper steered a careful course between several perceived errors. First, there was a general neglect of the sacraments, and especially baptism, among Dutch Protestants due to a creeping Zwinglianism, perhaps imported from American Methodists and Baptists, which emptied the sacraments of grace. Rationalism went a step further and emptied not just the sacrament but also Christianity of supernatural grace and replaced it with ethical pronouncements.[89] Roman Catholics and Lutherans, on the other hand, made the church the mediator of grace and wrongly taught that the sacrament worked regeneration (i.e., baptismal regeneration).[90] Finally, there was the error that Kuyper once made: "in our days Baptism is generally conceived of as being administered in hope of *subsequent* regeneration whereas Calvinists have always taught that Baptism of infants should be administered on the presumption that regeneration has preceded."[91] Correctly understood, Kuyper now said, regeneration came before baptism, and this greatly emphasized personal religious experience of the Spirit's hidden work of regeneration as a basis for baptism and deemphasized membership in the objective community. Or, in other words, regeneration came by a hidden work of the Spirit rather than by public ritual.

With this theology of baptism went a new, corresponding account of the social significance of baptism as a public sign distinguishing God's people from the world. Especially on this point Kuyper's revised theology of baptism argued against the social ethic of the national church. Kuyper began down the familiar logic of covenant. According to the rule of the covenant, God set election primarily in connection with families, and therefore the covenant included both believers and their children. Since baptism was the sacrament of the covenant, children ought to be baptized, or, in other words, baptism was an inherited and automatic benefit of the covenant. This rule simply stated, however, lent too much support to the faulty practices of the national church:

> This rule would mean that every child of whom it could be shown that one of his ancestors had ever confessed the Lord, would be considered as an elect and sealed with baptism. So in present day Europe, every living soul must be baptized....But this cannot be, because with this consequence every opposition between the church and the world would fall away; and simply birth of a woman, not the work of the Grace of God, would become the presupposition for baptism.[92]

Explaining which children should be baptized and why was, for Kuyper, at base the problem of distinguishing these two opposing societies: the church and the world. By *world* Kuyper meant something like Augustine's city of man, a society at odds with the church (not civil society, which included the church). Kuyper's criticism of the national church, including the conservatives, was not only about the work of grace in the sacrament. Doubtless many conservatives shared Kuyper's enthusiasm for orthodox Reformed scholastics like Voet, but Kuyper's criticism of the national church's baptismal policy extended deeper to the social relation implied in the sacrament. That was what distinguished his free church. Kuyper no longer took for granted that the Dutch nation was a Christian nation or that the church could make it so through baptism. As a voluntary institution in a plural civil society, the church could no longer indiscriminately baptize all who came into the house of baptism.[93]

Kuyper's explanation of who should be baptized included the logic of covenant but only indirectly, which led some in the Christian Reformed Church to say that Kuyper had abandoned covenant altogether. His rationale for presumptive regeneration made a subtle theological distinction, perhaps an overly subtle one, between the basis for baptizing children and presuming them to be regenerate. Children were baptized on their presumed regeneration, the Spirit's prior work implanting the potential to believe. But being a hidden and private work of the Spirit, the regeneration of any person could not be known with certainty—against the pretentions of the Anabaptists. If regeneration could not be known for sure, then might some reason be given for presuming upon it? Yes. Regeneration could be presumed on the basis of the centrality of families and generations in the covenant wherein the salvation of the elect was worked out.[94] The basis for baptism was not covenant membership, which Kuyper feared would lead back to the national church, but was regeneration. Regeneration, however, was presumed on the basis of covenant membership, thus, to Kuyper's mind, avoiding sectarianism.

Kuyper also took a more restricted view of covenant membership than he had before. Now, rather than taking Abraham's servants as precedent, he took Isaac and Ishmael. Not all of Abraham's descendants were circumcised, but only the children of the promise, which Kuyper understood to mean the members of the nuclear family, and in some extreme cases children of believing grandparents could be considered heirs of the covenant.[95]

The tragedy of infant mortality again figured into Kuyper's reasoning. He estimated that almost half of the children born died before their eighth birthday. God, whose election was worked out through covenant, would not forget those covenant promises to parents, as Dort had taught. Yet these children still suffered from Adam's sin. If God saved these children too young to come to mature faith, he did not withhold any of the benefits of salvation from them, including regeneration. Kuyper's reasonable conclusion was that if the church may presume the salvation of these children based on the covenant promises, their regeneration may likewise be presumed. And if the regeneration of 50 percent of the church's children may be presumed, then why not all? "With this, as you yourself also feel, the responsibility and the right of infant baptism is irrevocably established."[96]

This theology of baptism was critical for Kuyper and for generations of Dutch Protestants after, not only or primarily because of its account of the work of grace but also because it helped Kuyper explain how Reformed Protestants could retain their practice of infant baptism in a world that otherwise threatened to undo it. It did so by a paradoxical and potentially contradictory formula. Baptism, the seal of the covenant, was administered based on the private, subjective work of the Spirit in regeneration. The error of the national church was to suppose that the New Testament church was still a national church as Israel had been. In those cases, infants were initiated on the basis of external, tangible, and material factors.[97] But after Pentecost, the New Testament church was no longer a national church but a world church, and the covenant community marker given at Pentecost was the Spirit, whose work was not observable. Wholly different was the question of how this work of the Spirit might be known, or at least presumed, and that did require external and objective measures, found in the covenant family. Therefore, there was a disjunction between how one might be known to be a member of the community, and so initiated in baptism, and the basis of community membership itself, which was private.

The visible organic church, which had allowed Kuyper to delegitimize the institutional church, performed a similar function in his theology of baptism. During the course of his life, Kuyper ended up with three, not two, churches, each with their own requirements for membership, but the institutional church was certainly the most flimsy, and by definition prone to extinction, of the three. The first ecclesial body was the invisible, organic church, or Mystical Body of Christ. Membership in this body was only through regeneration and the receiving of a new ecclesial-corporal head, Christ in place of Adam.[98] Between the organic church and the institutional church, there was now another body that Kuyper introduced in his polemics for church reformation: the visible organic church.[99] Baptism made the invisible Mystical Body visible and signified membership in this body—a convenient point that relativized the importance of the institutional church in which one had been born and baptized.[100] "But meanwhile it absolutely does not follow that therefore he would already be a member in the institutional church...by his baptism."[101] What did make one a member of the institutional church, the key to membership, was voluntary confession. "The baptized child can only later, through his own voluntary action come to confession and entering into indispensible stipulations, through which they only then in the full sense appear personally as members of the institutional church."[102] Till that time such baptized, yet-to-confess members were "incomplete members" on the basis of their parents. On this reckoning, the institutional church had no more substantial warrant than labor guilds, political parties, private schools, or tennis clubs.

The external covenant had once been Kuyper's argument for the divine sanction for the church as institution. His delegitimization of the church institution was complete when he retracted the external covenant from the church's undergirding because it gave credibility to the state church.[103] After that it was not a far step to deny that the church was in any sense a *heilsinstituut*.[104] What was once the mother of the elect, ended up the chambermaid.

Conclusion

Churches are never purely private institutions, and baptism proves it. James Kennedy explains:

> In lands with a powerful state church, where church membership is almost equated with membership in the nation, baptism is seen as a public event because it is an entrance into a broader community. This was also once a shared understanding in Protestant Netherlands. J. A. Wormser [of the Netherlands Reformed Church] said, "Teach the nation to understand and esteem her baptism, and church and state will be saved."[105]

The separation of church and state changed things, as Kuyper recognized. Separate from the public institution of state, the churches became *de jure* private institutions, though of course it took some time to work out *de facto*. Even then, Kennedy points out, baptism was still a public event. "Even without a national church baptism can be a public event: here God let humanity see that this child belongs to God."[106] Contemporary Christians may think of their own public profession of faith every Sunday when they recite the Apostle's creed. This is held to be a public profession, because Christians are not simply confessing their faith to each other, not even only to God and each other but are also confessing their faith before the world, attempting to obey Jesus' command (Luke 12:8, Matthew 10:32). Likewise, baptism speaks not only to the church but also to the world.

The development of Abraham Kuyper's baptismal theology illustrates the challenge Reformed baptismal theology and practice face in modern society. Kuyper's secession church was a private church insofar as it rested on the private, voluntary support of its members instead of the public support of nation and state, yet baptism for Kuyper and the Reformed tradition generally retained (and retains) a very public significance: it distinguishes the church from the world. Baptism is more than a means or instrument of grace; it is a communal identity marker according to the Belgic Confession. By it, "we are received into the Church of God, and separated from all other people and strange religions."[107] Despite the church's new private status, this particular function of baptism is a very public one. The question Kuyper wrestled with was how to understand this public symbol in a private institution.

Baptism is also a means of grace, and modern civil society, which casts the church in the role of voluntary religious organization, presents no less a challenge to Reformed understandings of the efficacy of grace in the sacrament. In many respects, churches can act like one voluntary organization among others in civil society with little adverse effect. But infant baptism belies such action. Children are not baptized because they choose God; they are baptized because God chooses them. Secularists grasp this—probably better than anyone—when they protest that infant baptism forces children into a religious tradition not of their own choosing, which it undeniably does.

So modern society presented (and presents) a contradiction, but the contradiction is one already present in Reformed beliefs and practice. The practice of infant baptism tends toward a very broad church. Yet the very point of the sacrament is to distinguish the church from the world, little use if the whole world (or Europe at least) was already baptized.

6

Theologian of the Revolution: Abraham Kuyper's Radical Proposal for Church and State

The Herald adopts the ground principle of the Revolution.[1]

As far as the state is concerned, Kuyper remains with the Revolution.[2]

ABRAHAM KUYPER DEFINED himself by his opposition to the French Revolution.[3] His heirs continue to do so,[4] and so do historians such as Michael Wintle, for example, who places Kuyper at the culmination of the conservative movement in nineteenth-century Dutch Protestantism. Wintle contrasts Kuyper with progressive supporters of liberal and Enlightenment values.[5] Kuyper's contemporaries, however, did not see it this way. Philip Hoedemaker (Figure 6.2a) accused Kuyper of promoting the principles of the French Revolution in Kuyper's newspaper in *The Herald* (*De Heraut*). Moreover, if Kuyper did in fact oppose the French Revolution, as he claimed, he did not therefore see himself as a conservative. He derided religious conservatism, and in his sermon "Conservatism and Orthodoxy," preached at the distinguished conservative congregation of Utrecht, he set conservatism over against orthodoxy, an ironic contrast to J. Gresham Machen's *Christianity and Liberalism*.[6] And in 1886, the year of the Doleantie, the newspaper *De Uilenspiegel* portrayed Kuyper as a conspirator in fomenting revolution with modernist and ex-pastor Domela Nieuwenhuis (Figure 6.1). Hoedemaker was not alone in his estimate of Kuyper.

Abraham Kuyper was a revolutionary and a radical, his political mantra notwithstanding. The confusion is a semantic and historical one. What

108

Aan de vruchten kent men den boom.

D-m l- N-w nh-s. — Wij kunnen tevreden zijn, ex-collega!... het zaad dat wij gestrooid hebben, gij en ik, begint te kiemen en hier en daar zelfs reeds uit te loopen...
K-p-r. — Ach, ik vrees, broeder, dat het nog lang duren zal, vóórdat wij oogsten kunnen.   Men verstikt de kiemen met geweld!
D-m-l- N-w-nh-s. — Geen moedeloosheid, vriend!...   Laat men doen wat men wil.   Gij en ik blijven voortgaan met de zaden van onrust en beroering en van opstand tegen het gezag met volle handen uit te strooien ..

FIGURE 6.1 Kuyper the revolutionary cartoon. With modernist pastor F. Domela Nieuwenhuis. Caption: "The tree is known by its fruits." From the *Uilenspiegel* August 7, 1886. Collection Historisch Documentatiecentrum voor het Nederlands Protestantisme (1800-heden) VU University Amsterdam.

kind of revolutionary was he? Historians most often contrast Protestant modernism with theological conservatism, and Kuyper was certainly no modernist theologian. However, neither was he a religious conservative. He would not accept the existing order. The opposite of this kind of religious conservatism, which maintains and endorses the status quo, is not theological modernism but religious radicalism, the impulse to overturn existing structures and replace them with new ones, and that is the kind of radical Kuyper was. One might consider the respect that Kuyper cultivated for modernist Allard Pierson (Figure 6.2b) and compare Pierson's secession from the Netherlands Reformed Church with Kuyper's. Kuyper and Pierson took the same action, albeit from different motives, to achieve similar radical ends. They differed from the irenicals, as Kuyper contemptuously dubbed the national church conservatives, who pursued the peace and unity of the church at any theological price. For all the differences

FIGURE 6.2 Kuyper's rivals: (a) Conservative Philip Hoedemaker and (b) modernist Allard Pierson. Collection Historisch Documentatiecentrum voor het Nederlands Protestantisme (1800-heden) VU University Amsterdam.

between them, what the irenicals had, and what Kuyper lacked, was the commitment to a single, broad, national church at all costs. Kuyper's objection to this system constituted a revolutionary departure not only from Dutch tradition but also from the settlement of Western Christendom.

The matter of Kuyper's radicalism gets at the question of just what was new about Dutch neo-Calvinism. This question, John Bolt suggests, does not yet have a complete answer, though it has something to do with the church.[7] The new in Kuyper's neo-Calvinism was not a single idea or even a collection of doctrines but was an ethos that oriented his adjustment of Calvinism to the social situation of the nineteenth century wherein separation of church and state, religious pluralism, and democracy were ascendant, an ethos that not only tolerated but also even incorporated these features of modern society into Calvinism. This ethos was not simply a matter of this doctrine or that, but it came to especial poignancy in Kuyper's doctrine of the church. One place where this is clearly seen is Kuyper's proposal for church and state. By itself Kuyper's proposal for church and state was not the sum of neo-Calvinism, but it signaled a shift in the way Protestantism would do business in modern society and was close to the heart of the new religious and social synthesis that Kuyper envisioned. Kuyper put forth a vision of society that separated the Dutch nation and the Dutch state from any single institutional church and that allowed for a plurality of churches, or, in Kuyper's terms, the *pluriformity* of the church. He provided warrant for his account of the new social settlement by explaining the differing natures and roles of church and state, and here his doctrines of common and particular grace and the sovereignty of Christ played especially important roles. After examining these matters and others, this chapter then turns to Hoedemaker's critique, which brings Kuyper's ideas into sharper historical relief since Hoedemaker was an unquestioned Reformed conservative if ever there was one.

A host of literature has now arisen addressing the topics of natural law and two kingdoms theology in the Reformed and neo-Calvinist tradition.[8] As a work of historical theology, this chapter concerns itself with the meaning of Kuyper's theology in its own right, in its own day. While this chapter does not directly adjudicate contemporary debates, it occasionally gestures toward them and hopes to shed some light on them. Primarily, however, this chapter tries to make some historical sense of Kuyper's theology, if not to answer once and for all the question of what Kuyper said in minute detail then perhaps still to explain so what. In so doing, this chapter limits itself primarily to Kuyper's discussion of church and state in his three-volume work *Common Grace*, originally published serially in the *Herald*. When studying Kuyper, there is always the possibility (perhaps one should say the likelihood) that he says something different in some other place. That is the risk of this approach. Nonetheless, *Common Grace* is the fruit of Kuyper's mature thought and one of his most important contributions, and for those reasons it carries intrinsic interest. At twenty-eight chapters long, Kuyper's discussion of church and state is also quite an extensive statement. To appreciate the creativity of this proposal, it is helpful to begin by recalling the situation he found himself in.

The Travails of Church and State in the Nineteenth Century

The relationship of church and state in the Netherlands during the nineteenth century shifted and surged as the Netherlands moved toward a more modern arrangement. The Netherlands was never a confessional state in the manner of Scandinavian countries, but the Reformed church was unquestionably the dominant church. Since the Reformation, the Reformed church had been the public church, whose members alone could hold public office, for example, and which had preeminent public sanction. Formal disestablishment came with the rise of the French, revolutionary-inspired Batavian Republic in the 1790s, but under Napoleonic influence the Reformed church regained public prominence. Napoleon and his followers regarded it as more politically expedient to have religion and the churches on their side and under their oversight than against them, so once again the Reformed church took a prominent national place. Willem I, a true Dutch monarch, continued these trends centralizing, regulating, and consolidating the heretofore more loosely and locally organized Reformed church into the Netherlands Reformed Church (NHK) in 1816. Willem's son, Willem II, did not share his father's ecclesiastical concerns, and under his rule the liberal constitution of 1848 defined the separation of church and state for good. Until then, "Dutch Reformed ministers plausibly could claim that their church was the spiritual centre of the nation, cherished and protected by a monarch and a ministry that sought to give the church a prominent role in Dutch society."[9]

As it turned out, it was easier to separate church and state on paper than in actual practice. After 1848 various attachments between church and state remained, and many of the Reformed were loath to give them up. The churches continued to receive financial subsidy from the state, a practice not completely abolished until the 1980s (in one of the supposedly most secular and progressive countries in Europe). Ministers for the NHK were still educated at the public universities (*rijksuniversiteiten*), and *volkskerk* became the motto for many in the NHK. This post-1848 church is difficult to characterize. From an American perspective, the Netherlands may look to have been still firmly grounded in the ancien régime given the ongoing restrictions on Catholics, the public privilege of the *NHK*, and the antidemocratic sentiments circulating among the elites, but the old regime was weakening. There were, relatively speaking, more freedoms for Catholics and smaller communions and a growing sense of self-consciousness and self-determination among the people.

Charles Taylor offers a scheme for interpreting this peculiar transition and for defining the social changes that Kuyper's ecclesiology accounted accounted for. Generally, the nineteenth century moved from a "paleo-Durkheimian" situation to a "neo-Durkheimian" one, he says. Emile Durkheim recognized the close relationship between religion and society, so close that he proclaimed society to be the sacred. That is, the sacred is a purely social construction. Without succumbing to Durkheim's sociological reductionism, Taylor refers to the classic situation of one dominant societal church as paleo-Durkheimian, which consisted in two elements: a single dominant church; and a close relationship between that church and civil society—*cuius regio, eius religio* in Reformation-era terms. Responsible citizenship and the common good depended on participation in the one church and the close coordination and cooperation between church and state. The neo-Durkheimian situation experienced a degree of religious pluralization, but nonetheless religion, especially Christianity, was still presumed to be a public good. One might think of characterization of American religion as "Protestant, Catholic, Jew" or the appeal to "Judeo-Christian" values. One needn't be a Calvinist, Catholic, or Methodist in the neo-Durkheimian situation, but one had to be something. The religious pluralization that inaugurated the neo-Durkheimian era occurred preeminently in the nineteenth century. Correspondingly, Hugh McLeod says that the key to understanding nineteenth-century religious culture is pluralization, not just the proliferation of alternatives to Christianity but pluralization within Christianity itself.[10] In this situation, Abraham Kuyper's proposal for church and state called for the end of the paleo-Durkheimian framework, a framework that had oriented Western society since Constantine and that the Reformation had not overturned. In the Netherlands, even with its relative religious tolerance, this was a revolutionary call.

Abraham Kuyper's Radical Proposal

Abraham Kuyper viewed the problem of church and state in the nineteenth century in terms remarkably similar to Charles Taylor's. Kuyper observed that for most of medieval Christendom, there had been a close unity of church and state. The Great Schism between the East and the West and even the Reformation did not significantly alter this. The Reformers from Martin Luther and Huldrych Zwingli, John Calvin and Heinrich Bullinger, John Wycliffe and John Knox to Guido de Bres and Roman Catholics as well assumed the unity of the visible church and the coordination of church with the state. The Belgic Confession, written by de Bres and included in the Three Forms of Unity, made the common post-Constantinian and early Protestant assumption about the unity of church, state, and society. Article 36 of the confession charged the magistrates that "the government's task is not limited to caring for and watching over the public domain but extends also to upholding the sacred ministry, with a view to removing and destroying all idolatry and false worship of the Antichrist."[11] The chief hindrance to upholding this element of the confession in the nineteenth century, Kuyper said, was pluralism (in agreement with McLeod). "The relation of church and state undergoes no stronger change than through the splitting of the one visible church into many churches of different, even partly contradictory confession."[12] Was any government competent to decide among the myriad churches which was the one true church and which ones ought to be removed and destroyed? Kuyper asked.

Democratic governments, like that of the Netherlands, further complicated things. In Russia, the czar could at least establish the true church with little dispute, Kuyper observed, but in the Netherlands it would be the voters deciding. Kuyper worried that this would unleash an ecclesiastical civil war or, worse, that voters would confuse the prerogatives that belonged to them and those that belonged to God. Moreover, what would happen when the majority shifted in years to come and voted that a different church was the true church? Would the formerly true church then become a sect? Democracy was seeping through the walls, but "Christ's church is not judged by the majority of voices."[13] For this reason, article 36 was impossible to implement in the modern, plural world, and Kuyper proposed abolishing it altogether. That was not as simple as removing the offending clauses from the confession; it required a new logic of church, state, and society. This Kuyper provided in a series of articles under the heading of "Church and State" within his larger series on Common Grace (eventually appearing in volume 3 of *De Gemeene Gratie*).

As a preface to his theology of church and state, Kuyper's reordering of church and nation also clearly expressed his vision of a neo-Durkheimian society. Kuyper argued that though the invisible church had existed since creation, the church institution had not. There was no church institution under Israel. It was a new creation at Pentecost. As such, the institutional church had never been a single institutional unit even at the beginning, nor could it be. To think so was the error of Rome. Churches and confessions varied according to ethnic, historic, and local differences. "The Javanese are a different race than us; they live in a different region; they stand on a wholly different level of development; they are created differently in their inner life; they have a wholly different past behind them; and they have grown up in wholly different ideas. To expect of them that they should find the fitting expression of their faith in our Confession and in our Catechism is therefore absurd."[14] Such diversity was not a problem but part of the beauty of human life.

Neither did the division of churches correspond to the division of nations. Instead, Kuyper proposed the pluriformity of the church. He objected to the idea of a *volkskerk*, a single church institution for the Dutch nation, which had become popular in the NHK in the late nineteenth century.[15] He believed that the Dutch were a Christian and Protestant nation but that this might be expressed in different ecclesiastical institutions with diverse confessions. The church was thereby pluriform, plural in its external form.[16] The Reformation should have ended the one state, one church settlement, but here it failed to carry through its own principles. Further, Kuyper's construal of the church institution as a mechanical and artificial imposition permitted his doctrine of plurformity, which was itself a further development of the ecclesiological principles by which Kuyper legitimized his Doleantie churches alongside the more historically grounded NHK.[17] In retrospect, it seems that this plan paralleled the American denominational system.

Kuyper provided theological legitimation for his vision of a religiously plural society through his theology of church and state. In particular, his distinction between common and particular grace and his understanding of the mediatorship of Christ set these two institutions apart. The primary difference between the institutions of church and state depended on common grace and particular grace. In simplest terms, "the Church is from Particular Grace, and...the State...is an institution of Common Grace."[18] Common grace pertained to nature, and "the light necessary to form the state was none other than the light of nature."[19] Kuyper did allow that special revelation was of value in refining the state's role, but it was not strictly necessary. In contrast, the church was grounded in the supernatural, specifically in special revelation and regeneration.

With the pluriformity of the church, the responsibility of the state was not to judge which confession and which church were the true ones, a task for which the government had no competency as an institution of common grace. Instead, the state simply had to provide for the free movement of the churches under it. Nonetheless, the presence of churches within the state was a salutary thing, which the state ought not take for granted. Churches promoted civil order and virtue. While the state did not absolutely depend on the church, particular grace, or special revelation for its existence, the nation and the state were indisputably better for them.[20] In the pattern of church and society that Kuyper outlined, everyone did not have to be a member of a particular church, but everyone (or almost everyone) ought to be a member of some church.

This distinction between the church as institution of particular grace and the state as an institution of common grace also sorted out these two institutions as private and public, respectively. Common grace covered all of life, and consequently "the state comprehends *the whole* of our human race, the church only *a part*."[21] Consequently, common grace and the state were public entities insofar as they covered the common, shared elements of human life. In contrast, particular saving grace was not public, and, correspondingly, neither was the church. It was limited in scope and required voluntary consent.

Church and state also differed in their relation to the Son of God, and in explaining this Kuyper departed from his dictum of twenty years earlier (or at least as it is commonly interpreted[22]) that "there is not a thumb's breadth in the whole domain of our human existence over which Christ, who is Sovereign over all, does not cry: 'Mine!'"[23] Both church and state had their origin in the Son of God. Nevertheless, while the Son was mediator of creation for all people, he was Christ, mediator of redemption, only for the elect. Therefore, the Son was head of the church in his capacity as redemptive Messiah, Christ, "while in contrast, this Christ rules in the life of States, not as mediator of redemption, but as mediator of Creation, and thus as Son of God."[24] Strictly speaking then, Christ was not Christ for the state. As Messiah and Christ, he only could cry "Mine!" over the church, even if as Son of God he did so over all creation.

This point was so contentious that Kuyper returned to it again in his series on church and state. Apparently critics had responded that Christ ruled over not only the church but also all creation. Such a position, Kuyper said, led to a hopeless confusion over the roles of church and state. Confusing Christ's lordship in the visible and the invisible, over civil and ecclesiastical life, over common and particular grace led either to the state usurping the rights of the church or the church subjecting the state. Kuyper appealed to the Reformed Confessions. As mediator at God's right hand, Christ was never said to take up the providential work of God. "On the contrary, Christ is only spoken of in connection with Particular Grace in the great work of Redemption."[25]

Further differences between state and church concerned their scope and power, which directly correlated to these institutions as natural and supernatural, respectively. The sphere of the state was observable, natural life, whereas the church dealt with the heart. The state used coercive means in its ordering of natural life, whereas the church used spiritual means. Finally, the state was an institution that was given and whose authority was absolute even extending over life and death, as for example when the state called one to go to war. The church, on the other hand, was not given but voluntary and could not force anyone to become a member.[26]

Kuyper's proposal was no ivory tower abstraction. After the French Revolution and later the Batavian Revolution, King Willem I had reorganized the Reformed churches in the Netherlands in 1816 into the Netherlands Reformed Church following the Napoleonic model. Willem constructed an ecclesiastical hierarchy with its pinnacle in the national synod. Kuyper protested this intrusion of state power in church matters. He blamed the melding of church and state for various ills: the cooption of the church for state purposes, a lethargic spirituality induced by dependency on state handouts, and the use of the church by "wealthy young men of high standing, who use the gospel to strengthen their position and family influence."[27] Kuyper recognized what sociologists have confirmed a century later: the state church is a losing proposition in the modern world.[28]

Astutely attuned to the plural and disestablished character of modern society, this position involved a certain irony. A necessary correlate of the doctrine of pluriformity of the church was the priority of the subject over the corporate, institutional church. Kuyper interpreted the Reformation as the great turn to the subject, when doctrinal authority was transferred from the church to the people led by the Spirit.[29] Consequently, when it came to determining which church among the myriad churches was the true church, Kuyper left it up to the individual believer's judgment to compare and determine which church was the purer and the better.[30] So while Kuyper charged theological modernism with putting the human subject in the place of God, he put the subject in the place of the church.[31] Subjectivism thus appeared in Kuyper's theology, if not in his beliefs about the authority of Scripture then one step removed, in his theology of the church's right to interpret Scripture. Philip Hoedemaker was quick to point this out.

Hoedemaker's Critique

As a Protestant who held closely to the Reformed confessions, Hoedemaker is an unexpected opponent of Kuyper. After graduating with his Ph.D. in theology from the University of Utrecht, he made an odd mistake that would characterize the double bind he found himself in the rest of his life. Hoedemaker accepted the opportunity to preach in two different churches on the same Sunday, in the morning at a congregation of the Netherlands Reformed Church and in the evening in a congregation of the Christian Reformed Church (CGK), a church that had left the NHK in the secession of 1834 and had then existed more or less as a conservative Reformed sect.[32] Hoedemaker accepted the confessional theology of the CGK but cherished the broadness and the tradition of the NHK. The CGK, however, would not abide a preacher who made peace with its old ecclesiastical enemy, and they demanded that Hoedemaker choose.[33] He chose the NHK. Later, when Hoedemaker was appointed as a professor at Kuyper's Free University of Amsterdam (VU), he faced a similar dilemma. He joined the VU with the idea that it would be a bastion of Reformed orthodoxy for ministers of the NHK, but after Kuyper's secession from the NHK and the refusal of that church to ordain VU students it became clear that the VU and the NHK had different agendas and that Hoedemaker could not serve both of these masters. Again, Hoedemaker chose the NHK, with its national aspirations and its Dutch Reformed heritage. Hoedemaker was no less a critic of theological modernism and the cooption of the church by the state that had occurred under the 1816 arrangement, but he disagreed with Kuyper that secession was the right or only course. Subsequently, for all his other theological overlap with Kuyper, he opposed Kuyper with pen and paper on matters of church, state, and society.

Above all, Hoedemaker wanted one Reformed church for the Netherlands, and he detested Kuyper's tactics that endlessly divided party against party in church and in state. Hoedemaker represented an attempt to maintain the Reformation's paleo-Durkheimian situation in the modern age. Leaving aside for now the question of whose theology was more truly Reformed or biblical, Hoedemaker's or Kuyper's, Hoedemaker recognized Kuyper's reordering of church and society for what it was, an epoch-making overturning of the Reformation settlement and the Dutch Republic. Three topics in particular exhibit Kuyper's and Hoedemaker's differing approaches to church and society and their willingness, or not, to accommodate Reformed Protestantism to modern social trends: religious freedom in the form of the religious neutrality of the state; the democratization of Christianity; and the divorce of church and nation.

Abraham Kuyper had argued that although ideally the state should support the true church, in the contemporary situation, facing a plurality of churches, it was impossible for the state to determine which one was the true church. The only proper course was to permit all churches to operate freely. This, Hoedemaker said, was none other than the principle of the Revolution (i.e., the French Revolution) applied in the sphere of the state. This construal of religious freedom was an illegitimate religious neutrality foreign to the Reformed tradition. While Kuyper well knew that in the realm of ideas there was no neutrality, Hoedemaker understood better than Kuyper that institutional and social arrangements were never religiously or theologically neutral. When the state administered punitive judgments, for example, it did so on the basis of an idea of right and wrong and thus assumed a religious principle.[34] Further, Hoedemaker continued, Kuyper's concept of common grace supported this error. Kuyper too narrowly delimited the state as an institution of common grace without recourse to particular grace and special revelation:

> Special Revelation, we [i.e., Hoedemaker] opine, comprehends not only everything that stands in connection with reconciliation, that is, the restoration of fellowship between God and humanity, but everything that touches redemption in the broadest sense, namely the restoration, yes the glorifying of the first creation. And Particular grace does not fall so wholly together with the ministry of Word and Reconciliation that one can assign the terrain of the State to Common Grace and that of the church to Particular grace.[35]

It may seem as if Hoedemaker was out-Kuypering Kuyper. In fact, his critique illustrates just how much Kuyper's division of special and common grace and his application of these doctrines to church and state participated the modern project of separating the society into discrete spheres of activity and how it departed from the premodern vision of an organically interconnected society.

Hoedemaker likewise recoiled at Kuyper's democratization of Christianity in compensation for the state's incompetence in matters of religion. Since the state was not able to judge which church is the true church, the state had to rely on the voters, said Kuyper. The church had only an indirect influence on the state, via the people. In this way, Hoedemaker said, Kuyper treated doctrine as a matter public opinion, and he lost the principle that the church in its institutional appearance was the arbiter of doctrine. "Dr. Kuyper attacks the Confession in its essence, when he concludes that it is not a short synopsis of Holy Scripture (repetitio Sacrae Scripturae) but the echo of public opinion."[36] Closely related was Hoedemaker's criticism of Kuyper's partisan politics and the way this made church and state depend on the whims of the masses. In

Hoedemaker's system the state would be bound to the Word "not only through the conscience of the government officials, but through the conscience enlightened by the *public exposition of the Church* as established in the confession."[37] The state would rely on the church, not public opinion, for the right exposition of Scripture.

Finally, there was the nation. Both Kuyper and Hoedemaker exhibited the strong nationalist sentiments common to their day, and both viewed the Dutch as a Protestant nation by virtue of its history and the general character of the people. While Kuyper did not demand that this Protestant character be expressed in a single institutional church, Hoedemaker wanted to preserve the nation as a unified nation under a single Reformed church, not as a nation of disparate competing religious groups. "This [Protestant] character of the nation is connected with and finds one expression in the national church [*landskerk*], the revelation of the body of Christ in this land such as it manifests itself purified from deviations as *Reformed* Church."[38] Further, this one church would be the legal-public church, that is, recognized and supported by the state though not dominated by the state.

Kuyper supported his position by disconnecting the institutional church from nation in his biblical-theological interpretation. He claimed that the institutional church had not existed under Israel but came into existence only at Pentecost. It had, therefore, never been an institution chained to a single nation. Hoedemaker took the more traditional Reformed view and one more grounded in the Old Testament. The church had indeed existed under Israel. There one could find the ancestor of the New Testament Christian church, and, of course, the church under Israel was a national church.[39] Both views led to some ill-considered conclusions. Hoedemaker's close association between the Dutch nation and the one, true Reformed church resulted in an unsavory anti-Catholicism. Kuyper, for his part, tolerated a plurality of churches and made common cause with Catholics in a variety of political endeavors, but his antipathy for the national church apparently also hid some anti-Semitic feelings: "The national church as such is a parasitic Jewish plant that must be uprooted everywhere as a damaging weed."[40]

Conclusion

In protest to Hoedemaker's claims, Kuyper said that his idea of neutrality was not that of the men of the Revolution, by which he meant the French Revolution. Of course, it wasn't. Their neutrality, Kuyper pointed out, stemmed from the belief that religion was a private matter and that the church counted for nothing in the public domain. Against this, Kuyper championed the church as a part of national life and something that the government must honor. The crucial distinction lay in the concept of the church underlying Kuyper's and Hoedemaker's respective claims. Kuyper meant the invisible church and preinstitutional organic church manifested in pluriformity, while Hoedemaker thought of a particular, concrete institution, namely, the NHK. That allowed Kuyper to simultaneously affirm the public role of the church and deny the government the right to choose between churches.[41] But if Kuyper's theology was not that of the French Revolution, it was nonetheless a radical proposal.

Hoedemaker and Kuyper agreed on at least one thing: that Kuyper's proposal departed from historic Protestant beliefs and practices on church, state, and society. Kuyper viewed himself as carrying through the Reformation principle of freedom of conscience, which had gotten bogged down in Europe by the emergence of state churches. Hoedemaker, however, thought this was an essential element of the Reformation, and, not without some justification, he said that Kuyper's free-church ecclesiology was the child of Friedrich Schleiermacher, not the Reformation.[42] Regardless of who was right, Abraham Kuyper represented a new development in the Western understanding of church and society, one that in certain respects was more momentous than had occurred with the Reformation, to take both Kuyper's and Hoedemaker's words for it. Kuyper introduced an era characterized by the continuing dominance of Christianity in the public sphere but no longer by a single dominant church. How that could be needed explaining.

7

Private Church and Public Theology

Can there be a modern form of public religion that
does not aspire to being an "established," state or
societal church?
—José Casanova[1]

IN 1892 ABRAHAM KUYPER'S DOLEANTIE churches formalized an ecclesiastical union with the Christian Reformed Churches. The new church, the Reformed Churches in the Netherlands (Gereformeerde Kerken in Nederland), comprised almost 10 percent of the Dutch population. The national church declined, however, as a result not only of the Doleantie but also of the exit of other groups, including modernist Protestants newly empowered, after Kuyper's example, to leave the Netherlands Reformed Church. Kuyper was disappointed not to have led a larger exodus—only about a third of orthodox Calvinists in his Amsterdam parish followed him to the Doleantie.[2] As consolation, he did have the pure Calvinistic church he had dreamed of and stumped for. By August 1896, when he addressed the synod of the young church, he was months away from his sixtieth birthday. Perhaps some in the audience thought the church struggle was over, or at least Kuyper's part in it was. When they read the title of his message, "The Blessing of the Lord over Our Churches," perhaps they expected a benediction of sorts from an elder churchman and the passing of the baton to the next generation, but if they did they were disappointed. In fact, Kuyper said the battle for the church was only half over. Sure, a true Calvinistic institution had been achieved, but for just that reason a new task opened before the church organism. For "only where that Church as institute stands pure again, can she also act as organism, again shining light, enlivening, preserving."[3] Though the church's institutional form had been finalized, its cultural mission was just beginning.

The main analytical paradigm for this study has been the double distinction between the inner and outer aspects of the church and between
the church's ethic of purity and the ethic of universality—two continuums
derived from the work of Ernst Troeltsch and Stephen Sykes. The inner
aspects of the church include personal faith and commitment, and the
external aspects include the traditional, institutional features like office
and sacraments. Often a move along one of these two continuums corresponded with a necessary adjustment on the other as well. The struggle
to reconceive the church on both accounts was provoked by the changing social landscape, where the external side of the church was no longer
guaranteed by the state or other public entities and where religious diversity was increasing. The Dutch *volkskerk,* following the post-Reformation
Protestant hegemony and the unified pre-Reformation Christian cultural
settlement, pursued the ethic of universality so far as possible, but disestablishment disrupted this pursuit.

This study has addressed Kuyper's ecclesiology with these questions in
mind. It was found that early in his pastoral career, through the influence
of Calvin, Kuyper gained a new appreciation for the external forms of the
church, which he joined with an equal commitment to the sincerity of personal faith and practice. Yet his formula had several unresolved tensions.
On one hand, he called for cutting off the dead branches of the *volkskerk,*
a stricter adherence to the Reformed confessions, and greater discipline at
all levels of the church. On the other hand, his covenant theology taught a
broad application of baptism as instrument and means of grace—"Baptize
all who come into the house of baptism!" As far as the church's social
position, he championed the separation of church and state, but he also
proclaimed Christ's sovereignty over every thumb's breadth of creation.

Kuyper's early concept of a sacramental church eventually conflicted
with his church reform program, which stressed sincere participation and
separation from nation and state and located the true essence of the church
in its organic form. If Kuyper was going to break with the Netherlands
Reformed Church, the institution had to be delegitimized. To meet that
demand, Kuyper's ecclesiology shifted toward one that grounded the
church primarily in inward religious experience and the invisible organic
church, the believers' church, which allowed for greater flexibility in institutional forms and eventually a break with the church institution.

The peculiar circumstances of Kuyper's break-in at the New Church
in Amsterdam, the event that precipitated his break with the *volkskerk,*
embodied the dilemmas of his ecclesiology. Why would Kuyper go to such

extreme measures to hold onto church property if the true essence of the church was the believers, not the buildings? Kuyper was willing to fight for the New Church because though his assessment of the institution had diminished in importance compared with the organism, Kuyper never gave up on the church as institution. He continually upheld the church's external life while locating the source and essence of the church in its organic existence. We can surmise that the New Church also undoubtedly had personal meaning to Kuyper; he was not going to let go easily of the building where he had preached, baptized, and catechized his Calvinist flock.

More importantly, the New Church possessed immense symbolic weight. It was a monument of Dutch Protestantism, past and present and, as such, was a national symbol. Since 1814 it had been the church where Dutch Kings and Queens were crowned. Even if Kuyper did not want a national church, he did not intend for his free church to be but a small band of pilgrims. He still dreamed of a church that could gather the great majority of Dutch Protestants together, albeit on different terms than the *volkskerk* did. In the end he was disappointed. He lost the New Church, and the Doleantie did not catch on as well as he hoped. Kuyper thus lost his bid to represent Dutch Protestantism at large, yet when he addressed the synod in 1896 he had not given up his hope for Calvinism's broad cultural influence.

In view of the development of Kuyper's free church, discussions of his public theology must be reset. As Kuyper made clear in his address to the synod, public theology grew out of a matrix of ecclesiological concerns, not surprising since ecclesiology was Kuyper's most enduring theological interest. Ecclesiology bookended his theological career, from his master's thesis and doctoral dissertation to his last theological article in the *Herald*. On November 14, 1920, alongside Kuyper's obituary ran the sixty-eighth installment of his series "Concerning the Church,"[4] a fitting conclusion for one who once judged that the problem of the church was "none other than the problem of Christianity itself."[5]

Kuyper's public theology addressed a specific problem that his free church created in theory and practice: how to make a private church public. This chapter elucidates this problem of the public presence of the free church in terms of Kuyper's theology and of the historically unique position of his new church in Dutch society. Addressing Kuyper's public theology from this ecclesiological perspective, three theological distinctions appear by which Kuyper negotiated his public–private dilemma: between common public grace and private particular grace; between Calvinism as a public religion and the private Calvinistic church; and between the public organic church and the private institutional church.

The Problem of Public Theology

The ecclesiological problem of Kuyper's public theology can be glimpsed from several different but complementary angles. Three considerations highlight the multifaceted nature of the problem: the public–private distinction; Ernst Troeltsch's church-sect typology; and Kuyper's own historical and theological context.

The binary pair *public* and *private* is so variously used that some explanation of their use here must precede further discussion. Most basically, public refers to those aspects of religion or church that are shared, common, openly revealed, and, therefore, to some extent objective. The state, the nation as ethnic group, and society as the place of community outside of the state are public entities since they are shared, common entities, and they are the most important public entities Kuyper had to deal with. Private, in contrast, refers to things that are inner, hidden or withdrawn, not openly shared, and possibly subjective.[6] One's religious convictions, for example, are private. José Casanova says that "religion is a private affair" in two ways in the modern world. First, religion is a matter of conscience, and the freedom of conscience from the intrusion of public institutions like state or potentially church, is basic to modern liberal society. Religion is also private as a result of modernity's institutional differentiation—the separation of church and state—wherein secular spheres like government free themselves of ecclesiastical control and religious norms. "Religion was progressively forced to withdraw from the modern secular state and the modern capitalist economy and to find refuge in the newly formed private sphere."[7] This was an entirely novel situation, Casanova says.[8]

Further, these two senses in which religion is private are mutually interdependent when they are applied to the organizational forms of religion. To quote historians Joris van Eijnatten and Fred van Lieburg, "Orphaned by the withdrawing of the state and no longer obvious symbol of the existing order, she needed a new legitimation."[9] The church could no longer rely on the public support of the state, so the church's new legitimation became private conscience and voluntary support. Kuyper's believers' church, a church that "rested in human choices, decisions, and voluntary actions," was precisely this type of private institution.[10] Resting in private rather than public support is what it meant for the church to become a private institution.

One thing that private does not necessarily mean or imply is *individual* or *individualistic*. Private can refer to what is individual, over against what is collective, but that is not implied in the term as it is used here.[11] A church as a religious communion can be private and still be a corporate body. This was especially true for Abraham Kuyper. Although the institutional church was voluntary, Kuyper consistently resisted tendencies to individualistic and atomistic spirituality through his doctrine of the organic church. There was no sense, according to Kuyper, that a Christian was ever a lone Christian because being a Christian, whatever else it meant, meant participation in the Mystical Body of Christ, which was the organic church.

From these definitions the term *public theology*, a notoriously difficult concept to pin down, is derived. Martin Marty and Edith Blumhofer offer a definition of public theology that reflects the understanding of public and private given here: "the interpretive language of thinkers in the believing communities, when they direct themselves to the public good."[12] Public theology aims to speak to what is beyond the limited bounds and life of the religious community itself. In premodern societies, the term public theology would be redundant: "God was implicated in the very existence of society."[13] Theology, even when disputed, was public, and the public was theological. That is, the common, public sphere was shot through with transcendent meaning. At the Areopagus, Paul may have needed to make known to the Athenians who the one true God was, but he hardly needed to prove that such a god existed or that this god was concerned with their this-worldly affairs. One novelty of the modern public square, says Charles Taylor, is its secularity. It is not constituted by any transcendent laws or norms, just what some of Kuyper's Dutch liberal opponents advocated.[14] As modern private associations, churches do not have automatic, undisputed access or authority in the world outside their doors. Consequently Casanova says:

> The question that needs to be addressed...is whether the denomination [roughly what Kuyper's free church was], as the modern, voluntary form of religious association based on religious freedom and religious pluralism, can also assume a different kind of "publicity," a political one, in modern differentiated societies.[15]

Kuyper's public theology addressed that question. One thing that makes Kuyper's answer particularly interesting is its novelty on the European scene. The constitution of the Netherlands was one of the very first European constitutions to separate church and state (1848), so Abraham Kuyper stepped into largely uncharted territory when he went to explain how his private church could have a public impact.[16]

The public–private distinction resonates with one of Kuyper's best-known theological distinctions between *common* and *particular* grace. The Dutch term *particulier* in Kuyper's *particuliere genade* (i.e., particular grace) may, in fact, be rendered private as it is by contemporary Van Dale dictionaries. James Bratt renders Kuyper's *particulier* as "special" rather than as "particular" as this study does. That is fine as long as "special" is taken in the sense of specific, but the term *particulier* only inevitably conveys a higher rank or worth, as Bratt says, in the context of Kuyper's discussion. Otherwise, there is no lexical reason to think that *particulier* conveys the sense of a higher worth. The first two definitions (not including obsolete ones) of the 1915 edition of the *Woordenboek der Nederlandsche Taal* for the word *particulier* are: "belonging to one definite matter or person, or a number of matters of persons, but not with all or anyone," and "belonging to, undertaken or performed by, or having relation to one or more individual persons; private, not public."[17] At most *particulier* connotes a sense of special, better, or higher worth, but it does not denote that.

A few disclaimers must round out this discussion of public and private. First, public theology does not refer to political theology, though as Marty and Blumhofer acknowledge the latter may be a species of the former. Second, the public–private distinction is an analytical tool and heuristic device. Mary Douglas's proviso is now customary and obligatory in these kinds of discussions:

> Binary distinctions are an analytic procedure, but their usefulness does not guarantee that existence divides like that. We should look with suspicion on anyone who declared that there are two kinds of people, or two kinds of reality or process.[18]

Or indeed, two kinds of theology. All Christian theology at some point claims "for God so loved *the world*," and that is as public a theological claim as can be made. Even today, James Kennedy says, Dutch churches still have a public, if muted, presence.[19]

We may also view the problem of the private church in the terms that originally framed this study. Ernst Troeltsch's church–sect typology presumes a fundamental tension between two social ethics, the ethic of purity or holiness and the ethic of cultural dominance or universality. If a Christian communion pursues the ethic of universality as the church type does and attempts to bring the whole world under its wings, then purity will lack. Vice versa, the purifying process, which separates the silver from the dross, necessarily precludes claims to universality, so the ethic of purity sacrifices hopes of universality. Calvinism pleads for special consideration on this measure because it pursues both holiness and universality; it aims at the whole community and a holy one too. Amy Plantinga Pauw says that Jonathan Edwards and John Calvin, through their ecclesiologies, both "called for both breadth of membership and depth of spiritual transformation."[20]

Troeltsch regarded the European national churches as the most faithful followers of Calvin because they preserved Calvin's broad social vision. For Calvin and the national churches, the public relevance of the church and theology was undisputed, even unremarkable. All theology was public insofar as the church was part of the public social order. In Calvin's Geneva (and the whole of medieval Christendom, of which Troeltsch reckoned Calvin still a part), public theology would have been a distinction without a difference. In the case of the Dutch church, James Kennedy says, "Even after 1848 the churches continued to fulfill a public function and they were seen as essential parts of the public order," for, in the late nineteenth century the churches still had an "organic presence." Protestants viewed the nation in religious terms and ascribed the church the task of nurturing the people.[21] Philip Hoedemaker expressed this vision as "the whole church for the whole nation!"[22] But Abraham Kuyper, who otherwise had a strong theological affinity with Hoedemaker's confessional Calvinism, disagreed on this point, so strongly that Hoedemaker resigned his post at the Free University over these ecclesiological differences.[23]

Kuyper agreed that the national churches were in some respects the logical product of the Reformation, but he also believed that they represented a failure to carry out the Reformation completely. The Reformation broke the bonds of Rome's "world-church," but it stopped short of the goal, settling for the "territorial church" system.[24] Kuyper's attempt to push the Reformation through to completion with the free church was, among other things, an attempt to make the institutional church and theology less public. This attempt to depublicize the church occurred in various forms. For example, Kuyper protested against the synod as a creation of the state and against the department of public worship for the same reason. He rejected the need for a letter from the office of registry as a precondition for baptism[25] and did not agree that the state should have oversight in matters of doctrine.[26] Whereas Reformed theologians before him compared the church to the nation of Israel, Kuyper condemned that notion as support for a *volkskerk*. He wanted church property in local hands and Christian morals taken out of the public schools. Finally, when the police came to disrupt the ordination of one of his Free University students (one of the first actions of the Doleantie), we can be sure that Kuyper, more than ever, determined that church matters should be private matters.

Here Kuyper faced the dilemma of purity and universality. Kuyper's free church, like all free churches, demanded a high degree of purity, for example, in external forms like the church's confessions and personal commitment to the confessions, but he also cherished a famously universal social vision: "There is not a thumb's breadth in the whole domain of our human existence over which Christ, who is Sovereign over all, does not cry: 'Mine!'"[27] In terms of Troeltsch's purity–universality distinction, the question is whether a religious community that demands a high degree of purity and commitment (which is, after all, a concomitant of voluntarism) also engages society at large, when that society does not manifest the same level of purity and may even be hostile to it. Here Troeltsch's categories break down because, in fact, that was the strategy Kuyper pursued.

As a major area of study, Kuyper's public theology did not appear until late in his career, the *Lectures on Calvinism* in 1898, for example, and his three volumes on common grace beginning in 1895. Some of the elements had been there before, of course, but not in any concatenated system. The concept of the organic church, for example, dated far back in Kuyper's repertoire, though not as part of a program of public theology. The reason was that Abraham Kuyper did not develop a public theology (taken in the sense previously outlined, a theological reflection on the public or common good) until after the formation of his secession church because he did not need one until then. He needed a public theology because his new church was virtually a sect, as his opponents pointed out.[28] This was something Kuyper was sensitive to for many reasons, not least of all because he had consistently opposed sectarianism but also for the obvious reason that he was a very public figure—"Holland's foremost citizen," one American brochure announced.[29]

Yet Kuyper did sound like a sectarian, in certain respects. His doctrine of the antithesis sounded a clear come-out-from-them note. Kuyper argued that there was an absolute antithesis between the principles of redeemed and unredeemed humanity. Kuyper's 1892 rectoral address at the Free University, "The Blurring of the Boundaries," reconfirmed his commitment to the antithesis by contrasting the pantheism of the day with the God of the Bible who was *hammabdil*, distinct from creation. This address took aim at Friedrich Nietzsche's all-leveling, antimetaphysical philosophy the way "Uniformity" had at Bismark's social homogenization. "Our battle today has to be fought on the basis of principle....The clash between the basic theme of the Christian religion and that of our century cuts too deep to be left to the playful sparring of the apologists."[30] Kuyper's ecclesiology provided an ontological basis for the antithesis in his doctrine that the organic church was a human organism distinct from the rest of humanity due to its regenerate principle.[31] As for his more practical injunctions, Kuyper's agitating in the sphere of the church was considered schismatic. To this he responded that God had established the laws of what may be joined and what may not, and the story of the Bible was a long history of separation even to the point of fracture. His call for separating belief and unbelief followed God's own ordinances.[32]

Elsewhere the antithesis manifested itself in a variety of Reformed associations and organizations, including schools, a political party, and labor guilds. Kuyper faulted oldliners J. H. Gunning and A. W. Bronsveld, who besides not following Kuyper in the Doleantie also refused to support Kuyper's Calvinistic university for not carrying their Calvinistic principles into all spheres of life and therefore not recognizing that the antithesis applied to more than just Christian piety. They "tolerate the antithesis for the soul.... But not ecclesiastically. Not in society. Not in the Binnenhof [the Dutch parliament buildings]. Not in the university. Not in the terrain of art and science."[33] Though Kuyper's vision comprehended "every thumb's breadth," it was hardly a prescription for solidarity or cooperation.

Kuyper did, however, oppose sectarianism as withdrawal from the world in a way that, oddly enough, flowed from the same principles. As early as the 1870s, Kuyper had diagnosed the Reveil party as suffering from "politico-phobia."[34] Not only did they fail to carry their Calvinistic principles into politics; they also seemed to be afraid of politics altogether, partly due to the residual influence of the pietistic Reveil movement that had focused religion inward. Kuyper's actions in church and society, however, forced the hand of his opponents in the *volkskerk*. As Kuyper identified his own politics, his Hervormde opposition (i.e., which consisted of those remaining in the national church, the Netherlands Reformed Church) was forced to define its politics, in contrast. These opponents protested Kuyper's mixing religion and politics, but theirs was not so much a program as an antiprogram: anti-Kuyper, antisocialist, and anti-Catholic.[35] Kuyper, though, mobilized his Calvinist followers into active organizations and associations in every sphere of life, with a positive aim of building up Calvinist institutions.

Two years after the break in the church, in 1888, conservative Protestants also broke politically with Kuyper. They not only rejected mixing religion and politics but also resisted forming political parties altogether. Yet, though they were averse to political parties, Bronsveld and S. H. Buytendijk did form a Christian-historical voting union. The only principle was unity, but with few other principles or political planks there was little to anchor this unity. Yet the Hervormden did not withdraw from society. Instead of forming various Christian organizations, it made the institutional church directly engage society by transforming home missions and evangelism into social welfare tools.[36] They thus maintained a public role for the church, whereas Kuyper's church (the Gereformeerde church) was not only a private institution but also had a narrowly prescribed religious role, which minimized its public presence.

The differences between Kuyper's group and the Hervormden illustrate the difficulty and confusion of adjusting the Calvinist church to modern society.[37] Kuyper needed a rationale for his own social ethics. In 1896, having realized his vision of a free church in the formation of the Doleantie and then ecclesiastical union with the Christian Reformed Church, he addressed the synod with a new problem. Though they now had their desired church, Protestantism still languished in the modern world while modernism and Catholicism thrived. Protestantism seemed disoriented and dispirited. It had adopted the spirit of the age at just the time when the spirit of the age was hostile to it. Therefore,

> what Calvinism must do in our day is to set itself again at the head of Protestantism, and to do what neither Lutherans nor Anabaptists, what neither the Ethical mediating theologian nor Methodist zealot is able, that is, *to erect a life- and worldview composed from the root of Protestantism over against the wisdom of our age and partly over against Rome.*[38]

By Calvinism, Kuyper meant the confessional Calvinists of his free church, the church purified from unbelief. In fact, only such a church could be the foundation for true Christian engagement of society and the world:

> For whatever shall be Christian in the highest sense, its starting point *can* lie nowhere else than in Christ, and it must thus also always seek its focus *in his pure church*. Only where that Church as institute stands pure again, can she also act as organism, again shining light, enlivening, preserving.[39]

Kuyper laid the theological foundations for how his private church could have a broad, public radiance in the world in his *Common Grace* project (1895–1901) and in his Princeton Stone Lectures, the *Lectures on Calvinism* (1898).

Common Grace and the Antithesis: A Note on Some Secondary Sources

Kuyper is sometimes said to have passed through various intellectual stages: first the antithesis stage characterized by militant antimodernism and then the common grace stage characterized by a more charitable and accommodating attitude toward difference.[40] His American followers are commonly distinguished between those emphasizing common grace and those emphasizing the antithesis.[41] This historical division fails, however, to note the obvious antagonism Kuyper always nurtured against modernism and his consistent distinction between the church and the world, even in the so-called common grace period,[42] even in *Common Grace*.[43] The purpose of common grace was not to moderate the antithesis. The antithesis and common grace depended on each other. Kuyper would not have needed a theology of common grace if he had not had a theology of the antithesis. Certainly Kuyper's opponents in the national church who advocated a broad church had little use for one doctrine or the other. Common grace and the antithesis should not be conceived of as contrary doctrines[44] but as different tools in Kuyper's toolkit, a shovel and an axe perhaps. Using the axe did not imply that Kuyper had forsaken the shovel or was less enchanted by it than before. He may have simply been felling a tree instead of digging a ditch.

Making the Private Church Public Again

By the late 1890s, Kuyper had achieved most of his organizational plans, a free church, a free university, a political party, and a Christian school system, but his theological accounts for his community-organizing activities still lay scattered and disconnected in speeches here and sermons there. Kuyper needed to provide a theological account. His sermon to the general assembly in 1896 marked a change in theological strategy from securing the free church to explaining ground for the free church's social engagement. The church institution having been achieved, the church organism could go forth from a position of strength. Kuyper explained the public side of his private church by means of three distinctions that ran throughout his public theology: public grace and private grace; public worldview, private church; and the public organic church.

Public Grace and Private

With its insistence on private belief and separation from state and nation, Kuyper's free church faced the prospect of becoming a sect, closed off from the rest of the world. Addressing the perennial issue of the church and the world, Kuyper's doctrine of common grace prevented an unacceptable sectarian outcome by opening a public space for the church in the world and by proving the salutary influence the church could have on the world even while remaining separate from it. Common grace was the church's public grace.

Some elements of Kuyper's Calvinist theology did suggest the course of world withdrawal. The antithesis between regenerate and unregenerate humanity and the Calvinist doctrine of total depravity might lead one to believe that a clear distinction could be made between the evil works of the unbelieving world and the good works of Christians, but in practice such a distinction was nearly impossible. There was much beauty in the world and much ugliness in the church. "The sharp line that your confession drew between church and world thus turns out to be untenable."[45] This problem of delineating church and world also appeared when one considered which vocation to choose. If the whole world is under the curse of sin, and if the church is the only creation that bears eternal permanence, then shouldn't a person put all of his or her energy into the work of the church or the path of the ascetic? Yet again, in practice, this proved impossible:

> One person may be able to make a living in that way, as preacher . . . or missionary . . . . But what can never happen is that every member of

the church should give their earthly existence to that in order to wholly devote themselves to spiritual things.[46]

Even in the church, someone had to do the cooking and cleaning.

Kuyper described the false alternatives to the church's social ethic in terms similar to Troeltsch's typical church and sect. The *volkskerk* answered the problem of church and world by extending its wings over all of the nation and society. Late into the nineteenth century, "she held onto the idea of the church as guardian and tutor of the citizens of the Protestant fatherland," says Annemarie Houkes.[47] Kuyper agreed that the church was for the whole of society, but the *volkskerk* pursued this dream in the wrong way by indiscriminately bringing all of society into the church. Loose baptismal policies had been one way of doing this:

> Where you see the [national church] appear in her course through the world, she continually strives by flexibleness and indulgence and accommodation to entice everyone who belongs to a nation to holy Baptism, and not so long after, Christianity has become the religion of the whole nation.[48]

In contrast, Kuyper said, Christianity could benefit culture only if the institution was kept pure, which meant that baptism should be limited to believers and their offspring.[49]

The problem with the *volkskerk's* ethic was that in bringing the whole world into it, rather than leavening the world with grace, in fact the opposite happened. The world did not change. Instead it infiltrated the church. The "free-love" movement (apparently the kind that cropped up at Bloomsbury), which eroded marriage and instigated the state's usurpation of parental authority over children, indicated the waning influence of the church on society. Yet

> this development must be laid at the doorstep of the church. By acting as *volkskerk* almost everywhere, it has had to admit deception into its own bosom ....Today, it will even ally itself with the opponents of Christianity to frustrate those who argue in favor of Christian influence.[50]

The *volkskerk* in Kuyper's account adopted Troeltsch's universalist ethic: it "dominates the masses" and "desires to cover the whole life of humanity."[51] In accepting this model, however, the *volkskerk* had not anticipated the radical anti-Christian character of the modern world that it hoped to embrace.

There was another error that Kuyper wished to avoid, the opposite error to that of the *volkskerk*, which might aptly be called the sectarian extreme. This error limited God's work in the world to church life.[52] The church contained all of God's elect, and Christians needed not concern themselves with life outside it. Related to this was the "Anabaptist position" that confined religion and Christ to the inner, spiritual life. The Anabaptist may not withdraw from society, but "this way of thinking results in your living in two distinct circles of thought: in the very circumscribed circle of your soul's salvation on the one hand, and in the spacious, life-encompassing sphere of the world on the other."[53] Whether one withdrew in typical sectarian fashion or lived with the Anabaptist paradox, both assumed that God was not concerned with the world outside of the church, and such was not the case.

Kuyper searched for an alternative, some third way besides the church and sect, a way that did not admit the world into the church but did not withdraw the church from the world. He found this alternative through his distinction between common grace and particular grace. Particular grace was the saving grace that was limited to the church, specifically to the Mystical Body of Christ, while common grace was public grace available to the whole world. Thereby Kuyper hoped to "maintain both the essence of the church and the Christian character of society, through the simple distinction between the fruit of particular grace in 'the flock of the Lord,' and the fruit of common grace which is worked exactly through the appearance of the congregation."[54]

The notion of common grace, some salutary presence in the world beyond the circle of the elect, was present in the Reformed tradition but not in any systematic form. Kuyper found evidence of common grace in the Belgic Confession, where it spoke of a "few remains" of the original divine gifts still possessed by fallen humanity, and in the Canons of Dort, which affirmed that there is still "some of the light of nature" left over in humanity after the fall.[55] The simple fact of history also implied some form of common grace. Adam did not immediately die, nor did the world descend into irremediable chaos—sure evidence of common grace.[56] The biblical-theological *locus classicus* for common grace was the covenant with Noah, wherein God promised to restrain his anger against sin, symbolized in the rainbow.[57] In fact, Kuyper had hinted at the common grace in the Noah covenant as early as the 1870s, but not until much later did events call forth a deeper reflection on it.[58]

One other function of common grace was to provide a public space for the work of particular or special grace by restraining evil. Particular grace was the grace of salvation, salvific grace, experienced only by the elect. It worked through the benefits of salvation like regeneration, justification, and sanctification, and, ecclesiologically speaking, only the members of the Mystical Body of Christ, the invisible organic church, received this grace. Common grace, in contrast, was not limited to the elect, yet neither was it good for salvation. Rather, it restrained sin and evil in the world so that special grace could do its saving work. Common grace thereby created a broad space for special grace to work, and more than the elect benefited from the restraint of evil. Indeed, the field common grace created was as broad as history itself, for that was its task—to allow history to unfold.[59]

Particular grace and common grace differed, therefore, according to their function and according to their scope. The specificity of particular grace derived from its limited scope.[60] "The former, that is saving grace, which is in the nature of the case particular [or private] and restricted to God's elect. The second, *common* grace, is extended to the whole of our human life."[61] Kuyper's distinction between the scope of these two graces went to the root of his ecclesiological conundrum. Common grace retarded the progress and corruption of sin, thereby making civil (*burgelijk*) or extra-ecclesial (*buiten-kerkelijk*) life possible and even dignified.[62]

The source of common grace was the church. While particular grace and its saving effects were limited to the elect, particular grace still had broader, nonsaving effects. This public, nonsaving effect was common grace. Kuyper adapted the "city on a hill" metaphor to his own ends here. Such a city resided in the world but resisted the tide of the world to enter it. Instead, its light, the light of common grace, shone through open windows into the world around it.[63] Christianity's public influence came through the indirect leavening of the church in society via common grace; thereby the world was not brought into the church, yet the church remained in the world.[64]

Therefore, particular grace and common grace were, in some respects, not two graces but two effects of the same grace, and the common grace effects of particular grace worked in several ways. The church's means of grace, especially the preaching of the Word, became means of particular grace to the elect, working for their regeneration. To the nonelect, they became means of common grace. Thus, the means of grace had both the positive, particular grace effect of raising to new life as well as the negative, common grace effect of impeding the progress of evil.[65] In addition to working through the means of grace, common grace worked through the presence of the children of God in the world, the "presence of the church in this dispensation," and immediately through the work of the Holy Spirit directly on "natural persons."[66] These three effects of common grace produced a Christian society, in the true sense of the term:

> It is all human development, human refinement, human civiliza-
> tion, human enlightenment, human progress. They are altogether
> powers of the human nature that you see opened in the Christian
> nations.... Only where the Gospel enters the world and the church
> of Christ appears, does *human* progress begin.[67]

Christian societies were Christian because of the presence of the Christian church in them and because of the effects of the church on the surrounding society, not because the Church had control over every square inch of culture.

One of the challenges for religion's public appearance in modern society was to preserve freedom of conscience and religious tolerance. Conscience suffocated under an established church, or else it withdrew from reach of the dominant church as the sects were forced to do. Troeltsch may have overlooked the fact that the sects withdrew not only in pursuit of purity but also because they had no other options in the face of dominant, state-sanctioned churches. Disestablishment took much of the bite out of the dominant church's bark yet still a new way had to be devised to meet these demands. Common grace satisfied the requirements of freedom of conscience by reconceiving the nature of the church's public influence as indirect and moral rather than direct and coercive.[68] Whereas an established church might have direct influence in government, through governmental departments of public worship that sanctioned religious communities, common grace worked indirectly. Public officials went to church on Sunday; then they went to parliament on Monday, sanctified in some way by the means of grace. Further, common grace was not coercive in its power. It exercised a moral influence over the conscience. "By its influence on the state and civil society the church of Christ aims only at a *moral triumph*, not at the imposition of confessional bonds nor at the exercise of authoritarian control."[69]

Gerrit Schutte says that "theoretically [Kuyper] maintained, albeit in modernized forms, the old ideal of the theocratic Christian state, wherein the public life was normed according to biblical prescriptions,"[70] but that is far too facile an account. It is too simplistic, not because it misreads Kuyper's intentions but because it underestimates the great distance between the old ideal and the modernized form. So great is the difference between these two types of societies that Casanova says the question is whether religion can be public apart from an established church; in Kuyper's day there was no precedent or preprogrammed solution to this problem. In Kuyper's scheme, the rule of God, theocracy, pertained to Christian conscience and the church[71] and not directly to the state, as Schutte claims. Kuyper wanted neither a state church nor a church state.[72] (In any case, it is not much of a theocracy when God can be voted out.) This is, to be sure, a vision of a Christian society, but a vision adjusted for the great difference between the *ancien régime* and modern, democratic, plural, differentiated society.

Common grace also helped Kuyper maintain his dual devotion to the nation and to the church, in spite of the fact that he did not believe that the whole nation belonged in the church. So close were church and nation related in the mind of many Protestants that Kuyper's break with the *volkskerk* elicited accusations of treason. These charges demanded an answer but so did his own theology, because long ago in 1873 Kuyper had argued that the church was the source of the nation.[73] Yet his break with the national church seemed to contradict that belief, and his Calvinist *volks*-group could not claim to represent the nation or even the Protestant portion of it.[74] In fact, one of Kuyper's first applications of the doctrine of common grace, several years before he began his more extensive treatment, aimed at this dilemma of nation and church. The Christian, Kuyper said, was a member of two nations or "fatherlands," not one: a heavenly one and an earthly one. The earthly fatherland, one's nation, was the product of common grace, not saving grace.[75] It was an adaption of Augustine's two cities for the age of nation-states, says Johan Stellingwerff:

> While Augustine set the City of God over against the world ruled by Satan, Kuyper came with a third city. On the one side Zion or Jerusalem as the city of God in the heavenly Fatherland, on the other side Babylon the city of ruin in the evil world, and between those still a city of common grace in the national fatherland.[76]

The problem for the Dutch nation was the myriad ways the modern world pulled and seduced it, be it the communist, the Russian nihilist, the Paris Commune, or the "apotheosis of the state."[77] Kuyper lamented that religion no longer determined public life in the earthly fatherland, but he was not willing to accept the compromise of a territorial church.[78]

Although common grace did open the possibility of Christian influence on non-Christian society, it also had one ill effect. It fostered an extreme naiveté about Western cultural superiority. Consider the difference between "the Hottentot in his kraal and the life of highly refined family in European society," Kuyper said, to see the difference common grace made.[79] Looking back over a century of progress, he exclaimed, "The triumph of Christian Europe is a perfection."[80] If he could have instead looked forward over the bloodiest century in the history of the world, surely Kuyper's enthusiasm about common grace and the myth of progress it sponsored would have been attenuated.

Private Church, Public Worldview

Although Abraham Kuyper, in a sense, succeeded in privatizing the church, Calvinism was for him far more than a church. It was a *life system* or, in more contemporary terms,[81] a worldview, where *world* indicated the breadth of its gaze. *Calvinism*, Kuyper said, meant different things to different people. To Catholics in Catholic countries it had a derogatory, sectarian sense. To others Calvinism referred to a confessional commitment to divine sovereignty, and to still others it distinguished one denomination from another. But to Kuyper, Calvinism was more expansive than any of those uses indicated. Kuyper spoke of Calvinism in the "scientific" sense, by which he meant the kind of social-historical theory that Max Weber and Ernst Troeltsch after him (and perhaps because of him) also spoke of.[82] That kind of Calvinism was far broader than a set of theological principles or ecclesiastical forms. It was "the system of conceptions which, under the influence of the master-mind Calvin, raised itself to dominance in the several spheres of life," and following then historian of America George Bancroft, it was "'a theory of ontology, of ethics, of social happiness, and of human liberty, all derived from God.'"[83] If Kuyper's Calvinistic church looked sectarian, his Calvinism certainly did not.

According to Kuyper, a worldview began with a central animating principle. This principle radiated out from the center into all spheres of life to form a complete society.[84] Calvinism's basic principle was humanity's immediate relation to God, in contrast to Roman Catholicism's mediated relationship, for example.[85] In political society, Calvinism's principle produced democracy rather than aristocracy since all humans stood in equal relationship to God.[86] A worldview differed from a philosophy because a philosophy controlled the rationale aspects of life whereas a worldview was more comprehensive, controlling also one's practices and metanarratives.[87] It was nonetheless an intellectualist or idealist approach insofar as the principle at the root of a worldview was typically an idea. Kuyper's *Lectures on Calvinism* drew out this principle of Calvinism in all spheres of human culture: history, religion, politics, art, and science. It was an argument that Calvinism could not be kept at home or in the church. Rather, it was universal; it was public; it was a form of *cultuurprotestantisme*,[88] but crucially it was not a church.

Worldviews, according to Kuyper, provided fundamental orientation in three relationships: humanity and God; humans and other humans; and humanity and the world. The immediate relation to God and the egalitarian relations among humans ordered the first two; common grace ordered the last. Here Kuyper revisited the same arguments against the old national church and the medieval Roman Catholic Church. Such churches actually constrained the development of human potential by forcing all of life under their wings. Instead, "the church must withdraw again within its spiritual domain, and...in the world we should realize the potencies of God's common grace."[89] Calvinism reigned as a worldview rather than as an institutional church, and this permitted an important distinction. Kuyper's separation of church and state was absolute; separation of faith and politics, however, was impossible.

Religion was merely one product, one sphere of Kuyper's Calvinistic worldview (one chapter in the *Lectures on Calvinism*), and as a religion Calvinism produced a church. As the Christian social institution, the church elaborated in the *Lectures on Calvinism* was one of the most voluntaristic, republican, and unsacramental presentations of Kuyper's ecclesiology yet, perhaps tailored to his American audience but certainly highlighting the narrow scope of the institutional church in contrast to common grace's catholic privilege. Religion, Kuyper explained, was that domain of life pertaining to the worship of the Most High. The religion of the French Revolution, modern paganism, did not create a meaningful, ordered, religious life but "heaped together" a disparate, shallow "mysticism."[90] Calvinism, on the other hand, produced a definite social organization, one that was not a purely human contrivance. The earthly body was part of the larger heavenly body of Christ, and Holy Scripture was its constitution.

With this worldview system of the *Lectures on Calvinism*, Kuyper also presented a summary of his believers' church that had, if anything, gone further from its older sacramental moorings. The church on Earth was not, first of all, a preexisting institution but the gathering of confessors, who were obliged to follow God's commands for establishing an institutional church[91] so that it "rest[ed] in human choices, decisions and actions, consisting of members, offices, and help-means."[92] Gone from Kuyper's ecclesiology was the objective *ecclesia docens*, which he now denounced as a Lutheran error.[93] Gone, too, was the church as a mediator of grace. That was Rome's invention.[94] True religion was *"the inward, spiritual beauty of the worshipping soul."*[95]

The Public Organic Church

The institutional church was increasingly limited to moral and spiritual tasks in the late nineteenth century. In Kuyper's case, this was by design, and it coincided with his voluntaristic ecclesiology. The public reach of the institutional church, so far as it had one, was indirect, but there was more to the church than the institution. The organic church took up the church's public responsibilities and received the task of engaging the world directly, where the institution could act only indirectly.[96] So closely related was the organic church with Kuyper's cultural program that P. A. van Leeuwen said that Kuyper's doctrine of the organic church resembled a social philosophy more than an ecclesiology.[97]

While the institution was the church of particular, private grace, the organic church was the church that by virtue of common grace could act in every sphere of human life.[98] "The institute does not cover everything that is Christian.... This extra-institutional influence in society points us to the *church as organism*."[99] Kuyper discussed several possible terrains for common grace, one of which was "the terrain wherever the church as organism manifests itself, i.e., where personal confessors of Jesus in their own circle allow the life of common grace to be controlled by the principles of divine revelation."[100] This occurred when the organism, rooted as it was in particular grace, appropriated the benefits of common grace and called forth Christian endeavors in all areas of life, such as education, art, and science.[101] It was undoubtedly what Kuyper envisioned for his Reformed party (*volksdeel*) in the Netherlands, and in time it became a recipe for pillarization (*verzuiling*), wherein each ideological group in the Netherlands developed its own system of social structures and kept rigidly within them.[102]

In practice, the public work of the organic church took shape in the myriad parachurch Christian organizations that Kuyper helped establish.¹⁰³ This distinguished Kuyper from other Calvinist traditionalists like Hoedemaker, who wanted a distinctly Christian government, a state with the Bible.¹⁰⁴ Kuyper, in contrast, wanted a Christian political party, not a Christian government. The establishment of such organizations, be they political parties, Christian universities, or otherwise was not the responsibility of the church institution but of the organic church, the spontaneous actions of believers to establish Christian institutions. This tendency to Christian party-forming revolted Hoedemaker, who viewed the whole Dutch nation as a Christian-Protestant nation, not just one group within it.¹⁰⁵

José Casanova argues that one of the key failures of secularization theory is the failure to separate social differentiation, the separation of church and state, from its supposed effects on the practice of religion, namely, the supposed inevitable decline in religion. In fact, the separation of church and state has not uniformly led to the decline of religious practice, as is now well agreed. Already in the late nineteenth century, Kuyper believed that Christianity could thrive without establishment, based on his understanding of common grace and the organic church.¹⁰⁶ Kuyper argued that "secularization," by which he meant the separation of church and state, "is one of the most basic ideas of Calvinism."¹⁰⁷ He rejected the notion that the separation of church and state was part and parcel with the ideological secularism of the French Revolution. In fact, Kuyper envisioned a scenario more like the one that played out in the United States, where the separation of church and state worked for the good of religion, than what had actually occurred in the Netherlands and elsewhere in Western Europe, where the separation of church and state did contribute to sharp declines in religious practice.¹⁰⁸ No state church or established religion was necessary to ensure the vitality of Christianity, Kuyper believed, if the people themselves were Christian, that is, if society was permeated with the organic church. Kuyper's Christendom, in contrast to the medieval or Reformation-era synthesis, was a democratic, grassroots one: "Not a national church (*volkskerk*), but rather a church-people (*kerkvolk*)."¹⁰⁹

Making the Church Public

Casanova asks whether there can be a public form of religion that does not aspire to be an established or a societal church, and he concludes, "That the structural location any church occupies between state and society determines to a large extent the form which such a church assumes as a public religion."[110] This means that the nature of the church's relations with other societal institutions like the state, academy, or family determines the church's public form. If, for example, there is a constitutional separation between church and state, then the church's public political form must be something other than a direct, institutional connection with the political institutions. What Casanova found to be true of churches' concrete societal interactions, this study suggests is true of their theology as well. How one construes the church theologically determines how one construes the church's public role. In other words, public theology depends on ecclesiology. Abraham Kuyper's public theology was a public theology designed to meet the needs of his free church. This is not surprising if one considers that defining the church, the task of ecclesiology, gives the church the lines and contours of its form. This process of definition draws boundaries for the church, boundaries that determine what belongs to church and what does not. In large measure, the public and private facets of the church depend on how these boundaries are drawn.

Neither Troeltsch's ideal church nor the ideal sect could adequately answer Casanova's question. The ideal church, with its ethic of world dominance, was a societal church by definition and was excluded at the outset, not just by the way Casanova frames the question but by the real situation of disestablishment and religious pluralism that churches find themselves in. The ideal sect is likewise excluded since it does not pursue a robust, public presence but withdraws from society in pursuit of the ethic of purity. Kuyper's solution was to distinguish between different forms and manifestations of the church in society, some of which were public and some of which were not. Common grace, the organic church, and Kuyper's worldview philosophy were all ways by which the church might have a public life, while the institutional church with its tasks of worship and the means of grace was private. The necessity of such a flexible solution for the church arose directly from Kuyper's insistence on the separation of church and state, which made the institutional church a private institution. Kuyper's church was neither Troeltsch's church nor a sect, but a multiform reality, in some forms public and in other forms private.

If ecclesiology gives rise to a public theology, then the reverse must also be true: public theology implies an ecclesiology. This is one enduring lesson be taken seriously from Kuyper's ecclesiological reflections. Contemporary discussions of public theology can easily become disconnected from the concrete Christian community, whereas Kuyper's example teaches that ecclesiology ought to be a first principle of public theology.

Once we have an account of the church, then we can give an account of its public role. Especially with regard to the institutional church, we may find, as Kuyper did, that its role is more modest than we wish.

Yet it is not too modest. There is also a negative lesson to draw from Kuyper's ecclesiology. Kuyper's private church, grounded as it was in conscience, circumscribed by group identity and relativized as a modern organization, obscured the public mandate that the institutional church does have. Kuyper's proposal marginalized the institutional church, yet this church is the church for the world. Its mandate cannot be truncated by any social arrangements, modern or ancient. The preaching of the Word and the sacraments of the Lord, not Christian political parties or colleges or school systems, proclaim a message of hope to the world, the announcement of a light to lighten the Gentiles and the glory of the people Israel—a public mission if ever there was one.

Notes

1. In fact, no saw was used. The term *panel-sawing* was meant to associate Kuyper
   with a notorious burglar of the day, Lavertu, who did use a saw to break into
   houses. The popular political cartoon "Church-trouble in Amsterdam" pictured
   Kuyper and his band as Lavertu, saw in hand. For the cartoon and a brief account
   of events see Jan de Bruijn, *Abraham Kuyper: Een Beeldbiografie* (Amsterdam: Bert
   Bakker, 2008), 165–168. Frank Vanden Berg, *Abraham Kuyper* (Grand Rapids, MI:
   Eerdmans, 1960), 134–149, offers an account in English with loads of detail.
2. Mark Noll, *The Old Religion in the New World: The History of North American
   Christianity* (Grand Rapids, MI: Eerdmans, 2002), 249. Americans in particular
   celebrate Kuyper's legacy of Christian engagement in public life; for example,
   Clifford Blake Anderson, "A Canopy of Grace: Common and Particular Grace
   in Abraham Kuyper's Theology of Science," *Princeton Seminary Bulletin* 24
   (2003): 123–140; Vincent E. Bacote, *The Spirit in Public Theology: Appropriating
   the Legacy of Abraham Kuyper* (Grand Rapids, MI: Baker Academic, 2005); John
   Bolt, *A Free Church, A Holy Nation: Abraham Kuyper's American Public Theology*
   (Grand Rapids, MI: Eerdmans, 2000); John R. Bowlin, "Some Thoughts on Do-
   ing Theology in Public," *Princeton Seminary Bulletin* 28 (2007): 235–243; James
   Bratt, "Abraham Kuyper's Public Career," *Reformed Journal* 37 (1987): 9–12; J.
   Budziszewski, ed., *Evangelicals in the Public Square: Four Formative Voices on Po-
   litical Thought and Action* (Grand Rapids, MI: Baker Academic, 2006); Wayne
   A. Kobes, "Sphere Sovereignty and the University: Theological Foundations of
   Abraham Kuyper's View of the University and Its Role in Society" (Ph.D. diss.,
   Florida State University, 1993); George M. Marsden, "Introduction: Reformed
   and American," in *Reformed Theology in America*, ed. David Wells (Grand Rapids,
   MI: Baker, 1997); John Witte Jr., *The Reformation of Rights: Law, Religion, and
   Human Rights in Early Modern Calvinism* (Cambridge: Cambridge University
   Press, 2007); Nicholas Wolterstorff, "Abraham Kuyper on Christian Learning,"

in *Educating for Shalom: Essays on Christian Higher Education,* ed. Clarence W. Joldersma and Gloria Goris Stronks (Grand Rapids, MI: Eerdmans, 2004).

3. Kuyper, *Lectures on Calvinism* (Grand Rapids, MI: Eerdmans, 1931), 62.

4. Kuyper, "De Ontwikkeling der Pauselijke Macht onder Nicolaas I (1859)," in *Kuyper Archief* (Amsterdam: Historisch Documentatiecentrum voor het Nederlands Protestantisme); Kuyper, "Van de Kerk," *De Heraut* 1919–1920; Abraham Kuyper, *Abraham Kuyper's Commentatio (1860): The Young Kuyper about Calvin, A Lasco, and the Church,* ed. Jasper Vree and Johan Zwaan, vol. 2, Brill's Series in Church History (Leiden: Brill, 2005).

5. Kuyper, "Conservatism and Orthodoxy: False and True Preservation (1870)," in *Abraham Kuyper: A Centennial Reader,* ed. Bratt (Grand Rapids, MI: Eerdmans, 1998), 69.

6. Joris van Eijnatten and Fred van Lieburg, *Nederlandse Religiegeschiedenis* (Hilversum: Verloren, 2005), 271.

7. Claude Welch, *Protestant Thought in the Nineteenth Century, 1870–1914,* vol. 2 (New Haven, CT: Yale University Press, 1985), 213. Welch says that the dominant theological problem of culture was the secularization of the European mind, not the secularization of the state and society.

8. The term *conventionally necessary* is suggested by Stephen Sykes's account of another nineteenth-century ecclesiological debate over the outward and the inward between Anglicans J. B. Lightfoot and R. C. Moberly. Moberly criticized Lightfoot for taking the view that the externals of the church, namely, priesthood, are conventionally necessary (i.e., the normal requirements of human sociality) but not necessary sacerdotal mediation between God and humanity. Moberly contended that the inner and outer are instead like body and spirit, mutually related aspects of a single person. Moberly described Lightfoot's position (which Moberly disagreed with) this way: "while the inward is essentially necessary for the reality of the outward, the outward is only conventionally necessary for the reality of the inward." Leaving aside the question of the adequacy of Moberly's interpretation of Lightfoot, the distinction Moberly makes is quite appropriate for describing the changes in Kuyper's ecclesiology. At different times Kuyper believed that the external forms were "essentially necessary" to the church; then once outside of the national church, with the necessity of delegitimizing the institution, Kuyper presented the external forms as only conventionally necessary. R. C. Moberly, *Ministerial Priesthood: Chapters (Preliminary to a Study of the Ordinal) on the Rationale of Ministry and the Meaning of Christian Priesthood,* 2nd ed. (London: John Murray, 1910), xxxviii; Stephen Sykes, *The Identity of Christianity: Theologians and the Essence of Christianity from Schleiermacher to Barth* (Philadelphia: Fortress, 1984), 45–50.

9. See the illustration in Jeroen Koch, *Abraham Kuyper: Een Biografie* (Amsterdam: Uitgeverij Boom, 2006), unnumbered pages.

10. Karel Blei, *The Netherlands Reformed Church, 1571–2005,* trans. Allan J. Janssen, The Historical Series of the Reformed Church in America (Grand Rapids, MI: Eerdmans, 2006), 6–7, 25.

11. van Eijnatten and van Lieburg, *Nederlandse Religiegeschiedenis*, 174.

12. "The Belgic Confession," in *The Creeds of Christendom*, ed. Philip Schaf (Grand Rapids, MI: Baker, 1993), art. 36, 432.

13. Peter van Rooden, "Long-Term Religious Developments in the Netherlands, c. 1750–2000," in *The Decline of Christendom in Western Europe, 1750–2000*, ed. Hugh McLeod and Werner Ustorf (Cambridge: Cambridge University Press, 2003), 115.

14. Further, "It is seen—or at least views itself—more as the leading representative of what is particular to the nation than as the representative of a particular, well-defined faith perspective." Blei, *The Netherlands Reformed Church*, 2. Also Blei, "Volkskerk," in *Christelijke Encyclopedie*, ed. George Harinck et al., vol. 3 (Kampen: Kok, 2006), 1819. The *volkskerk* was not a populist, grassroots church, as the English translation "people's church" might imply. It was controlled by elites. The secession churches like the 1834 Afscheiding church and Kuyper's Doleantie turned out to be the churches that were actually of and for the people.

15. Annemarie Houkes, *Christelijke Vaderlanders: Godsdienst, Burgerschap, en de Nederlandse Natie (1850–1900)* (Amsterdam: Wereldbibliotheek, 2009), 182.

16. Cf. Dag Thorkildsen, "Scandanavia: Lutheranism and National Identity," in *The Cambridge History of Christianity: World Christianities c. 1815–1914*, ed. Sheridan Gilley and Brian Stanley, vol. 8 (Cambridge: Cambridge University Press, 2006), 342–358.

17. N. B. Eric Hobsbawm says there were various concepts of nation and various forms of nationalism circulating in the nineteenth century. He calls the American version a "revolutionary-democratic" kind, whereas toward the late nineteenth century another form came to emphasize especially ethnic and linguistic features. Kuyper fits this latter definition better, though not every part. Hobsbawm is less perceptive as to the religious aspects of national identity. Ernest Gellner, *Nations and Nationalism* (Ithaca, NY: Cornell University Press, 1983), 1; Hobsbawn, *Nations and Nationalism since 1780: Programme, Myth, Reality* (Cambridge: Cambridge University Press, 1990).

18. Vree, "De Herziening van het Hervormde Algemeen Reglement (1846–1852)," in *Om de Toekomst van het Protestantse Nederland. De Gevolgen van de Grondwetsherziening van 1848 voor Kerk, Staat en Maatschappij*, ed. G. J. Schutte and Vree (Zoetermeer: Meinema, 1998), 44, 52.

19. Quoted in Blei, *The Netherlands Reformed Church*, 33.

20. George Harinck and Lodewijk Winkeler, "De Negentiende Eeuw," in *Handboek Nederlandse Kerkgeschiedenis*, ed. Herman J. Selderhuis (Kampen: Kok, 2006), 609–611.

21. van Rooden, "Long-Term Religious Developments," 119.

22. Vree, "De Herziening."

23. James C. Kennedy, *Stad op een Berg: De Publieke Rol van Protestantse Kerken* (Zoetermeer: Boekencentrum, 2009), 43.

24. van Rooden, "Long-Term Religious Developments," 121.

25. Houkes, *Christelijke Vaderlanders*, 145–183.

26. Kuyper, *Confidentie: Schrijven aan den Weled. Heer J.H. van der Linden* (Amsterdam: Höveker & Zoon, 1873), 55.

27. Michael Wintle, *An Economic and Social History of the Netherlands, 1800–1920: Demographic, Economic, and Social Transition* (Cambridge: Cambridge University Press, 2000), 252–256; van Eijnatten and van Lieburg, *Nederlandse Religiegeschiedenis*, 275; Vree, "More Pierson and Mesmer, and Less Pietje Baltus: Kuyper's Ideas on Church, State, and Culture during the First Years of his Ministry (1863–1866)," in *Kuyper Reconsidered: Aspects of His Life and Work*, ed. Cornelis van der Kooi and Jan de Bruijn (Amsterdam: VU Uitgeverij, 1999), 299–309.

28. Hugh McLeod, *Secularization in Western Europe, 1848–1914* (New York: St. Martin's, 2000), 28. McLeod refers to Jeffery Cox, *The English Churches in a Secular Society* (New York: Oxford University Press, 1982); Thomas Kselman, "The Varieties of Religious Experience in Urban Modern France," in *European Religion in the Age of the Great Cities, 1830–1930*, ed. McLeod (London: Routledge, 1995), 165–190. See also Peter Berger, "Secularization Falsified," *First Things*, no. 180 (2008): 23–27.

29. Joris van Eijnatten and Fred van Lieburg, *Nederlandse Religiegeschiedienis* (Hilversum: Verloren, 2005), 271–274, here 274; Schutte, *Het Calvinistisch Nederland: Mythe en Werkelijkheid* (Hilversum: Verloren, 2000), 125–128.

30. Quoted in A. J. Rasker, *De Nederlandse Hervormde Kerk vanaf 1795* (Kampen: Kok, 1974), 117.

31. Willem van der Schee, "Kuyper's Archimedes Point: The Reverend Abraham Kuyper on Election," in *Kuyper Reconsidered: Aspects of His Life and Work*, ed. Cornelis van der Kooi and Jan de Bruijn, *VU Studies on Protestant History* (Amsterdam: VU Uitgeverij, 1999), 105.

32. Petrus Antonius van Leeuwen, *Het Kerkbegrip in de Theologie van Abraham Kuyper* (Franeker: Wever, 1946), 21–22.

33. L. W. E. Rauwenhoff, "De Kerk," *Theologisch Tijdschrift* 1 (1867): esp. 1–5.

34. Quoted in Cornelis Augustijn, "Kerk en Godsdienst 1870–1890," in *De Doleantie van 1886 en haar Geschiedenis*, ed. Wim Bakker (Kampen: Kok, 1986), 58–62.

35. J. van den Berg, "Oplossing der Kerk in de Maatschappij? Modernen, Ethischen en de Toekomstvisie van Richard Rothe," in *Ad Interim: Opstellen over Eschatologie, Apocalyptic en Ethiek*, ed. T. Baarda et al. (Kampen: Kok, 1976), 151–167.

36. Ernst Troeltsch, *The Social Teaching of the Christian Churches*, trans. Olive Wyon, vol. 2, Library of Theological Ethics (Louisville, KY: Westminster/John Knox, 1960), 796–797.

37. Michael Wintle, *Pillars of Piety: Religion in the Netherlands in the Nineteenth Century, 1813–1901*, Occasional Papers in Modern Dutch Studies (Hull: Hull University Press, 1987), 22–23.

38. See Vree, "'Het *Reveil*' en 'Het (neo-)Calvinisme' in hun onderlinge samenhang (1856–1896)," in *Abraham Kuyper: Vast en Veranderlijk: De Ontwikkeling van zijn Denken*, ed. Augustijn and Vree (Zoetermeer: Meinema, 1998), 54–85.

39. Rasker, *Nederlandse Hervormde Kerk*, 53.

40. Vree, "Petrus Hofstede de Groot and the Christian Education of the Dutch Nation (1833–1861)," *Nederlands Archief voor Kerkgeschiedenis* 78 (1998): 75.

41. "Algemeen Reglement voor het bestuur der Hervormde Kerk in het Koningrijk der Nederlanden," (1816), http://www.kerkrecht.nl/main.asp?pagetype=Literatuur&item=90&subitem=.

42. Vree, "Historical Introduction," in *Abraham Kuyper's Commentatio (1860): The Young Kuyper about Calvin, A Lasco, and the Church*, vol. 1, *Brill's Series in Church History* (Leiden: Brill, 2005), 39–40.

43. Rasker, *Nederlandse Hervormde Kerk*, 64, gives an extended quotation from the official articles of separation.

44. On the *Afscheiding* see Blei, *The Netherlands Reformed Church*, 55–70; Rasker, *Nederlandse Hervormde Kerk*, 64–66.

45. Kuyper gave up on Gunning and Saussaye, he recalled, because they were "too relative, too uncertain of definition, to fluid and accommodating, too bubbling and drifting to give my spirit stability." Kuyper, "Confidentially (1873)," in *Abraham Kuyper: A Centennial Reader*, ed. Bratt (Grand Rapids, MI: Eerdmans, 1998), 57.

46. van Leeuwen, *Het Kerkbegrip*, 36–37.

47. For a useful comparison of Kuyper and Gunning, see Vree, "Gunning en Kuyper: Een Bewogen Vriendschap rond Schrift en Kerk in de Jaren 1860–1873," in *Noblesse Oblige: Achtergrond en Actualiteit van de Theologie van J. H. Gunning Jr.*, ed. Theo Hettema and Leo Mietus (Gorinchem: Ekklesia, 2005), esp. 62–65.

48. Heiko Oberman, "Calvin's Legacy: Its Greatness and Limitations (Revised version of the Kuyper Lectures, 1986, Free University of Amsterdam)," in *The Two Reformations: The Journey from the Last Days to the New World*, ed. Donald Weinstein (New Haven, CT: Yale University Press, 2003), 117.

49. Troeltsch, *Social Teaching of the Christian Churches*, vol. 1, 331.

50. Kuyper, "Conservatism and Orthodoxy."

51. J. C. Rullmann, *Kuyper-Bibliographie*, vol. 2 ('s-Gravenhage/Kampen: Js. Bootsma/J.H. Kok, 1923–1940), 135.

52. Cf. D. G. Hart, *Defending the Faith: J. Gresham Machen and the Crisis of Conservative Protestantism in Modern America* (Baltimore: Johns Hopkins University Press, 1994), 1–5.

53. Bratt, *Abraham Kuyper: A Biography* (unpublished), chapter 8, "Church Reformer."

54. Perhaps the closest contemporary analogy is the Anglican Church, which contains those who hold basic Christian beliefs like the Trinitarian God and the divinity of Jesus Christ and those who do not. The factor uniting these groups is

not a set of shared religious beliefs but a commitment to a particular ecclesiastical heritage and apparatus.

55. W. Balke, *Gunning en Hoedemaker: Samen op Weg* ('s-Gravenhage: Boekencentrum, 1985), 64–65.

56. Rullmann, *De Strijd voor Kerkherstel in de Nederlandsch Hervormde Kerk der XIXe Eeuw* (Amsterdam: W. Kirchner, 1915), 204–207.

57. Kuyper, "Vredelievden in de Besturen," in *Het Conflict Gekomen* (Amsterdam: J.H. Kruyt, 1886), 45.

58. On the history of confessional subscription see D. Nauta, *De Verbindende Kracht van de Belijdenis Schriften: Verhandeling over de Formulierkwestie in de Negentiende Eeuw in Nederland* (Kampen: Kok, 1969); Rasker, *Nederlandse Hervormde Kerk*, 184; C. H. W. van den Berg, "De Ontstaangeschiedenis van de Doleantie te Amsterdam," in *De Doleantie van 1886 en Haar Geschiedenis*, ed. Bakker et al. (Kampen: J.H. Kok, 1986).

59. Andreas Havinga, "Church Authorities Not to Discipline Dutch 'Atheist' Pastor," *Ecumenical News International* (2009), http://www.eni.ch/featured/article.php?id=2861.

60. David Bos, *In dienst van het Koninkrijk: Beroepsontwikkeling van Hervormde Predikanten in Negentiende-Eeuws Nederland* (Amsterdam: Bert Bakker, 1999), 61–62.

61. Kuyper, "De Doopskwestie," *De Heraut*, October 7, 1870.

62. Kuyper, "Referaat over de Belijdenis (1870)," in *Revisie der Revisie-Legende* (Amsterdam: J.H. Kruyt, 1879), 56. NB A forthcoming Kuyper bibliography states that this lecture was actually given in 1870, not in 1869 as stated.

63. Quoted in Vree, *Kuyper in de Kiem: De Precalvinistische Periode van Abraham Kuyper, 1848–1874* (Hilversum: Uitgeverij Verloren, 2006), 11.

64. Ibid., 18.

65. Kuyper, "Confidentially (1873)," 46–47.

66. Kuyper, "De Ontwikkeling der Pauselijke Macht onder Nicolaas I," in *Kuyper Archief* (Amsterdam: Historisch Documentatiecentrum voor het Nederlands Protestantisme (1800-heden)), 13.

67. See Kuyper's 1859 correspondence with his fiancée Jo Schaay in George Puchinger, *Abraham Kuyper: De Jonge Kuyper (1837–1867)* (Franeker: Weaver, 1987), 113–114.

68. Vree, "Historical Introduction," 49–53; Vree, "Gunning en Kuyper," 62–63.

69. Kuyper, *Commentatio*, ss. 179, 322, emphasis mine.

70. Ibid., ss. 175, page 312; ss. 188, 335.

71. Vree, "Historical Introduction," 49–61; Henry Zwaanstra, "Abraham Kuyper's Conception of the Church," *Calvin Theological Journal* 9 (1974): 153–154.

72. Kuyper, "Confidentially (1873)," 50–51.

73. Puchinger, *Abraham Kuyper: His Early Journey of Faith*, ed. Harinck, trans. Simone Kennedy (Amsterdam: VU Press, 1998), 14–15.

74. Puchinger, *De Jonge Kuyper*, 183.

75. Kuyper, "Confidentially (1873)," 54–55, emphasis mine.

76. Puchinger, *De Jonge Kuyper*, 176, 209–210.

77. Kuyper, "Confidentially (1873)," 55–56.

78. Kuyper, "(Letter to the Editor)," *De Bazuin* 1895.

79. Charles Taylor, *A Secular Age* (Cambridge, MA: Harvard University Press, 2007), 143; Frances Knight, *The Church in the Nineteenth Century*, I.B. Tauris History of the Christian Church (London: I.B. Tauris, 2008), xvi; John McManners, "Enlightenment: Secular and Christian (1600–1800)," in *The Oxford Illustrated History of Christianity*, ed. John McManners (Oxford: Oxford University Press, 1990).

80. Quoted in Oberman, "Calvin's Legacy," 124–125, emphasis mine.

81. Puchinger, *De Jonge Kuyper*; Puchinger, *Abraham Kuyper: His Early Journey of Faith*.

82. Koch does concede, however, that Kuyper preserved the public–private distinction in one place, his theology of common grace. Well, yes, and we might likewise conclude that Martin Luther was practically a Pelagian, save his theology of justification by grace. Koch, *Biografie*, 62–64. Peter S. Heslam, "Review of *Abraham Kuyper: Een Biographie*, by Jeroen Koch," *Documentatieblad voor de Nederlandse Kerkgeschiedenis na 1800* 65 (2006).

83. van Leeuwen, *Het Kerkbegrip*; Zwaanstra, "Abraham Kuyper's Conception of the Church."

84. Johan Zwaan, "Sociale Bewogenheid in een Jeugdwerk van Abraham Kuyper," in *Een Vrije Universiteitsbibliotheek: Studies over Verleden, Bezit en Heden van de Bibliotheek der Vrije Universiteit*, ed. Johannes Stellingwerf (Assen: Van Gorcum, 1980).

85. Kuyper, *Commentatio*.

86. Kuyper, "Confidentially (1873)"; Puchinger, *De Jonge Kuyper*; Vree, "More Pierson and Mesmer"; Vree, *Kiem*.

87. Harinck, "'Men zal met een serieuze analyse moeten beginnen.' Jasper Vree en Abraham Kuyper," *Documentatieblad voor de Nederlandse Kerkgeschiedenis na 1800* 29 (2006): 51–60.

88. Vree, "Abraham Kuyper in de Jaren 1848–1874: Een Briljante, Bevlogen Branie," *Documentatieblad voor de Nederlandse Kerkgeschiedenis na 1800* 29 (2006): 27–49.

89. Augustijn and Vree, eds., *Abraham Kuyper: Vast en Veranderlijk: De Ontwikkeling van zijn Denken* (Zoetermeer: Meinema, 1998).

90. Zwaanstra, "Abraham Kuyper's Conception of the Church," 150.

91. van Leeuwen, *Het Kerkbegrip*; Vree, "Organisme en Instituut: De Ontwikkeling van Kuypers Spreken over Kerk-Zijn (1867–1901)," in *Abraham Kuyper: Vast en Veranderlijk: De Ontwikkeling van Zijn Denken* (Zoetermeer: Meinema, 1998).

92. C. H. W. van den Berg, "Kuyper en de Kerk," in *Abraham Kuyper: Zijn Volksdeel, Zijn Invloed*, ed. Augustijn et al. (Delft: Meinema, 1987).

93. Bratt, *Abraham Kuyper*, see chapter 3 "The Pastor" and chapter 4 "The Young Politician."

94. Peter S. Heslam, *Creating a Christian Worldview: Abraham Kuyper's Lectures on Calvinism* (Grand Rapids, MI: Eerdmans, 1998); Arie L. Molendijk, "Neo-Calvinist Culture Protestantism: Abraham Kuyper's *Stone Lectures*," *Church History and Religious Culture* 88 (2008); Cornelius Van Til, *Common Grace and the Gospel* (Nutley: Presbyterian and Reformed, 1977); J. Douma, *Algemeene Genade: Uiteenzetting, Vergelijking en Beoordeling van de Opvatting van A. Kuyper, K. Schilder, en Joh. Calvijn over 'Algemeene Genade'* (Goes: Oosterbaan & Le Cointre, 1976).

95. Kuyper, *Lectures on Calvinism*, 11, emphasis original.

96. Kuyper, "De Sleutelen," in *Uit het Woord. Stichtelijke Bijbelstudiën*, vol. 2 (Amsterdam: J.A. Wormser, n.d.), 42, emphasis original; Kuyper, "Confidentially (1873)."

97. Welch, *Protestant Thought Vol. 2*, x.

98. Welch, *Protestant Thought in the Nineteenth Century*, vol. 1, 1799–1870 (New Haven, CT: Yale University Press, 1972), 7.

99. Troeltsch, *Social Teaching*, 656.

100. Kennedy, *Stad op een Berg*, 13.

101. Troeltsch, *Social Teaching*, 25.

102. Theodore M. Steeman, "Church, Sect, Mysticism, Denomination: Periodological Aspects of Troelsch's Types," *Sociological Analysis* 36 (1975): 184–185; Troeltsch, *Social Teaching*, 34.

103. Welch, *Protestant Thought Vol. 2*, 294.

104. Troeltsch, *Social Teaching*, 25–30.

105. Rodney Stark and William S. Bainbridge, "Of Churches, Sects, and Cults: Preliminary Concepts for a Theory of Religious Movements," *Journal for the Scientific Study of Religion* 18, no. 2 (1979).

106. Troeltsch, *Social Teaching*, 34.

107. Steeman, "Church, Sect, Mysticism, Denomination," 182.

108. For example, Kuyper, *De Leer der Verbonden*, vol. 5, Uit Het Woord. Stichtelijke Bijbelstudiën (Kampen: Kok, 1909), 189; Kuyper, "Common Grace (1895–1901)," in *Abraham Kuyper: A Centennial Reader*, ed. Bratt (Grand Rapids, MI: Eerdmans, 1998), 189–191.

109. Sykes, *Identity of Christianity*, 4.

110. Troeltsch, *Social Teaching*, 338.

111. Ibid., 331.

112. Kuyper decries conservatism that "swears by the status quo." Kuyper, "Conservatism and Orthodoxy," 71.

113. Troeltsch, *Social Teaching*, 339.

114. Ibid.

115. For example, Jose Casanova complains that Troeltsch did not anticipate denominations. José Casanova, *Public Religions in the Modern World* (Chicago: University of Chicago Press, 1994), 52.

116. Kuyper, *Drie Kleine Vossen* (Kampen: J.H. Kok, 1901), 46 and here 49.

117. Dietrich Bonhoeffer, *Sanctorum Communio: A Theological Study of the Sociology of the Church*, ed. Wayne Whitson Floyd Jr., vol. 1, Dietrich Bonhoeffer Works (Minneapolis: Fortress, 1998), 253–257, 268.

118. Steeman, "Church, Sect, Mysticism, Denomination," 202; Troeltsch, *Social Teaching*, 670.

119. Casanova, *Public Religions in the Modern World*, 250–251. Citing H. Richard Niebuhr, *The Social Sources of Denominationalism* (New York: Henry Holt and Company, 1929), 24. It is true that Niebuhr described denominationalism as the secularization of the church, but he attributed it to economic factors of the modern "caste" system not to the differentiation of society.

120. Troeltsch, *Social Teaching*, 656–657.

121. Casanova, *Public Religions in the Modern World*, 52, 250–251.

122. For example, Kuyper, "Sphere Sovereignty (1880)," in *Abraham Kuyper: A Centennial Reader*, ed. Bratt (Grand Rapids, MI: Eerdmans, 1998); Kuyper, "Calvinism: Source and Stronghold of Our Constitutional Liberties (1874)," in *Abraham Kuyper: A Centennial Reader*, ed. Bratt (Grand Rapids, MI: Eerdmans, 1998).

123. Lewis Mudge, "Searching for Faith's Social Reality," *Christian Century*, September 22, 1976, 784.

124. George M. Marsden, "Christianity and Cultures: Transforming Niebuhr's Categories," *Insights: The Faculty Journal of Austin Seminary* 115 (1999): 7.

125. Bonhoeffer, *Sanctorum Communio*, 256, 268.

126. Roger Haight S.J., *Christian Community in History: Historical Ecclesiology*, vol. 1 (New York: Continuum, 2004), 26.

127. Kuyper, *Encyclopaedie der Heilige Godgeleerdheid*, vol. 1 (Amsterdam: J.A. Wormser, 1894), vi; Martien E. Brinkman and Cornelis van der Kooi, "Het Calvinisme van Kuyper en Bavinck," in *Het Calvinisme van Kuyper en Bavinck*, ed. Martien E. Brinkman and Cornelis van der Kooi (Zoetermeer: Uitgeverij Meinema, 1997), 10.

128. Robert Wuthnow, *After the Baby Boomers: How Twenty- and Thirty-Somethings Are Shaping the Future of American Religion* (Princeton, NJ: Princeton University Press, 2007), xiv.

129. John L. Austin, *How to Do Things with Words* (Oxford: Oxford University Press, 1962); Quentin Skinner, *Visions of Politics: Regarding Method*, vol. 1 (Cambridge: Cambridge University Press, 2002), 88.

130. Haight, *Christian Community in History: Historical Ecclesiology, Vol. 1*, 26–35; Haight, *Christian Community in History: Comparative Ecclesiology*, vol. 2 (New York: Continuum, 2005).

131. Cf. Haight, "Comparative Ecclesiology," in *The Routledge Companion to the Christian Church*, ed. Gerard Mannion and Mudge (New York: Routledge, 2008).

132. James Ginther, "The Church in Medieval Theology," in *The Routledge Companion to the Christian Church*, ed. Mannion and Mudge (London: Routledge, 2008), 49–50.

133. Haight, *Christian Community in History: Comparative Ecclesiology, Vol. 2*, 1.

134. See Princeton Seminary Special Collections Finding Aid for Kuyper cartoons. See also the dozens of cartoons included in de Bruijn, *Beeldbiografie; Dr. Kuyper in de Caricatuur* (Amsterdam: Van Holkema & Warendorp, 1909).

135. The literary journal *The Netherlands Spectator* furnished one; so did the satirical newsweekly *Uilenspiegel*. For a sampling of cartoons dealing with the *Doleantie* of 1886 see "Kerkberoerte te Amsterdam," *De Nederlandsche Spectator* 2 (1886); de Bruijn, *Beeldbiografie*, 166, 172, 175; Rullmann, *De Strijd voor Kerkherstel*, 288, 293.

136. Rullmann, *De Strijd voor Kerkherstel*, 282–286.

137. G. J. Vos, *Het Keerpunt in de Jongste Geschiedenis van Kerk en Staat: De Eerste Bladzijde der Tweede Afscheiding* (Dordrecht: J.P. Revers, 1887), 139, italics in original. The consistory, the classis, and the provincial board were the various ecclesiastical courts, in ascending order, of the Netherlands Reformed Church. See text for further explanation.

138. Ibid., 140–141.

139. Rasker, *Nederlandse Hervormde Kerk*, 184.

140. Ibid., 182; van den Berg, "De Ontstaangeschiedenis van de Doleantie te Amsterdam," 96–98.

CHAPTER 2

1. Abraham Kuyper, "Confidentially (1873)," in *Abraham Kuyper: A Centennial Reader*, ed. James Bratt (Grand Rapids, MI: Eerdmans, 1998), 54–55.

2. See George Puchinger, *Abraham Kuyper: De Jonge Kuyper (1837–1867)* (Franeker: Weaver, 1987), 205–243; George Puchinger, *Abraham Kuyper: His Early Journey of Faith*, ed. George Harinck, trans. Simone Kennedy (Amsterdam: VU Press, 1998); Jasper Vree, "More Pierson and Mesmer, and Less Pietje Baltus: Kuyper's Ideas on Church, State, and Culture during the First Years of his Ministry (1863–1866)," in *Kuyper Reconsidered: Aspects of his Life and Work*, ed. Cornelis van der Kooi and Jan de Bruijn (Amsterdam: VU Uitgeverij, 1999), 209–309; Vree, *Kuyper in de Kiem: De Precalvinistische Periode van Abraham Kuyper, 1848–1874* (Hilversum: Uitgeverij Verloren, 2006), 129–162.

3. See chapter 1 on Ernst Troeltsch's heuristic definitions. On Kuyper's low view of the church up to 1865 including his views as a university student and his evolving views especially with respect to baptism, see John Halsey Wood Jr., "Church, Sacrament, and Society: Abraham Kuyper's Early Baptismal Theology, 1859–1874," *Journal of Reformed Theology* 2 (2008): 275–296.

4. Kuyper, "Een Wandel in 't Licht: De Grondslag van alle Gemeenschap in de Kerk van Christus, August 9, 1863," in *Archief Kuyper* 152 (Amsterdam: Historisch Documentatiecentrum voor het Nederlands Protestantisme), 13.

5. Ibid., 8.

6. As Bratt also recognizes. Kuyper, "Confidentially (1873)," 56–57; Bratt, *Abraham Kuyper: A Biography* (unpublished, 2004).

7. Kuyper, "Heidelbergsche Catechismus, Zondag 21, de Kerk, Februari 7, 1864," in *Archief Kuyper* 161 (Amsterdam: Historisch Documentatiecentrum voor het Nederlands Protestantisme), 5.

8. Ibid., 8.

9. Ibid., 13.

10. Ibid., 14–15.

11. Kuyper, "De Wedergeboorte, May 1, 1864," in *Kuyper Archief* 153 (Amsterdam: Historisch Documentatiecentrum voor het Nederlands Protestantisme), 5–6.

12. Though they were written in 1865, these articles were not published until 1869. See Vree, "The Marnix-Vereeniging: Abraham Kuyper's First National Organization (1868–89)," *Dutch Review of Church History* 84 (2004): 388–475, esp. 399.

13. Cf. Vree, "More Pierson and Mesmer," 303.

14. Kuyper, "De Eeredienst der Hervormde Kerk en de Zamenstelling van Haar Kerkboek," in *Geschiedenis der Christelijke Kerk in Nederland, in Tafereelen*, ed. B. ter Haar and W. Moll, vol. 2 (Amsterdam: Portielje & Zoon, 1869), 89.

15. Ibid., 90–91.

16. On the Victorian frame of mind see Bratt, "Abraham Kuyper: Puritan, Victorian, Modern," in *Religion, Pluralism, and Public Life: Abraham Kuyper's Legacy of the Twenty-First Century*, ed. Luis E. Lugo (Grand Rapids, MI: Eerdmans, 2000), 3–21; Norman Cantor, *The American Century: Varieties of Culture in Modern Times* (New York: Harper Collins, 1997), 15–27.

17. See Allard Pierson, *Dr. A. Pierson aan Zijne Laatste Gemeente* (Arnhem: D.A. Thieme, 1865); J. Trapman, "Allard Pierson en Zijn Afscheid van de Kerk," *Documentatieblad voor de Nederlandse Kerkgeschiedenis na 1800* 19 (1996): 15–27.

18. Kuyper, "Humanisme en Christendom, November 26, 1865," in *Archief Kuyper* 154 (Amsterdam: Historisch Documentatiecentrum voor het Nederlands Protestantisme).

19. See Kuyper, "The Blurring of the Boundaries (1892)," in *Abraham Kuyper: A Centennial Reader*, ed. Bratt (Grand Rapids, MI: Eerdmans, 1998), 363–402; Vree, "Palingenesie bij Abraham Kuyper: Een Levensproces dat door Heel de Schepping Gaat," in *Protestants Nederland tussen Tijd en Eeuwigheid* (Zoetermeer: Meinema, 2000), 154–171.

20. Kuyper, "Humanisme en Christendom," 10–11.

21. George Harinck and Lodewijk Winkeler, "De Negentiende Eeuw," in *Handboek Nederlandse Kerkgeschiedenis*, ed. Herman J. Selderhuis (Kampen: Kok, 2006), 629.

22. Emphasis mine. Kuyper, "De Sleutelmacht," in *Uit het Woord. Stichtelijke Bijbel-studiën*, vol. 2 (Amsterdam: J.A. Wormser, n.d.), 120. N.B. Puchinger, *De Jonge Kuyper*, 209–213, also referred to this group as "mystics."

23. Kuyper, "Pietje Baltus (*De Standaard*, March 30, 1914)," in *Abraham Kuyper: A Centennial Reader*, ed. Bratt (Grand Rapids, MI: Eerdmans, 1998), 58–59; Kuyper, "Confidentially (1873)," 55–61.

24. Kuyper, "De Openbare Godsvereering en het Bestaan der Kerk, December 3, 1864," in *Archief Kuyper* 154 (Amsterdam: Historisch Documentatiecentrum voor het Nederlands Protestantisme), esp. 9–10.

25. Kuyper, "Het Gemeenschapleven der Menschheid, Einddoel van Jezus' Kerk en Middel Harer Ontwikkeling, December 11, 1865," in *Kuyper Archief* 154 (Amsterdam: Historisch Documentatiecentrum voor het Nederlands Protestantisme), 6.

26. Vree, "Gunning en Kuyper: Een Bewogen Vriendschap rond Schrift en Kerk in de Jaren 1860–1873," in *Noblesse Oblige: Achtergrond en Actualiteit van de Theologie van J. H. Gunning Jr.*, ed. Theo Hettema and Leo Mietus (Gorinchem: Ekklesia, 2005), 63.

27. Kuyper, "Wandel in 't Licht," 25.

28. Ibid., 29.

29. Ibid., 25.

30. As Vree explains, "As far as Kuyper was concerned, the separation between church and state did not need to be brought to a head." Vree, *Kiem*, 130.

31. Kuyper, "De Kerk," 5.

32. Kuyper, "De Eerste Kerkvergadering of De Vestiging onzer Hervormde Kerk, en de Strijd om Haar Zelfstandig Bestaan, 1550–1618," in *Geschiedenis der Christelijke Kerk in Nederland in Tafereelen*, ed. B. ter Haar and W. Moll, vol. 2 (Amsterdam: G. Portielje & Zoon, 1869), 80.

33. Ibid.

34. Kuyper, "Humanisme en Christendom, November 26, 1865," in *Archief Kuyper* 154 (Amsterdam: Historisch Documentatiecentrum voor het Nederlands Protestantisme), 9–10.

35. On Kuyper's social concern and the possible personal sources thereof, see Bratt, *Abraham Kuyper: A Biography*, chapter 3, "The Preacher"; Vree, "The Marnix-Vereeniging: Abraham Kuyper's First National Organization (1868–89)," 400; Vree, *Kiem*, 16–18, 133, 136, 150–153, 366; Johan Zwaan, "Sociale Bewogenheid in een Jeugdwerk van Abraham Kuyper," in *Een Vrije Universiteitsbibliotheek: Studies over Verleden, Bezit en Heden van de Bibliotheek der Vrije Universiteit*, ed. Johannes Stellingwerf (Assen: Van Gorcum, 1980), 203–219.

36. Kuyper, "Humanisme en Christendom," 11–12.

37. Kuyper, "Gemeenschapleven der Menschheid," 9.

38. Ibid., 10–11.

39. Ibid., 12.

40. Ibid., 13.

41. L. W. E. Rauwenhoff, "De Kerk," *Theologisch Tijdschrift* 1 (1867): 1–37, here 19; J. van den Berg, "Oplossing der Kerk in de Maatschappij? Modernen, Ethischen en de Toekomstvisie van Richard Rothe," in *Ad Interim: Opstellen over Eschatologie, Apocalyptic en Ethiek*, ed. T. Baarda et al. (Kampen: Kok, 1976), 151–167; A. van Toorenenbergen, "De Kerk," *Waarheid in Liefde* (1867): 513–568. NB Although Toorenenbergen was a supernaturalist, he clearly fits what Richard Niebuhr called the "Christ of Culture" type with his Abelardian view of the atonement and this-worldly mission of the church as chief educator of the people.

42. Kuyper, "De Menschwording Gods: Het Levensbeginsel der Kerk (1867)," in *Predicatiën, in de jaren 1867 tot 1873, tijdens zijn Predikantschap in het Nederlandsch Hervormde Kerkgenootschap, gehouden te Beesd, te Utrecht, en te Amsterdam* (Kampen: Kok, 1913), 259.

43. Ibid., 260.

44. Friedrich Schleiermacher, *The Christian Faith* (New York: T&T Clark, 1999), 525.

45. Kuyper, "De Menschwording Gods," 272.

46. Ibid.

47. Troeltsch, *The Social Teaching of the Christian Churches*, trans. Olive Wyon, vol. 2, Library of Theological Ethics (Louisville, KY: Westminster/John Knox, 1960), 656.

CHAPTER 3

1. Quoted in Theo van Tijn, *Twintig Jaren Amsterdam: De Maatschappelijke Ontwikkeling van de Hoofdstad, van de Jaren '50 der Vorige Eeuw tot 1876* (Amsterdam: Scheltema & Holkema, 1965), 385, emphasis mine; Abraham Kuyper, "Complot en Revolutie," in *Het Conflict Gekomen* (Amsterdam: J.H. Kruyt, 1886).

2. Kuyper, "Calvinism: Source and Stronghold of Our Constitutional Liberties (1874)," in *Abraham Kuyper: A Centennial Reader*, ed. James Bratt (Grand Rapids, MI: Eerdmans, 1998), 313.

3. Ibid., 315; Kuyper, *Kerkvisitatie te Utrecht in 1868 met het Oog op den Kritieken Toestand Onzer Kerk* (Utrecht: J.H. van Peursem, 1868), 1–6.

4. Eric Hobsbawn, *The Age of Revolution, 1789–1848* (Cleveland: World, 1962), 53.

5. Mark Noll, *The Civil War as a Theological Crisis* (Chapel Hill: University of North Carolina, 2007).

6. Kuyper, "Conservatism and Orthodoxy: False and True Preservation (1870)," in *Abraham Kuyper: A Centennial Reader*, ed. Bratt (Grand Rapids, MI: Eerdmans, 1998), 69, emphasis mine.

7. Hugh McLeod, *Secularization in Western Europe, 1848–1914* (New York: St. Martin's, 2000), 28.

8. See Kuyper, "Modernism: A *Fata Morgana* in the Christian Domain (1871)," in *Abraham Kuyper: A Centennial Reader*, ed. Bratt (Grand Rapids, MI: Eerdmans,

1998), 87–124; Jasper Vree, *Kuyper in de Kiem: De Precalvinistische Periode van Abraham Kuyper, 1848–1874* (Hilversum: Uitgeverij Verloren, 2006), 335–337.

9. Kuyper, *Confidentie: Schrijven aan den Weled. Heer J.H. van der Linden* (Amsterdam: Höveker & Zoon, 1873), 103.

10. Cited in van Tijn, *Twintig Jaren Amsterdam*, 386.

11. Kuyper, "Confidentially (1873)," in *Abraham Kuyper: A Centennial Reader*, ed. Bratt (Grand Rapids, MI: Eerdmans, 1998), 61.

12. Cf. Bratt, "The Context of Herman Bavinck's Stone Lectures: Culture and Politics in 1908," in *A Pearl and a Leaven: Herman Bavinck for the Twenty-First Century* (Calvin College: unpublished paper, 2008); Max Weber, "The Principle Characteristics of Charismatic Authority and Its Relations to Forms of Communal Organization," in *The Theory of Social and Economic Organization*, ed. Talcott Parsons (New York: Free Press, 1947), 358–359.

13. Annemarie Houkes, *Christelijke Vaderlanders: Godsdienst, Burgerschap, en de Nederlandse Natie (1850–1900)* (Amsterdam: Wereldbibliotheek, 2009), chapter 5.

14. Kuyper, *Confidentie*, 52; Vree, *Kiem*, 209.

15. Kuyper, *Confidentie*, 55.

16. Ibid., 58.

17. Vree, *Kiem*, 173, 204–209. The state paid for ten of the Utrecht pastors, and problems arose when an eleventh was to be added because the church would have to foot the bill.

18. See pamplets like Kuyper, *Vrijmaking der Kerk* (Amsterdam: H. de Hoogh, 1869); Kuyper, *De Kerkelijke Goederen* (Amsterdam: H. Höveker, 1869).

19. Quoted in van Tijn, *Twintig Jaren Amsterdam*, 385, italics in original.

20. See Walter H. Conser Jr., *Church and Confession: Conservative Theologians in Germany, England, and America, 1815–1866* (Macon, GA: Mercer University Press, 1984); McLeod, *Secularization in Western Europe*, 31–51.

21. Kuyper, *Vrijmaking der Kerk*.

22. Vree, *Kiem*, 301–302.

23. Kuyper, *Kerkvisitatie*, 6–9; Vree, *Kiem*, 294, 320.

24. Vree, *Kiem*, 307–308; Kuyper, *De Leer der Onsterfelijkheid en de Staatsschool* (Amsterdam: H. de Hoogh, 1870).

25. Kuyper, "Conservatism and Orthodoxy," 69.

26. Stephen Sykes, *The Identity of Christianity: Theologians and the Essence of Christianity from Schleiermacher to Barth* (Philadelphia: Fortress, 1984), 4.

27. Kuyper, "Conservatism and Orthodoxy," 81.

28. Roger Haight S.J., *Christian Community in History: Comparative Ecclesiology*, vol. 2 (New York: Continuum, 2005), 364.

29. Kuyper, "De Menschwording Gods: Het Levensbeginsel der Kerk (1867)," in *Predicatiën, in de jaren 1867 tot 1873, tijdens zijn Predikantschap in het Nederlandsch Hervormde Kerkgenootschap, gehouden te Beesd, te Utrecht, en te Amsterdam* (Kampen: Kok, 1913), 256–257 and here 260.

30. Ibid., 258.

31. Quoted in J. C. Rullmann, *Kuyper-Bibliographie*, vol. 1 ('s-Gravenhage/Kampen: Js. Bootsma/J.H. Kok, 1923–1940), 26–27. Later, interpreter P. A. van Leeuwen suggested that the incarnational model indicated the residual influence of some form of modernist theology, and he showed that Kuyper's model resembled that of his contemporary J. H. Gunning, who used the incarnational model to reconcile the immanent and the transcendent aspects of the church. Petrus Antonius van Leeuwen, *Het Kerkbegrip in de Theologie van Abraham Kuyper* (Franeker: Wever, 1946), 101–106.

32. Ephesians 3:17.

33. Avery Dulles, *Models of the Church* (New York: Doubleday, 1987), 60.

34. Kuyper, "Conservatism and Orthodoxy," 82.

35. Kuyper, "Geworteld en Gegrond (1870)," in *Predicatiën, in de jaren 1867 tot 1873, tijdens zijn Predikantschap in het Nederlandsch Hervormde Kerkgenootschap, gehouden te Beesd, te Utrecht, en te Amsterdam* (Kampen: Kok, 1913), 329, italics in original.

36. Ibid.

37. Ibid.

38. J. Cramer, "Vrijmaking der Kerk, Waardoor? en Wanneer?," *Stemmen voor Waarheid en Vrede* 7 (1870): 410.

39. Kuyper, *Confidentie*, 58.

40. Sykes, *Identity of Christianity*, 236–237.

41. Dulles, *Models of the Church*, 60.

42. Kuyper, "Conservatism and Orthodoxy," 82.

43. R. C. Moberly, *Ministerial Priesthood: Chapters (Preliminary to a Study of the Ordinal) on the Rationale of Ministry and the Meaning of Christian Priesthood*, Second ed. (London: John Murray, 1910), 39–40, 52.

44. Kuyper, "Geworteld en Gegrond," 335.

45. Ibid., 330.

46. Sykes, *Identity of Christianity*, 236.

47. Vree showed that the terms *organism* and *institute* did not show up again until 1883, in Kuyper's *Tractaat van de Reformatie der Kerken*. The idea, if not the terms, that the church consisted of a mutually edifying form and essence, an inner and outer aspect, which the organism–institute formula expressed, was the core of his free-church ecclesiology. Vree, "Organisme en Instituut: De Ontwikkeling van Kuypers Spreken over Kerk-Zijn (1867–1901)," in *Abraham Kuyper: Vast en Veranderlijk: De Ontwikkeling van Zijn Denken* (Zoetermeer: Meinema, 1998), 86–108.

48. *Pace* James K. A. Smith, *Introducing Radical Orthodoxy: Mapping a Post-Secular Theology* (Grand Rapids, MI: Baker Academic, 2004), 238, note 221. Smith says Kuyper's ecclesiology is "flattened" and "unsacramental" compared with Calvin's. *Sacramental* is my term, not Kuyper's, but compare Haight, *Christian*

Community in History, vol. 2, 107, who describes Calvin's ecclesiology as "sacramental" for the same reasons I describe Kuyper's that way: "Ultimately the eternal Word of God alone rules and governs the church. But within history the Word of God, by God's own design, requires human agents or ministers to become channeled or mediated to people's lives. Departing from Calvin's language here, but not his conception, this could be called the sacramental principle: the church is the sacrament of God's Word in history. God uses ministers, sacraments, and organizations instrumentally."

49. Dulles, *Models of the Church,* 66–67.

50. Kuyper, "Modernism: A *Fata Morgana* in the Christian Domain (1871)," 89; Kuyper, "Calvinism: Source of Our Constitutional Liberties," 314.

51. For example, Edmund Burke, *Reflections on the Revolution in France,* ed. F. G. Selby (New York: McMillan, 1890), 105.

52. Kuyper, "Het Mystieke Lichaam van Christus," *Zondagsblad (van De Standaard)* 1875, no. 69.

53. Ibid., no. 70.

54. Ibid.

55. Ibid., no. 71.

56. Ibid., no. 70.

57. Kuyper, "De Uitverkiezing," in *Uit het Woord. Stichtelijke Bijbelstudiën,* vol. 2, *Uit het Woord* (Amsterdam: J.A. Wormser, n.d.), 170.

58. Kuyper, "De Sleutelen," in *Uit het Woord. Stichtelijke Bijbelstudiën,* 6 vols., vol. 2 (Amsterdam: J.A. Wormser, n.d.), 44.

59. Ibid., 45.

60. Ibid., 62.

61. Kuyper, "Individualisme en Kerk, September 26, 1868," in *Archief Kuyper* 157 (Amsterdam: Historisch Documentatiecentrum voor het Nederlands Protestantisme), 16–17.

62. Kuyper, "De Sleutelmacht," in *Uit het Woord. Stichtelijke Bijbelstudiën,* vol. 2 (Amsterdam: J.A. Wormser, n.d.), 99.

63. Ibid., 102.

64. Kuyper, "Confidentially (1873)," 59–60.

65. Kuyper, "De Sleutelen," 43.

66. Kuyper, "Mystieke Lichaam," no. 74.

67. Ibid.

68. Kuyper, "De Uitverkiezing," 189.

69. Kuyper, "Individualisme en Kerk," 13. On the *Reveil* and its later adherents, see James H. Mackay, *Religious Thought in Holland during the Nineteenth Century* (London: Hodder and Stoughten, 1911), 1–43, 112–130.

70. Kuyper, "Wedergeboorte en Bekeering," in *Uit Het Woord. Stichtelijke Bijbelstudiën,* vol. 3 (Amsterdam: Höveker & Wormser, n.d.), 34, 37.

71. Friedrich Schleiermacher, *The Christian Faith* (New York: T&T Clark, 1999), 103.

72. George Harinck and Lodewijk Winkeler, "De Negentiende Eeuw," in *Handboek Nederlandse Kerkgeschiedenis*, ed. Herman J. Selderhuis (Kampen: Kok, 2006), 610.

73. All features common to free-church ecclesiology according to Veli-Matti Kärkkäinen, *An Introduction to Ecclesiology: Ecumenical, Historical and Global Perspectives* (Downers Grove: InterVarsity, 2002), 59–67.

74. Kuyper, "Vrijheid: Bevestigingsrede van Dr. Ph. S. van Ronkel (1873)," in *Predicatiën, in de jaren 1867 tot 1873, tijdens zijn Predikantschap in het Nederlandsch Hervormde Kerkgenootschap, gehouden te Beesd, te Utrecht, en te Amsterdam* (Kampen: Kok, 1913), 405.

75. Kuyper, *Vrijmaking der Kerk.*

76. Kuyper, *Confidentie*, 86–91.

77. "The Belgic Confession," in *The Creeds of Christendom*, ed. Philip Schaf (Grand Rapids, MI: Baker, 1993), III.432.

78. Kuyper, "Vrijheid," 400.

79. Kuyper, "Een Wandel in 't Licht: De Grondslag van alle Gemeenschap in de Kerk van Christus, August 9, 1863," in *Archief Kuyper* 152 (Amsterdam: Historisch Documentatiecentrum voor het Nederlands Protestantisme), 25.

80. Kuyper, "De Autonomie der Gemeente," *De Standaard*, September 20, 1874.

81. Ibid. See also Kuyper, "Eenheid: Rede, ter Bevestiging van een Dienaar des Woords, Gehouden 31 Augustus 1873 in de Nieuwe Kerk te Amsterdam," in *Predicatiën, in de jaren 1867 tot 1873, tijdens zijn Predikantschap in het Nederlandsch Hervormde Kerkgenootschap, gehouden te Beesd, te Utrecht, en te Amsterdam* (Kampen: Kok, 1913), 442.

82. Kuyper, *Confidentie*, 84–85.

83. Ibid., 98; Kuyper, *Kerkvisitatie*, 1–6; van Tijn, *Twintig Jaren Amsterdam*, 385.

84. Kuyper, *Confidentie*, 92–93; Kuyper, "Vrijheid," 409–410.

85. Kuyper, *Confidentie*, 80–81.

86. Kuyper, "Vrijheid," 400–401.

87. Kuyper, *Confidentie*, 86–91.

88. Ibid., 84.

89. Bonhoeffer had difficulty describing the church sociologically, distinguishing between the senses in which the church is a compulsory organization, a voluntary association, a community, a society, and a divinely established community. Dietrich Bonhoeffer, *Sanctorum Communio: A Theological Study of the Sociology of the Church*, ed. Wayne Whitson Floyd Jr., vol. 1, Dietrich Bonhoeffer Works (Minneapolis: Fortress, 1998), 252.

90. Troeltsch's definitions were ideal types and not as inflexible as Bonhoeffer portrayed them. See the discussion in chapter 1. "The Free Church system is the destruction of the mediaeval and early Protestant idea of a social order welded together by one uniform State Church ....This meant that the question of Church membership now became a matter of individual choice, and that, at

least outwardly, the form of Church-order becomes that of a voluntary association, even though theologically the community which thus comes into being
may still continue to be considered as an objective, ecclesiastical institution."
Ernst Troeltsch, *The Social Teaching of the Christian Churches*, trans. Olive Wyon,
vol. 2, Library of Theological Ethics (Louisville, KY: Westminster/John Knox,
1960), 656.

91. Kuyper, "Vrijheid," 406.

92. Ibid., 398.

93. See Kuyper's citations of Alexis de Tocqueville, ibid., 399, 407.

94. Jaroslav Pelikan, *Credo: Historical and Theological Guide to Creeds and Confessions
of Faith in the Christian Tradition* (New Haven, CT: Yale University Press, 2003),
486–497.

95. Vree, "De Drie Formulieren van Enigheid: Een Vondst van Abraham Kuyper,"
Historisch Tijdschrift GKN 13 (2007): 3–17; R. A. Flinterman, "Toorenenbergen,
Johan Justus van," in *Biografisch Lexicon voor de Geschiedenis van het Nederlands
Protestantisme*, ed. D. Nauta, et al., vol. 2 (Kampen: Kok, 1983), 421–424; D. Nau-
ta, *De Verbindende Kracht van de Belijdenis Schriften: Verhandeling over de Formu-
lierkwestie in de Negentiende Eeuw in Nederland* (Kampen: Kok, 1969), 84–91.

96. Kuyper, "Tweede Annexe: Referaat over de Belijdenis," in *Revisie der Revisie
Legende* (Amsterdam: J.H. Kruyt, 1879), 56–68, here 57, emphasis mine.

97. Kuyper, *Confidentie*, 52; Vree, *Kiem*, 209.

98. On the revision of the Church Order, see Vree, "De Herziening van het Hervormde Algemeen Reglement (1846–1852)," in *Om de Toekomst van het Protestantse Nederland. De Gevolgen van de Grondwetsherziening van 1848 voor Kerk,
Staat en Maatschappij*, ed. Schutte and Vree (Zoetermeer: Meinema, 1998),
22–63.

99. Kuyper, *Confidentie*, 79.

100. Kuyper, *Wat Moeten Wij Doen: Het Stemrecht aan ons zelven Houden of den Kerkeraad Machtigen? Vraag bij de Uitvoering van art. 23 Toegelicht* (Culemborg: A.J.
Blom, 1867), 15. See also Kuyper, *Confidentie*, 74–80.

101. Kuyper, *Confidentie*, 80.

102. Kuyper, *Wat Moeten Wij Doen*, 8.

103. Houkes, *Christelijke Vaderlanders*, 145–183.

104. Quoted in Bratt, *Abraham Kuyper: A Centennial Reader* (Grand Rapids, MI:
Eerdmans, 1998), 141. See also Hans Krabbendam, "Zielenverbrijzelaars en
Zondelozen: Reacties in de Nederlandse Pers op Moody, Sankey, en Pearsall Smith, 1874–1878," *Documentatieblad voor de Nederlandse Kerkgeschiedenis
na 1800* 34 (1991): 39–55; Bratt, *Abraham Kuyper: A Biography* (unpublished),
chapter 5 "Brighton and Breakdown."

105. On the exchange between Gunning and Kuyper, see J.H. Gunning, Jr., *Lijden en
Heerlijkheid* (Amsterdam: B. van den Land, 1875); Gunning, "Antwoord aan Dr.
A. Kuyper van J. H. Gunning (1876)," in *De Weg ter Godzaligheid* (Zwolle: J.P.

van Dijk, 1877); Kuyper, "Aan Ds. J. H. Gunning," in *De Weg ter Godzaligheid* (Zwolle: J.P. van Dijk, 1875).

106. Krabbendam, "Zielenverbrijzelaars en Zondelozen," 50–51.

107. Kuyper, "Mystieke Lichaam," no. 74.

108. Vree, "Historical Introduction," in *Abraham Kuyper's Commentatio (1860): The Young Kuyper about Calvin, A Lasco, and the Church*, vol. 1, Brill's Series in Church History (Leiden: Brill, 2005), 39–42.

109. Kuyper, *Wat Moeten Wij Doen*, 9.

110. Kuyper, *Confidentie*, 104.

111. James C. Kennedy, *Stad op een Berg: De Publieke Rol van Protestantse Kerken* (Zoetermeer: Boekencentrum, 2009), 43–44.

112. Kuyper, *Confidentie*, 62.

113. Ibid., 70.

114. Ibid., 66.

115. Kennedy, *Stad op een Berg*, 42–49.

116. Quoted in Houkes, *Christelijke Vaderlanders*, 177. See also Harinck, "Een Leefbare Oplossing: Katholieke en Protestantse Tradities en de Scheiding van Kerk en Staat," in *Ongewenste Goden: De Publieke Rol van Religie in Nederland*, ed. Marcel ten Hooven and Theo de Wit (Amsterdam: Sun, 2006), 106–130; Peter van Rooden, "Long-Term Religious Developments in the Netherlands, c. 1750–2000," in *The Decline of Christendom in Western Europe, 1750–2000*, ed. Hugh McLeod and Werner Ustorf (Cambridge, UK: Cambridge University Press, 2003), 113–129.

117. Kuyper, '*Het Rede op het Volksgeweten': Rede ter Opening van de Algemeene Vergadering der 'Vereeniging voor Christelijk Nationaal-Schoolonderwijs,' Gehouden te Utrecht, den 18 Mei 1869* (Amsterdam: B.H. Blankenberg Jr., 1869); Cornelis Augustijn, "Kuypers Theologie van de Samenleving," in *Abraham Kuyper: Vast en Veranderlijk*, ed. Augustijn and Vree (Zoetermeer: Meinema, 1998), 34–35; Jeroen Koch, "Abraham Kuyper tussen Gereformeerde Natie en Gereformeerde Zuil," *Tijdschrift voor Geschiedenis* 120 (2007): 527–528.

118. Kuyper, *Confidentie*, 66–70.

119. Kuyper, "Sphere Sovereignty (1880)," in *Abraham Kuyper: A Centennial Reader*, ed. Bratt (Grand Rapids, MI: Eerdmans, 1998), 463–472.

120. Kuyper, *Confidentie*, 63–66.

121. Kuyper, "Sphere Sovereignty," 472–473; Kuyper, "Uniformity: The Curse of Modern Life (1869)," in *Abraham Kuyper: A Centennial Reader*, ed. Bratt (Grand Rapids, MI: Eerdmans, 1998).

122. See footnote 5 in Kuyper, "Calvinism: Source of our Constitutional Liberties," 284.

123. Kuyper, "De Uitverkiezing," 127. Also Kuyper, *Confidentie*, 69–70.

124. Kuyper, "Calvinism: Source of our Constitutional Liberties," 296. And Kuyper was not wholly mistaken: see John Witte Jr., *The Reformation of Rights: Law,*

Religion, and Human Rights in Early Modern Calvinism (Cambridge, UK: Cambridge University Press, 2007).

125. Bratt, *Abraham Kuyper*, chapter 7 "Political Theorist."

126. John Bolt, *A Free Church, A Holy Nation: Abraham Kuyper's American Public Theology* (Grand Rapids, MI: Eerdmans, 2000), 448–452; Troeltsch, *Social Teaching*, 656–661.

127. Cf. Harinck, "Een Leefbare Oplossing," 106–130; Houkes, *Christelijke Vaderlanders*, 25–46; Augustijn, "Kerk en Godsdienst 1870–1890," in *De Doleantie van 1886 en haar Geschiedenis*, ed. Wim Bakker (Kampen: Kok, 1986), 41–75.

128. Kuyper, *Confidentie*, 80.

129. Peter Berger et al., *Religious America, Secular Europe? A Theme and Variations* (Aldershot: Ashgate, 2008), 34.

CHAPTER 4

1. Johannes Stellingwerff, *Dr. Abraham Kuyper en de Vrije Universiteit* (Kampen: Kok, 1987), 121.

2. See Charles Taylor, *A Secular Age* (Cambridge, MA: Harvard University Press, 2007), 423–472; George Harinck and Lodewijk Winkeler, "De Negentiende Eeuw," in *Handboek Nederlandse Kerkgeschiedenis*, ed. Herman J. Selderhuis (Kampen: Kok, 2006), 676–721; Joris van Eijnatten and Fred van Lieburg, *Nederlandse Religiegeschiedenis* (Hilversum: Verloren, 2005), 278–290.

3. A. J. Rasker, *De Nederlandse Hervormde Kerk vanaf 1795* (Kampen: Kok, 1974), 182.

4. C. H. W. van den Berg, "De Ontstaangeschiedenis van de Doleantie te Amsterdam," in *De Doleantie van 1886 en Haar Geschiedenis*, ed. W. Bakker et al. (Kampen: J.H. Kok, 1986), 98–99; James Bratt, *Abraham Kuyper: A Biography* (unpublished), chapter 8 "Church Reformer."

5. For a brief history of these events, see Rasker, *De Nederlandse Hervormde Kerk.*

6. Abraham Kuyper, *Het Conflict Gekomen* (Amsterdam: J.H. Kruyt, 1886), III.45.

7. Ibid., III.7–12.

8. Kuyper, *Tractaat van de Reformatie der Kerken, aan de Zonen der Reformatie Hier te Lande op Luther's Vierde Eeuwfeest Aangeboden* (Amsterdam: Höveker & Zoon, 1883). Kuyper also summarized his main ecclesiological points in Kuyper, *Stellingen in den Professorenkrans der "Vrije Universiteit"* (1884); Kuyper, "(Main Points of Ecclesiology)," *De Heraut*, December 4, 1884.

9. For brief discussions of the "believers' church," see Veli-Matti Kärkkäinen, *An Introduction to Ecclesiology: Ecumenical, Historical and Global Perspectives* (Downers Grove, IL: InterVarsity, 2002), 59–67; Miroslav Volf, *After Our Likeness: The Church as the Image of the Trinity* (Grand Rapids, MI: Eerdmans, 1998), 1–18.

10. van den Berg, "De Ontstaangeschiedenis van de Doleantie te Amsterdam," 94–96; Rasker, *Nederlandse Hervormde Kerk*, 183; Vree, "De Drie Formulieren

van Enigheid: Een Vondst van Abraham Kuyper," *Historisch Tijdschrift GKN* 13 (2007): 8–9.

11. Kuyper, *Tractaat van de Reformatie der Kerken*, Introduction. I have also used Herman Hoeksema's English translation of the *Tract*, which appeared as installments in *The Standard Bearer* (1978–1987), but all translations are my own. Kuyper, "A Pamphlet on the Reformation of the Churches (trans. Herman Hoeksema)," *The Standard Bearer* 54–63 (1978–1987). For the sake of convenience, I have provided citations of the *Tract* according to chapter numbers ("ss.") so that interested readers can find the cited material in either English or the original Dutch.

12. This response appeared in *De Heraut* no. 330 and is quoted at length in J. C. Rullmann, *Kuyper-Bibliographie* ('s-Gravenhage/Kampen: Js. Bootsma/J.H. Kok, 1923–1940), II.97–98.

13. Ibid., 97.

14. Roger Haight S.J., *Christian Community in History: Comparative Ecclesiology*, vol. 2 (New York: Continuum, 2005), 306–307; Dennis M. Doyle, "Möhler, Schleiermacher, and the Roots of Communion Ecclesiology," *Theological Studies* 57, no. 3 (1996): esp. 474–475. One of the notable differences between Friedrich Schleiermacher and Möhler, according to Doyle, was that no particular concrete institutional form of the church was essential for Schleiermacher, while Möhler's central argument was that the Roman Catholic Church was the essential form of the church.

15. Vree, "Organisme en Instituut: De Ontwikkeling van Kuypers Spreken over Kerk-Zijn (1867–1901)," in *Abraham Kuyper: Vast en Veranderlijk: De Ontwikkeling van Zijn Denken* (Zoetermeer: Meinema, 1998), 95.

16. Petrus Antonius van Leeuwen, *Het Kerkbegrip in de Theologie van Abraham Kuyper* (Franeker: Wever, 1946), 146; Vree, "Organisme en Instituut," 97; Kuyper, "(Untitled Series on Baptism and the Visible Church)," *De Heraut* 1887–1888. See also H. J. Langman, *Kuyper en de Volkskerk: Een Dogmatisch-Ecclesiologische Studie* (Kampen: Kok, 1950), 81. NB "Cuper," or "Cooper" in English, is a form of Kuyper.

17. Kuyper, *Tractaat van de Reformatie der Kerken*, ss. 14, italics in original.

18. Kuyper, "(Main Points of Ecclesiology)," paragraph 5. Also "a gathering possesses the essence of the church, even though its officers do not yet function"; Kuyper, *Tractaat van de Reformatie der Kerken*, ss. 14, italics in original.

19. Kuyper, "Locus de Ecclesia," in *Dictaten Dogmatiek*, vol. 4 (Grand Rapids, MI: J.B. Hulst, n.d.), 107–108.

20. Kuyper, *Tractaat van de Reformatie der Kerken*, ss. 14.

21. Kuyper, "Confidentially (1873)," in *Abraham Kuyper: A Centennial Reader*, ed. Bratt (Grand Rapids, MI: Eerdmans, 1998), 57; van Leeuwen, *Het Kerkbegrip*, 15–38; Vree, "Gunning en Kuyper: Een Bewogen Vriendschap rond Schrift en Kerk in de Jaren 1860–1873," in *Noblesse Oblige: Achtergrond en Actualiteit van de*

Theologie van J. H. Gunning Jr., ed. Theo Hettema and Leo Mietus (Gorinchem: Ekklesia, 2005).

22. Kuyper, "Geworteld en Gegrond (1870)," in *Predicatiën, in de jaren 1867 tot 1873, tijdens zijn Predikantschap in het Nederlandsch Hervormde Kerkgenootschap, gehouden te Beesd, te Utrecht, en te Amsterdam* (Kampen: Kok, 1913), 335.

23. Ibid., 329, italics in original.

24. Kuyper, *Tractaat van de Reformatie der Kerken*, 14; Kuyper, "(Main Points of Ecclesiology)," paragraph 5; Kuyper, "Locus de Ecclesia," 112.

25. Kuyper, *Lectures on Calvinism* (Grand Rapids, MI: Eerdmans, 1931), 21.

26. Kuyper, "Locus de Ecclesia," 108.

27. Stephen Sykes, *The Identity of Christianity: Theologians and the Essence of Christianity from Schleiermacher to Barth* (Philadelphia: Fortress, 1984), 232–233.

28. R. C. Moberly, *Ministerial Priesthood: Chapters (Preliminary to a Study of the Ordinal) on the Rationale of Ministry and the Meaning of Christian Priesthood*, 2d ed. (London: John Murray, 1910); Sykes, *Identity of Christianity*, 45–50.

29. Kuyper, "Locus de Ecclesia," 113.

30. Ibid., 108.

31. Kuyper, *Stellingen in den Professorenkrans*, here 9, also 4; Kuyper, *Tractaat van de Reformatie der Kerken*, ss. 15; Kuyper, *Separatie en Doleantie* (Amsterdam: J.A. Wormser, 1890), 6, italics in original.

32. Kuyper, "(Main Points of Ecclesiology)," 4, 6, 7.

33. Kuyper, *Tractaat van de Reformatie der Kerken*, ss. 3.

34. For example, Kuyper, "Geworteld en Gegrond."

35. Dietrich Bonhoeffer, *Sanctorum Communio: A Theological Study of the Sociology of the Church*, ed. Wayne Whitson Floyd Jr., vol. 1, Dietrich Bonhoeffer Works (Minneapolis: Fortress, 1998), 268. Nevertheless, in the same breath Bonhoeffer admitted that some Christian communities ("sects" he called them) did place excessive emphasis on the inner experience of believers, which in fact did have consequences for the social forms.

36. Kuyper, *Tractaat van de Reformatie der Kerken*, ss. 10–13.

37. Ibid., ss. 13.

38. Ibid., ss. 14.

39. Ibid., ss. 16.

40. Ibid., ss. 17.

41. Kuyper, *Lectures on Calvinism*, 22–28.

42. Kuyper, *Tractaat van de Reformatie der Kerken*, ss. 13.

43. Ibid., ss. 14.

44. Ibid.

45. Ibid., ss. 15.

46. Ibid., ss. 2.

47. Ibid., ss. 15.

48. Ibid., ss. 4.

49. Ibid., ss. 36.
50. Ibid., ss. 35, emphasis original.
51. For example, Theo van Tijn, *Twintig Jaren Amsterdam: De Maatschappelijke Ontwikkeling van de Hoofdstad, van de Jaren '50 der Vorige Eeuw tot 1876* (Amsterdam: Scheltema & Holkema, 1965), 397.
52. Kuyper, *Tractaat van de Reformatie der Kerken*, ss. 4, emphasis original.
53. Cornelis Augustijn, "De Spiritualiteit van de Dolerenden," in *Abraham Kuyper: Vast en Verandelijk: De Ontwikkeling van zijn Denken*, ed. Augustijn and Vree (Zoetermeer: Meinema, 1998), 186.
54. Bratt, *Abraham Kuyper*, chapter 8 "Church Reformer."
55. Kuyper, *Het Conflict Gekomen*, III.45, italics in original.
56. Kuyper, *Tractaat van de Reformatie der Kerken*, ss. 38, also ss. 37.
57. Ibid., ss. 40.
58. Ibid., ss. 49, 50. Cf. Langman, *Kuyper en de Volkskerk*, 80.
59. Kuyper, *Tractaat van de Reformatie der Kerken*, ss. 49.
60. Ibid., ss. 50.
61. Ibid., ss. 54.
62. Ibid., ss. 51.
63. Ibid.
64. Ibid., ss. 55, 56.
65. Ibid., ss. 55, 58. NB These chapters are a critical part of Kuyper's argument, but—let the reader beware—Herman Hoeksema's English translation is occasionally misleading. Hoekema, for example, translates *kerkverband*, which Kuyper uses to denote unions of congregations like a synod, as "denomination." If, however, Kuyper had meant denomination, he likely would have used the term *kerkgenootschap*.
66. Ibid., ss. 56.
67. Ibid., ss. 57.
68. Ibid., ss. 58.
69. Ibid., ss. 59.
70. Ibid., ss. 53.
71. John Williamson Nevin, *The Anxious Bench* (Chambersburg: Publication Office of the German Reformed Church, 1844).
72. Bratt, ed., *Abraham Kuyper: A Centennial Reader* (Grand Rapids, MI: Eerdmans, 1998), 142. See also Hans Krabbendam, "Zielenverbrijzelaars en Zondelozen: Reacties in de Nederlandse Pers op Moody, Sankey, en Pearsall Smith, 1874–1878," *Documentatieblad voor de Nederlandse Kerkgeschiedenis na 1800* 34 (1991): 39–55.
73. See Kuyper, "Calvinism: Source and Stronghold of Our Constitutional Liberties (1874)," in *Abraham Kuyper: A Centennial Reader*, ed. Bratt (Grand Rapids, MI: Eerdmans, 1998), 279–322.
74. Kuyper, *Het Conflict Gekomen*, I.36, 38–40.

75. Haight, *Christian Community in History*, 364–365.

76. B. A. Gerrish, "Continuity and Change: Friedrich Schleiermacher on the Task of Theology," in *Tradition and the Modern World: Reformed Theology in the Nineteenth Century* (Chicago: University of Chicago Press, 1978), 41. Gerrish's point is illustrated by the Table of Contents of Schleiermacher's *Brief Outline of the Study of Theology*, which places dogmatics in the field of "The Historical Knowledge of the Present Condition of Christianity." Friedrich Schleiermacher, *Brief Outline of the Study of Theology*, trans. William Farrer (London: T&T Clark, 1850).

77. E. Brooks Holifield, *Theology in America: Christian Thought from the Age of the Puritans to the Civil War* (New Haven, CT: Yale University Press, 2003), 291–305. Grant Wacker describes this as Pentecostalism's "primitivist" impulse; Grant Wacker, *Heaven Below: Early Pentecostals and American Culture* (Cambridge, MA: Harvard University Press, 2001), 10–14.

78. Owen Chadwick, *From Bossuet to Newman: The Idea of Doctrinal Development* (Cambridge, UK: Cambridge University Press, 1957), 139–163.

79. NB Although the term *narrative* is appropriate, it is also anachronistic. Kuyper would have almost certainly regarded it as too flimsy for his purposes. The dispute between him and the NHK was over real historical events and their meanings. Any suggestion of artificial construction would probably have been considered weakness. John Bolt, *A Free Church, A Holy Nation: Abraham Kuyper's American Public Theology* (Grand Rapids, MI: Eerdmans, 2000), 43; Bratt, *Abraham Kuyper*, chapter 7 "The Political Theorist"; Arie L. Molendijk, ""Mine": The Rhetorics of Abraham Kuyper," *Journal for the History of Modern Theology/ Zeitschrift für Neuere Theologiegeschichte* 15 (2008), italics in original.

80. W. Nijenhuis, "De Nederlandse Hervormde Kerk en de Doleantie," in *De Doleantie van 1886 en Haar Geschiedenis*, ed. Wim Bakker et al. (Kampen: Kok, 1986), 185.

81. Kuyper, *Tractaat van de Reformatie der Kerken*, ss. 63.

82. Ibid.

83. Michael Wintle, *Pillars of Piety: Religion in the Netherlands in the Nineteenth Century, 1813–1901*, Occasional Papers in Modern Dutch Studies (Hull: Hull University Press, 1987), 18–19.

84. Kuyper, *Afwerping van het Juk der Synodale Hierarchie* (Amsterdam: J.A. Wormser, 1886), 5.

85. Kuyper, *Het Conflict Gekomen*, 46.

86. Kuyper, *Afwerping van het Juk der Synodale Hierarchie*, 6.

87. Ibid.; Kuyper, *Separatie en Doleantie*, 36.

88. All quotes from Kuyper, "It Shall Not Be So among You (1886)," in *Abraham Kuyper: A Centennial Reader*, ed. Bratt (Grand Rapids, MI: Eerdmans, 1998), 126–131.

89. Kuyper, *Afwerping van het Juk der Synodale Hierarchie*, 3.

90. Kuyper, *Tractaat van de Reformatie der Kerken*, ss. 63.

91. J. van Gelderen, "Op Weg naar de Vereniging van 17 Juni 1892," in *De Vereniging van 1892 en haar Geschiedenis*, ed. L. J. Wolthuis and Vree (Kampen: Kok, 1992), 45.

92. H. Bavinck, "Review of *Tractaat van de Reformatie van der Kerken*, by Abraham Kuyper," *De Vrije Kerk* 9 (1883): 554.

93. Kuyper, *Tractaat van de Reformatie der Kerken*, ss. 55.

94. Bavinck, "Review of *Tractaat*," 557–558.

95. Kuyper, *Tractaat van de Reformatie der Kerken*, ss. 32; Kuyper, *Separatie en Doleantie*, 12.

96. Kuyper, *Separatie en Doleantie*, 62–65.

97. Rullmann provides an extended quote from *The Herald*, Rullmann, *Kuyper-Bibliographie*, II.100.

98. Kuyper, *Tractaat van de Reformatie der Kerken*, ss. 64; Bavinck, "Review of *Tractaat*," 560–561.

99. Kuyper, *Separatie en Doleantie*, 61, italics in original.

100. Ibid., 9, 62–63.

101. Ibid., 62–63, 68.

102. Kuyper, *Tractaat van de Reformatie der Kerken*, ss. 18.

103. Ibid., ss. 26. NB English translations of the Belgic Confession often speak of the "duty" of believers where the Dutch speaks of the *ambt* of believers. *Ambt*, like the German *amt*, is the term for office.

104. Kuyper, *Separatie en Doleantie*, 25–28.

105. Kuyper, *Tractaat van de Reformatie der Kerken*, ss. 12; Kuyper, "Van het Kerkelijk Ambt," *De Heraut* 1887–1888, no. 508.

106. Kuyper, *Tractaat van de Reformatie der Kerken*, ss. 26.

107. Ibid., ss. 12.

108. Ibid., ss. 26, 12, 20; Kuyper, *Separatie en Doleantie*, 28–29.

109. Kuyper, *Tractaat van de Reformatie der Kerken*, ss. 26, emphasis mine.

110. Kuyper, *Separatie en Doleantie*, 28–30.

111. Kuyper, *Tractaat van de Reformatie der Kerken*, ss. 12.

112. Ibid., ss. 18.

113. Ibid., ss. 20, 28, 29, 30. *Executive* and *judicial* are my terms, not Kuyper's, but they are suggested by Kuyper's description of Christ's power as "legislative" (*wetgevend*), and they compare with Calvin's concept of office. See Eduardus van der Borght, *Theology of Ministry: A Reformed Contribution to an Ecumenical Dialogue*, Studies in Reformed Theology (Leiden: Brill, 2007), 88–89.

114. Kuyper, *Tractaat van de Reformatie der Kerken*, ss. 18.

115. Ibid., ss. 20.

116. Ibid., ss. 26.

117. Ibid., ss. 20.

118. Kuyper, *Separatie en Doleantie*, 9–10.

119. Kuyper, *Confidentie: Schrijven aan den Weled. Heer J.H. van der Linden* (Amsterdam: Höveker & Zoon, 1873), 14.

120. Volf, *After Our Likeness*, 16.
121. Kuyper, *Stellingen in den Professorenkrans*, paragraph 1.
122. Kuyper, *Tractaat van de Reformatie der Kerken*, ss. 2.
123. This social ontology and its relation to the church are explained best in Kuyper, *Stellingen in den Professorenkrans*, paragraphs 1 and 2; Kuyper, "Locus de Ecclesia," 26–27. NB The *Stellingen* were a short list of the main ecclesiological points of the *Tractaat*, and they were also published in *De Heraut*, Kuyper, "(Main Points of Ecclesiology)."
124. Kuyper, *Tractaat van de Reformatie der Kerken*, ss. 2, 7.
125. Jeroen Koch, "Abraham Kuyper tussen Gereformeerde Natie en Gereformeerde Zuil," *Tijdschrift voor Geschiedenis* 120 (2007): 528.
126. Jeroen Koch, *Abraham Kuyper: Een Biografie* (Amsterdam: Uitgeverij Boom, 2006), 107. Bratt, *Abraham Kuyper*, chapter 8 "Church Reformer," also observes this problem.
127. Descriptions of Calvin's view of church and state, often according to the passions of the author. "Separate but cooperating spheres" seems to be a suitable shorthand description. See Haight, *Christian Community in History*, 125; John Witte Jr., *The Reformation of Rights: Law, Religion, and Human Rights in Early Modern Calvinism* (Cambridge, UK: Cambridge University Press, 2007), 70–76.
128. Kuyper's point is driven home by a quote from Servetus to the effect that heretics should be put to death. Kuyper, "Calvinism: Source of Our Constitutional Liberties," 304. On Calvin see Philip Benedict, *Christ's Churches Purely Reformed: A Social History of Calvinism* (New Haven, CT: Yale University Press, 2002), 105. Benedict says that the idea that the civil government should use capital punishment for heretics was "scarcely controversial among either Switzerland's leading theologians or much of the Genevan population."
129. Kuyper, *Tractaat van de Reformatie der Kerken*, ss. 62.
130. Ibid., italics in original.
131. Kuyper, *Separatie en Doleantie*, 49.
132. Let those who have ears hear! In his articles on office from 1887, Kuyper contracted his well-known declaration in "Sphere Sovereignty," where he said that Jesus Christ ruled over all spheres. In 1887 Kuyper said that Jesus Christ ruled the church; the king ruled the state. Kuyper, "Van het Kerkelijk Ambt," no. 508; Kuyper, "Sphere Sovereignty (1880)," in *Abraham Kuyper: A Centennial Reader*, ed. Bratt (Grand Rapids, MI: Eerdmans, 1998), 488.
133. Kuyper, *Tractaat van de Reformatie der Kerken*, ss. 19.
134. van der Borght, *Theology of Ministry: A Reformed Contribution to an Ecumenical Dialogue*, 101.
135. Kuyper, *De Gemeene Gratie*, 3 vols. (Kampen: Kok, 1931–1932), 288–294; Peter S. Heslam, *Creating a Christian Worldview: Abraham Kuyper's Lectures on Calvinism* (Grand Rapids, MI: Eerdmans, 1998), 136–139. See chapter 6 for a further discussion of Kuyper's concept of pluriformity.

136. National churches cease to be "churches" when they cease to be compulsory, coercive, monopolistic institutions, says José Casanova, *Public Religions in the Modern World* (Chicago: University of Chicago Press, 1994), 47.

137. James C. Kennedy, *Stad op een Berg: De Publieke Rol van Protestantse Kerken* (Zoetermeer: Boekencentrum, 2009), 43.

138. Kuyper's group was one movement that shattered the unity of the Protestant nation in the late 1800s and mobilized the masses based on religious differences. See Peter van Rooden, "Secularization in the Netherlands," *Kirchliche Zeitschrift* 11 (1998): 34–41.

CHAPTER 5

1. Cf. Richard J. Mouw, "Baptism and the Salvific Status of Children: An Examination of Some Intra-Reformed Debates," *Calvin Theological Journal* 41 (2006).

2. Abraham Kuyper, *De Gemeene Gratie*, 3 vols. (Kampen: Kok, 1931–1932), 261–263.

3. Dietrich Bonhoeffer, *Sanctorum Communio: A Theological Study of the Sociology of the Church*, ed. Wayne Whitson Floyd Jr., vol. 1, Dietrich Bonhoeffer Works (Minneapolis: Fortress, 1998), 258, 268.

4. For a more detailed discussion of Kuyper's theology of baptism as a preparatory means of grace, see John Halsey Wood Jr., "Church, Sacrament, and Society: Abraham Kuyper's Early Baptismal Theology, 1859–1874," *Journal of Reformed Theology* 2 (2008).

5. Ernst Troeltsch, *The Social Teaching of the Christian Churches*, trans. Olive Wyon, vol. 1, Library of Theological Ethics (Louisville, KY: Westminster/John Knox, 1960), 338.

6. As Fink and Stark's "supply side" theories of religious participation suggest; cf. Roger Finke and Rodney Stark, *The Churching of America, 1776–2005: Winners and Losers in Our Religious Economy*, 2d ed. (New Brunswick, NJ: Rutgers University Press, 2005).

7. David Martin, "Comparing Different Maps of the Same Ground," in *Reflections on Sociology and Theology* (Oxford: Clarenden Press, 1997), 80–81.

8. See also Peter Berger et al., *Religious America, Secular Europe? A Theme and Variations* (Aldershot, UK: Ashgate, 2008), 114–116.

9. William Young, "Historic Calvinism and Neo-Calvinism," *Westminster Theological Journal* 36 (1974): 48–64, 156–173.

10. George Harinck and Lodewijk Winkeler, "De Negentiende Eeuw," in *Handboek Nederlandse Kerkgeschiedenis*, ed. Herman J. Selderhuis (Kampen: Kok, 2006), 686; Jan Veenhof, "A History of Theology and Spirituality in the Dutch Reformed Churches (Gereformeerde Kerken), 1892–1992," *Calvin Theological Journal* 28 (1993): 270.

11. For example, Jan Veenhof, "Geschiedinis van Theologie en Spiritualiteit in de Gereformeerde Kerken," in *100 Jaar Theologie: Aspecten van een Eeuw Theologie*

in de Gereformeerde Kerken in Nederland (1892–1992), ed. Martien E. Brinkman (Kampen: J.H. Kok, 1992); Veenhof, "A History of Theology and Spirituality in the Dutch Reformed Churches (Gereformeerde Kerken), 1892–1992."

12. E. Smilde, *Een Eeuw van Strijd over Verbond en Doop* (Kampen: Kok, 1946).

13. C. Graafland, "De Doop als Splijtzwam in de Gereformeerde Gezindte," in *Rondom De Doopvont*, ed. Willem van 't Spijker (Goudriaan, The Netherlands: De Groot, 1983).

14. Willem H. Velema, *De Leer van de Heilige Geest bij Abraham Kuyper* ('s-Gravenhage: Van Keulen, 1957), 208.

15. J. Kamphuis, *Een Eeuwig Verbond* (Haarlem: Uitgeverij Vijlbrief, 1984), 27–30.

16. David Bos, *In dienst van het Koninkrijk: Beroepsontwikkeling van Hervormde Predikanten in Negentiende-Eeuws Nederland* (Amsterdam: Bert Bakker, 1999), 59–63; R. F. Vulsma, *Burgerlijke Stand, Bevolkingsregister en Genealogie* (Naarden: Boekencentrum, 1968), 8–10. On the intertwining of the *volkskerk* and society generally see Cornelis Augustijn, "Kerk en Godsdienst 1870–1890," in *De Doleantie van 1886 en haar Geschiedenis*, ed. Wim Bakker (Kampen: Kok, 1986), 41–75.

17. Vree, "De Herziening van het Hervormde Algemeen Reglement (1846–1852)," in *Om de Toekomst van het Protestantse Nederland. De Gevolgen van de Grondwetsherziening van 1848 voor Kerk, Staat en Maatschappij*, ed. G. J. Schutte and Vree (Zoetermeer: Meinema, 1998), 44, 52.

18. Kuyper, *Ons Program (met Bijlagen)* (Amsterdam: J. H. Kruyt, 1879), 1129.

19. J. van den Berg, "Oplossing der Kerk in de Maatschappij? Modernen, Ethischen en de Toekomstvisie van Richard Rothe," in *Ad Interim: Opstellen over Eschatologie, Apocalyptic en Ethiek*, ed. T. Baarda et al. (Kampen: Kok, 1976).

20. "Itaque ex evangelii mente baptisma et Coena symbolicae dicendae sunt actiones, quae in gloriosam Domini nostri memoriam institutae ecclesiae unitatem promovent, simul quoque pungunt nos atque incitant, ut Christum toto corde amplectamur et tenerrimum erga fratres foveamus amorem." Kuyper, *Abraham Kuyper's Commentatio (1860): The Young Kuyper about Calvin, A Lasco, and the Church*, ed. Vree and Johan Zwaan, vol. 2, Brill's Series in Church History (Leiden: Brill, 2005), ss. 179, 322, emphasis mine.

21. Ibid., ss. 175, 312, ss. 188, 335.

22. Kuyper, "Confidentially (1873)," in *Abraham Kuyper: A Centennial Reader*, ed. James Bratt (Grand Rapids, MI: Eerdmans, 1998), 54–55.

23. See chapter 2 and Vree, *Kuyper in de Kiem: De Precalvinistische Periode van Abraham Kuyper, 1848–1874* (Hilversum: Uitgeverij Verloren, 2006), 371–373; Vree, "More Pierson and Mesmer, and Less Pietje Baltus: Kuyper's Ideas on Church, State, and Culture during the First Years of his Ministry (1863–1866)," in *Kuyper Reconsidered: Aspects of his Life and Work*, ed. Cornelis van der Kooi and Jan de Bruijn (Amsterdam: VU Uitgeverij, 1999).

24. Kuyper, "De Eeredienst der Hervormde Kerk en de Zamenstelling van Haar Kerkboek," in *Geschiedenis der Christelijke Kerk in Nederland, in Tafereelen*, ed. B. ter Haar and W. Moll, vol. 2 (Amsterdam: Portielje & Zoon, 1869), 89.

25. Ibid., 87–113, here 189–190; Kuyper, "De Eerste Kerkvergadering of De Vestiging onzer Hervormde Kerk, en de Strijd om Haar Zelfstandig Bestaan, 1550–1618," in *Geschiedenis der Christelijke Kerk in Nederland in Tafereelen*, ed. Haar and Moll, vol. 2 (Amsterdam: G. Portielje & Zoon, 1869), 71–86.

26. Kuyper, "Review of J. I. Doedes, *De Heid. Cat. in zijne eerste Levensjaren, 1563–1567, Hist. Bibliogr. nalezing, met 26 facsimilé's*," in *Godgeleerde Bijdragen voor 1867* (Utrecht: Kenmink en Zoon, 1867), 403–422; Kuyper, *Wat Moeten Wij Doen: Het Stemrecht aan ons zelven Houden of den Kerkeraad Machtigen? Vraag bij de Uitvoering van art. 23 Toegelicht* (Culemborg: A.J. Blom, 1867). On Kuyper's historical work during this period see Vree, "The Marnix-Vereeniging: Abraham Kuyper's First National Organization (1868–89)," *DRCH* 84 (2004): 388–475, esp. 394–412.

27. Kuyper, *Kerkvisitatie te Utrecht in 1868 met het Oog op den Kritieken Toestand Onzer Kerk* (Utrecht: J.H. van Peursem, 1868); Vree, *Kiem*, 210–218.

28. Kuyper, "Referaat over de Belijdenis (1870)," in *Revisie der Revisie-Legende* (Amsterdam: J.H. Kruyt, 1879), 56.

29. Bos, *Dienst*, 61–62.

30. Kuyper, "De Naam in de Heilige Schrift," in *Uit het Woord. Stichtelijke Bijbelstudiën*, vol. 1 (Amsterdam: J.A. Wormser, n.d.), 37. See also Kuyper, ed., *Aan de Kerkeraden der Nederduitsche Hervormde Gemeenten in Nederland* (Utrecht: Kemink en Zoon, 1868); Kuyper, "De Spitse der Openbaring," in *Uit Het Woord. Stichtelijke Bijbelstudiën*, vol. 1 (Amsterdam: J.A. Wormser, n.d.), 261–279; Kuyper, "De Doopskwestie," *De Heraut*, October 7, 1870, 2.

31. Kuyper, *Kerkvisitatie*, 14–16; Vree, *Kiem*, 246.

32. Kuyper, *Kerkvisitatie*, 6–7.

33. Kuyper, "Conservatism and Orthodoxy: False and True Preservation (1870)," in *Abraham Kuyper: A Centennial Reader*, ed. Bratt (Grand Rapids, MI: Eerdmans, 1998).

34. NB Rome was a *volkskerk* according to Kuyper. Kuyper, *Confidentie: Schrijven aan den Weled. Heer J.H. van der Linden* (Amsterdam: Höveker & Zoon, 1873), 83.

35. Ibid., 55.

36. Kuyper, "De Doopskwestie," *De Heraut* 1870.

37. Kuyper, "Wedergeboorte en Bekeering," in *Uit Het Woord. Stichtelijke Bijbelstudiën*, vol. 3 (Amsterdam: Höveker & Wormser, n.d.), 33.

38. Kuyper, "Heilsfeit en Heilswoord," in *Uit het Woord. Stichtelijke Bijbelstudiën*, vol. 1 (Amsterdam: J.A. Wormser, n.d.), 66–69, 74–75.

39. Ibid., 73.

40. Ibid., 75–76, emphasis mine.

41. Ibid., 76.

42. Ibid., 76–77.

43. Vree, *Kiem*, 331.

44. Kuyper does not specifically name Doedes, but his criticisms precisely match Doedes's views. J. I. Doedes, *De Leer der Zaligheid: Volgens het Evangelie* (Utrecht:

Kemink en Zoon, 1868), 333–340; Kuyper, "De Spitse der Openbaring," 263–270, italics in original.

45. The series, titled "The Pinnacle of Revelation" (*"De Spitse der Openbaring,"* June 1872), appeared in *De Standaard* rather than in the ecclesiastical weekly *De Heraut*, which had been discontinued in April 1872.

46. Kuyper, "De Spitse der Openbaring," 268.

47. Ibid., 276–277, italics in original.

48. Ibid., 278.

49. Though the Word may also come in other, unusual circumstances beyond preaching in church. Kuyper, "De Uitverkiezing," in *Uit het Woord. Stichtelijke Bijbelstudiën*, vol. 2, *Uit het Woord* (Amsterdam: J.A. Wormser, n.d.), 186.

50. Ibid., 173.

51. Kuyper, "Wedergeboorte en Bekeering," 21. It is not true, as Kuyper may have implied, that the Groningen theologians did not have any concept of conversion to salvation, though even with Petrus Hofstede de Groot, a chief representative, this doctrine was not always obvious, especially in his theological writings. See Vree, "'Want Hij weet wat Maaksel Wij Zijn, Gedachtig Zijnde dat Wij Stof Zijn': Het Publieke en het Persoonlijke Geloofsleven van P. Hofstede de Groot," in *De Kunst van het Ontfermen. Studies voor Gerben Heitink*, ed. Alma Lanser et al. (Kampen: Kok, 2003), 147–169.

52. See Vree, "Petrus Hofstede de Groot and the Christian Education of the Dutch Nation (1833–1861)," *Nederlands Archief voor Kerkgeschiedenis* 78 (1998): 70–93. Also Petrus Antonius van Leeuwen, *Het Kerkbegrip in de Theologie van Abraham Kuyper* (Franeker: Wever, 1946), 9–14.

53. A. van Toorenenbergen, "De Kerk," *Waarheid in Liefde* (1867): 513–568.

54. Kuyper, "Wedergeboorte en Bekeering," 34.

55. Ibid., 37.

56. Ibid.

57. Ibid., 35, italics in original. "'De erfzonde is ook door den Doop *niet ganschelick* weggenomen', t.w., gelijk uit het vervolg des Artikels blijkt, wel weggenomen ten opzichte van de toerekenbaarheid der *erfschuld*, maar niet weggenomen als *wortel* der latere zonden." NB The syntactical nuance that Kuyper appeals to in the Belgic Confession is not apparent in some English translations. Although Kuyper does not give his source for this view of baptismal efficacy, it was common among the Reformed Scholastics such as Amandus Polanus and Leonardus Riisenius, see Heinrich Heppe, *Reformed Dogmatics: Set Out and Illustrated from the Sources*, ed. Ernst Bizer, trans. G. T. Thomson (Grand Rapids, MI: Baker, 1950), 619, italics in original.

58. Chapter 10, "Wedergeboren zonder het te weten" ("Regeneration without Knowing It") in Kuyper, "Wedergeboorte en Bekeering," 51–55. NB At this early stage there was apparently little criticism from the *Christelijke Gereformeerde Kerk* in response to Kuyper's ideas about regeneration; see J. C. Schaeffer, *De Plaats van*

Abraham Kuyper in 'De Vrije Kerk' (Amsterdam: Buijten & Schipperheijn, 1997), 13–60.

59. On Kuyper's experience with infant mortality and its effects on his theology, see A. van Egmond, "Kuyper's Dogmatic Theology," in *Kuyper Reconsidered: Aspects of his Life and Work*, ed. Cornelis van der Kooi and Jan de Bruijn (Amsterdam: VU Uitgeverij, 1999), 87; Vree, "Abraham Kuyper in de Jaren 1848–1874: Een Briljante, Bevlogen Branie," *DNK* 65 (2006): 28.

60. Kuyper, "Wedergeboorte en Bekeering," 47. See "The Canons of the Synod of Dort," in *The Creeds of Christendom*, ed. Philip Schaff, vol. 3 (New York: Harper & Brothers, 1905), art. I.17, 585.

61. *Westminster Confession of Faith*, 10.3.

62. Kuyper, "Wedergeboorte en Bekeering," 35.

63. Kuyper, *Dat de Genade Particulier Is*, 6 vols., vol. 4, Uit Het Woord. Stichtelijke Bijbelstudiën (Kampen: Kok, 1909). In English, Kuyper, *Grace Is Particular*, trans. Marvin Kamps (Granville, MI: Reformed Free Publishing Association, 2001).

64. Maarten Aalders, *125 Jaar Faculteit der Godgeleerdheid aan de Vrije Universiteit* (Meinema: Zoetemeer, 2005), 31–32; Johannes Stellingwerff, *Dr. Abraham Kuyper en de Vrije Universiteit* (Kampen: Kok, 1987), 109.

65. "Notulen, April 10, 1880," in *Archief Curatoren, Ingekomen Stukken* (Amsterdam: Historisch Documentatiecentrum voor het Nederlands Protestantisme).

66. Kuyper, *De Leer der Verbonden*, vol. 5, Uit Het Woord. Stichtelijke Bijbelstudiën (Kampen: Kok, 1909), 176–177.

67. Ibid., 178–182. In fact, Kuyper distinguishes between essential and apparent covenant members. Essential covenant members are the elect, but they are unknown except in God's hidden counsel and at the end of history. The apparent covenant members, Kuyper's main concern and the body that makes up the church, is a group of wheat and chaff that cannot be winnowed by any human ingenuity.

68. Ibid., 195.

69. Ibid., 185–186.

70. Kuyper, "Practijk in de Bediening," in *Practijk der Godzaligheid*, Uit Het Woord. *Stichtelijke Bijbelstudiën* (Kampen: J.H. Kok, 1909), 37.

71. Kuyper, *De Leer der Verbonden*, 186.

72. Ibid., 194.

73. Ibid., here 187, also 187–192.

74. *Heidelberg Catechism*, question and answer 65.

75. Kuyper, *De Leer der Verbonden*, 197–207.

76. Ibid. Kuyper quoted from J. C. Appelius, *Brief Behelzende de Voornaamste Gronden, en de Byzondere Mening van de Hedendaagsche Nieuwe Lere der Sacramenten: Neffens de Voornaamste Bewyzen, Tegen Dezelve: als ook eene Oplossing van Hare Voornaamste Tegenwerpingen* (Groningen: Wed. I. Spandaw, 1768).

77. Bos, *Dienst*, 59–60; Kuyper, "De Eeredienst der Hervormde Kerk," 89; Vree, *Kiem*, 245.

78. Kuyper, "Practijk in de Bediening," 35–36.

79. Ibid., 37. See also Kuyper, *De Leer der Verbonden*, 198–202.

80. Kuyper, "Practijk in de Bediening," 37.

81. On this prehistory, of the *Doleantie* see C. H. W. van den Berg, "De Ontstaange-schiedenis van de Doleantie te Amsterdam," in *De Doleantie van 1886 en Haar Geschiedenis*, ed. Bakker et al. (Kampen: J.H. Kok, 1986), 93–104.

82. Kuyper, "Practijk in de Bediening," 32, 37.

83. Kuyper, "(Letter to the Editor)," *De Bazuin* 1895.

84. Like so much of Kuyper's theology, this commentary ran first as a serial publication in the *Herald* from 1886 to 1894 and was later collected into four volumes. The chapters on the sacraments began at the end of 1889.

85. Vree, "De Drie Formulieren van Enigheid: Een Vondst van Abraham Kuyper," *Historisch Tijdschrift GKN* 13 (2007).

86. Kuyper, *E Voto Dordraceno: Toelichting op den Heidelbergschen Catechismus* (Kampen: J.H. Kok, 1892–1895), 2.465.

87. Kuyper, "Wedergeboorte en Bekeering," 34.

88. Kuyper, *E Voto*, 2.404–405. Also Kuyper, "Practijk in de Bediening," 37–38.

89. Kuyper, *E Voto*, 2.405.

90. Ibid., 2.484.

91. Kuyper, "Calvinism and Confessional Revision," *Presbyterian and Reformed Review* 2 (1891): here 388, emphasis mine; Kuyper, *E Voto*, 2.463–491.

92. Kuyper, *E Voto*, 3.39.

93. Ibid., 3.40–41. Cf. Kuyper, "Practijk in de Bediening," 37.

94. Kuyper, *E Voto*, 3.47–48. Here Kuyper summarizes this argument, which he has been making since the beginning of this volume.

95. Ibid., 3.34 and 45–46.

96. Ibid., 3.5–14, here 19.

97. Ibid., 3.31.

98. Kuyper, *Separatie en Doleantie* (Amsterdam: J.A. Wormser, 1890), 14. Many of the points made here are presented neatly in Kuyper's apologetic pamphlet for breaking with the national church and plea for union with the *Christian Reformed Church*, titled *Separation and Doleantie*, which was published the same year as his account of baptism in *E Voto*.

99. See chapter 4.

100. Abraham Kuyper, "(Untitled Series on Baptism and the Visible Church)," *De Heraut* 1887–1888.

101. Kuyper, *Separatie en Doleantie*, 14.

102. Ibid., 15.

103. Abraham Kuyper, "Locus de Foedere," in *Dictaten Dogmatiek* (Grand Rapids, MI: B. Sevensma, 1910), 153–154. Cf. Kuyper, *De Leer der Verbonden*, 182–187.

104. Harinck and Gerard Dekker, "The Position of the Church as Institute in Society: A Comparison between Bonhoeffer and Kuyper," *Princeton Seminary Bulletin* 28, no. 1 (2007); Kuyper, *Lectures on Calvinism* (Grand Rapids, MI: Eerdmans, 1931).

105. James C. Kennedy, *Stad op een Berg: De Publieke Rol van Protestantse Kerken* (Zoetermeer: Boekencentrum, 2009), 24. Kennedy quotes from A. J. Rasker, *De Nederlandse Hervormde Kerk vanaf 1795* (Kampen: Kok, 1974), 254.

106. Kennedy, *Stad op een Berg*, 24.

107. Belgic Confession, chapter 34. See also Heidelberg Catechism question and answer 74: "by baptism, as sign of the covenant, [infants] must be grafted into the Christian church and distinguished from the children of unbelievers."

Chapter 6

1. Philip J. Hoedemaker, *Artikel XXXVI: Onzer Nederduitsche Geloofsbeleidenis tegenover Dr. A. Kuijper Gehandhaafd* (Amsterdam: J.H. van Dam, 1901), 172.

2. Philip J. Hoedemaker, *Dr. A. Kuyper in Tegenspraak met Groen van Prinsterer; een Waarschuwend Woord voor de Verkiezingen in Juni 1891 door een Hervormd Predikant* (Amsterdam: Egeling, 1891), 13. Quoted in H. van Spanning, "Hoedemaker en de Antirevolutionairen," in *Hoedemaker Herdacht*, ed. G. Abma and Jan De Bruijn (Baarn: Ten Have, 1989), 236.

3. A version of this chapter appears in *Kingdoms Apart: Engaging the Two Kingdoms Perspective*, ed. Ryan McIlhenny (Phillipsburg: Presbyterian and Reformed, 2012), 155–171.

4. For example, Nicholas Wolterstorff, "Abraham Kuyper (1827–1920)," in *The Teachings of Modern Protestantism, on Law, Politics, and Human Nature*, ed. John Witte Jr. and Frank S. Alexander (New York: Columbia University Press, 2007), 32–33.

5. Michael Wintle, *Pillars of Piety: Religion in the Netherlands in the Nineteenth Century, 1813–1901*, Occasional Papers in Modern Dutch Studies (Hull: Hull University Press, 1987), xiii, 40.

6. Abraham Kuyper, "Conservatism and Orthodoxy: False and True Preservation (1870)," in *Abraham Kuyper: A Centennial Reader*, ed. James D. Bratt (Grand Rapids, MI: Eerdmans, 1998); J. Gresham Machen, *Christianity and Liberalism*, intro Carl R. Trueman (Grand Rapids, MI: Eerdmands, 2009). See also Kuyper, "Dr. Kuyper's Democracy," in *A Free Church, A Holy Nation: Abraham Kuyper's American Public Theology*, ed. John Bolt (Grand Rapids, MI: Eerdmans, 2001).

7. Bolt, *A Free Church, A Holy Nation: Abraham Kuyper's American Public Theology* (Grand Rapids, MI: Eerdmans, 2000), 443–464. In this appendix, Bolt mentions several others including Ernst Troeltsch and F. M. Ten Hoor, who like Hoedemaker viewed Kuyper as a liberal and a not as a conservative Calvinist.

8. For example, David VanDrunen, "Abraham Kuyper and the Reformed Natural Law and Two Kingdoms Traditions," *Calvin Theological Journal* 42 (2007): 283–307; Bolt, "The VanDrunen-Kloosterman Debate on 'Natural Law' and

'Two Kingdoms' in the Theology of Herman Bavinck," *Bavinck Society Discussion* 1 (2010), http://bavinck.calvinseminary.edu/wp-content/uploads/2010/06/ Discussion_1_VanDrunen-Kloosterman_debate.pdf.

9. James C. Kennedy, "Dutch Political Developments and Religious Reform," in *Political and Legal Perspectives*, ed. Keith Robbins (Leuven: Leuven University Press, 2010), 131. The brief history of church and state here depends largely upon Kennedy's work, but readers may also consult George Harinck and Lodewijk Winkeler, "De Negentiende Eeuw," in *Handboek Nederlandse Kerkgeschiedenis*, ed. Herman J. Selderhuis (Kampen: Kok, 2006), 597–721.

10. Hugh McLeod, *Secularization in Western Europe, 1848–1914* (New York: St. Martin's, 2000), 28.

11. Guido de Bres, "The Belgic Confession (1561)," in *Creeds and Confessions of Faith in Christian Tradition*, ed. Jaroslav Pelikan and Valerie Hotchkiss (New Haven, CT: Yale University Press, 2003), 424.

12. Kuyper, *De Gemeene Gratie* (Kampen: Kok, 1931–1932), 3.231–232.

13. Ibid., 3.253–255. Curiously, Kuyper did not explain how this could be harmonized with his own arguments for democratic polity in the church, such as Abraham Kuyper, *Wat Moeten Wij Doen: Het Stemrecht aan ons zelven Houden of den Kerkeraad Machtigen? Vraag bij de Uitvoering van art. 23 Toegelicht* (Culemborg: A.J. Blom, 1867).

14. Kuyper, *De Gemeene Gratie*, 3.237.

15. See Annemarie Houkes, *Christelijke Vaderlanders: Godsdienst, Burgerschap, en de Nederlandse Natie (1850–1900)* (Amsterdam: Wereldbibliotheek, 2009).

16. Kuyper's revised theology of the institutional church as a "mechanical" and "artificial" imposition permitted such a view.

17. Kuyper, *De Gemeene Gratie*, 3.103–105, 288–289. Compare the notion in *Common Grace* of the church institution as artificial with Kuyper's earlier view of the institutional form of the church in *Confidentially* wherein he portrayed the institution, not as an accretion of spiritual life but as a precondition and necessity for it. "Exactly the unconscious life of every individual demands that the church, as mother of believers, must offer conscious form, that can bring the yet embryonic life to clearer consciousness." Kuyper, *Confidentie: Schrijven aan den Weled. Heer J.H. van der Linden* (Amsterdam: Höveker & Zoon, 1873), 58.

18. Kuyper, *De Gemeene Gratie*, 3.104.

19. Ibid., 3.109, see also 289.

20. Ibid., 3.129–144, 260–267.

21. Ibid., 3.105, italics in original.

22. Richard J. Mouw, *Abraham Kuyper: A Short and Personal Introduction* (Grand Rapids, MI: Eerdmans, 2011), 57–58.

23. Kuyper, *Soevereiniteit in Eigen Kring. Rede ter Inwijding van de Vrije Universiteit, den 20sten Oktober 1880 Gehouden, in het Koor der Nieuwe Kerk te Amsterdam* (Amsterdam: J.H. Kruyt, 1880), 35.

24. Kuyper, *De Gemeene Gratie*, 3.123, see also point 125 on 290. The same logic is at work in Kuyper's earlier work; Kuyper, "Van het Kerkelijk Ambt," *De Heraut* 1887–1888, nos. 519–533.

25. Kuyper, *De Gemeene Gratie*, 3.274–281, here 279.

26. Ibid., 3.105–107, 109–114, also points 106 and 108 on 290.

27. Ibid., 3.259, also 252.

28. Ibid., 3.257, and, much earlier, Kuyper, *Confidentie*, 86–91.

29. Kuyper, *De Gemeene Gratie*, 3.239–245.

30. Ibid., 3.272–273.

31. Kuyper, "Modernism: A *Fata Morgana* in the Christian Domain (1871)," in *Abraham Kuyper: A Centennial Reader*, ed. Bratt (Grand Rapids, MI: Eerdmans, 1998), 103. Kuyper did recognize that the church was not simply a voluntary organization. The practice of infant baptism proved that, but he did not fully explain this point in Common Grace. His argument for presumptive regeneration as the basis for infant baptism was his attempt to marry his otherwise highly subjective ecclesiology with traditional reformed practice.

32. On Hoedemaker's life see Jan de Bruijn, "Philippus Jacobus Hoedemaker: Een Biografische Schets," in *Hoedemaker Herdacht*, ed. G. Abma and Jan De Bruijn (Baarn: Ten Have, 1989), 11–29. Here I mean the term *sect* in the general sociological sense that Ernst Troeltsch used the term and not as a derogatory term.

33. Lest anyone think the CGK overly divisive, it should be noted that the CGK had faced various injustices more or less directly at the hands of the NHK, beginning with but not limited to the quartering soldiers in their homes.

34. Hoedemaker, *Artikel XXXVI*, 16, 63–64. Various articles discuss Hoedemaker's critique of Kuyper's neutrality; see Abma, "Hoe Neutraal Is Neutraal? Hoedemaker en de Politiek," in *Hoedemaker Herdacht*, ed. Abma and Bruijn (Baarn: Ten Have, 1989), 188–215; van Spanning, "Hoedemaker en de Antirevolutionairen," 234–245.

35. Hoedemaker, *Artikel XXXVI*, 55.

36. Ibid., 87, see also 73, 88–89.

37. Ibid., 76, see also 56.

38. Ibid., 76; van Spanning, "Hoedemaker en de Antirevolutionairen," 236–238.

39. See Hoedemaker, "De Kerk en de Staat Onder het Oude Verbond," *Troffel en Zwaard* 1 (1898): 142–162; Hoedemaker, "Kerk en Staat in Israel," *Troffel en Zwaard* 1 (1898): 208–237.

40. Kuyper, *Encyclopaedie der Heilige Godgeleerdheid*, 3 vols. (Amsterdam: J.A. Wormser, 1894), 3.286. See also Abma, "Hoe Neutraal Is Neutraal?," 198–199.

41. Kuyper, *De Gemeene Gratie*, 3.286–288.

42. Hoedemaker, *Artikel XXXVI*, 16; Vree, "Historical Introduction," in *Abraham Kuyper's Commentatio (1860): The Young Kuyper about Calvin, A Lasco, and the Church*, vol. 1, Brill's Series in Church History (Leiden: Brill, 2005), 49–51.

CHAPTER 7

1. José Casanova, *Public Religions in the Modern World* (Chicago: University of Chicago Press, 1994), 51.
2. James Bratt offers a few statistics on the size of Kuyper's *doleantie* church; see Bratt, *Abraham Kuyper: A Biography* (unpublished), chapter 6 "Church Reformer."
3. Abraham Kuyper, *De Zegen des Heeren over onze Kerken: Rede ter Inleiding op het Gebed voor het Samenkomen der Gereformeerde Kerken in Generale Synode Gehouden in de Noorderkerk te Middelburg, op 10 Augustus 1896* (Amsterdam: J.A. Wormser, 1896), 23.
4. Kuyper, "Van de Kerk," *De Heraut* 1919–1920.
5. Kuyper, "Conservatism and Orthodoxy: False and True Preservation (1870)," in *Abraham Kuyper: A Centennial Reader*, ed. Bratt (Grand Rapids, MI: Eerdmans, 1998), 68. See also Kuyper, "De Sleutelen," in *Uit het Woord. Stichtelijke Bijbelstudiën*, vol. 2 (Amsterdam: J.A. Wormser, n.d.), 41–42.
6. See the use of these terms, for example, in James C. Kennedy, *Stad op een Berg: De Publieke Rol van Protestantse Kerken* (Zoetermeer: Boekencentrum, 2009), 20–21; Martin E. Marty and Edith L. Blumhofer, "Public Religion in America Today," http://divinity.uchicago.edu/martycenter/research/publicreligion_today.shtml.
7. Casanova, *Public Religions in the Modern World*, 40.
8. Ibid., 51.
9. Joris van Eijnatten and Fred van Lieburg, *Nederlandse Religiegeschiedenis* (Hilversum: Verloren, 2005), 271.
10. Kuyper, *De Gemeene Gratie*, vol. 2 (Kampen: Kok, 1931–1932), 254.
11. Marty and Blumhofer, "Public Religion in America Today," n.d.
12. Ibid.
13. Further, "A kingdom could only be conceived as grounded in something higher than mere human action in secular time." Charles Taylor, *A Secular Age* (Cambridge, MA: Harvard University Press, 2007), 25.
14. Ibid., 191–196; Jeroen Koch, *Abraham Kuyper: Een Biografie* (Amsterdam: Uitgeverij Boom, 2006), 65.
15. Casanova, *Public Religions in the Modern World*, 55.
16. Claude Welch says that the really new cultural conundrum that Christianity faced in the late nineteenth century was the degree to which the "religious view of life began to be displaced." Even the idea of the unity of church and state was still generally accepted in Europe. This is where Kuyper and the Netherlands offer a new and important lesson. While the secularization of the European mind certainly happened here as well, the Netherlands was on the leading edge as far as the separation of church and state, and theologians had to deal with the problems arising from that, which were first of all ecclesiological. Welch, *Protestant Thought in the Nineteenth Century, 1870–1914*, vol. 2 (New Haven, CT: Yale University Press, 1985), 212–214.

17. See "particulier" in Van Dale Groot Woordenboek: Engels Nederlands, Nederlands Engels Ver. 2.1, Van Dale Lexicographie, Utrecht/Antwerpen. Also ""Particulier" in *De Geïntegreerde Taal-Bank*, 2009, no. December 11 (2007–2009), http://gtb.inl.nl/iWDB/search?actie=article&wdb=WNT&id=M0524 14&lemmodern=particulier; Kuyper, "Common Grace (1895–1901)," in *Abraham Kuyper: A Centennial Reader*, ed. Bratt (Grand Rapids, MI: Eerdmans, 1998), 166.

18. Mary Douglas, "Judgments on James Frazier," *Daedelus* 107 (1978): 161.

19. Kennedy, *Stad op een Berg*, 11, 39.

20. Amy Plantinga Pauw, "Practical Ecclesiology in John Calvin and Jonathan Edwards," in *John Calvin's American Legacy*, ed. Thomas J. Davis (New York: Oxford University Press, 2010).

21. Cf. Annemarie Houkes, *Christelijke Vaderlanders: Godsdienst, Burgerschap, en de Nederlandse Natie (1850–1900)* (Amsterdam: Wereldbibliotheek, 2009).

22. Hoedemaker, *Heel de Kerk en Heel het Volk!: Een Protest tegen het Optreden der Gereformeerden als Partij, en een Woord van Afscheid aan de Confessioneele Vereeniging* (Sneek: J. Campen, 1897).

23. Vree, "'Onvermijdelijk Was Zeker Isolement…'. Hoedemaker als Hoogleraar aan de Vrije Universiteit (1880–1887)," in *Hoedemaker Herdacht*, ed. Abma and Bruijn (Ten Have: Passage, 1989).

24. Kuyper, "Vrijheid: Bevestigingsrede van Dr. Ph. S. van Ronkel (1873)," in *Predicatiën, in de jaren 1867 tot 1873, tijdens zijn Predikantschap in het Nederlandsch Hervormde Kerkgenootschap, gehouden te Beesd, te Utrecht, en te Amsterdam* (Kampen: Kok, 1913), 405. Cf. Kuyper, "De Sleutelmacht," in *Uit het Woord. Stichtelijke Bijbelstudiën*, vol. 2 (Amsterdam: J.A. Wormser, n.d.), 101.

25. Kuyper, *Ons Program (met Bijlagen)* (Amsterdam: J.H. Kruyt, 1879), 1129.

26. Kuyper, "Vrijheid," 400; Kuyper, *De Gemeene Gratie*, 92–294.

27. Kuyper, *Soevereiniteit in Eigen Kring. Rede ter Inwijding van de Vrije Universiteit, den 20sten Oktober 1880 Gehouden, in het Koor der Nieuwe Kerk te Amsterdam* (Amsterdam: J.H. Kruyt, 1880), 35. In English, Kuyper, "Sphere Sovereignty (1880)," in *Abraham Kuyper: A Centennial Reader*, ed. Bratt (Grand Rapids, MI: Eerdmans, 1998), 488.

28. Kuyper said that the main charge leading to his ouster from the national church was sectarianism; Kuyper, "Common Grace," 191.

29. See a photocopy of the brochure in Koch, *Biografie*, unnumbered pages.

30. Kuyper, "The Blurring of the Boundaries (1892)," in *Abraham Kuyper: A Centennial Reader*, ed. Bratt (Grand Rapids, MI: Eerdmans, 1998), 368.

31. Kuyper, *Stellingen in den Professorenkrans der "Vrije Universiteit"* (1884), paragraphs 1, 2.

32. Kuyper, *Ijzer en Leem: Rede ter Inleiding op het Gebed voor De Eenige Hoogschool Hier te Lande, Die op Gods Woord Gegrond Staat* (Amsterdam: J.H. Kruyt, 1885), esp. 11–15.

33. Kuyper, "De Heelen en de Halven," *De Standaard*, June 17, 1885; Kuyper, *Ijzer en Leem: Rede ter Inleiding op het Gebed voor De Eenige Hoogschool Hier te Lande, Die op Gods Woord Gegrond Staat.*

34. Vree, "'Het Reveil' en 'Het (neo-)Calvinisme' in hun onderlinge samenhang (1856–1896)," in *Abraham Kuyper: Vast en Veranderlijk: De Ontwikkeling van zijn Denken*, ed. Cornelis Augustijn and Vree (Zoetermeer: Meinema, 1998), 61–67.

35. Houkes, *Christelijke Vaderlanders*, 250.

36. On the *Hervormde* social ethics and activity see ibid., 231–250.

37. See also, for example, the disputes within Kuyper's new church over how the free church should relate to the free university; Vree, "Hoe de Citadel Onstand: De Consolidatie der Vereniging 1892–1905," in *Abraham Kuyper: Vast en Veranderlijk, De Ontwikkeling van Zijn Denken*, ed. Augustijn and Vree (Zoetermeer: Meinema, 1998), 209–214.

38. Kuyper, *De Zegen des Heeren*, 22, italics in original.

39. Ibid., 23, italics in original.

40. For example, Clifford Blake Anderson, "A Canopy of Grace: Common and Particular Grace in Abraham Kuyper's Theology of Science," *Princeton Seminary Bulletin* 24 (2003); Johannes Stellingwerff, *Dr. Abraham Kuyper en de Vrije Universiteit* (Kampen: Kok, 1987); Bratt, *Dutch Calvinism in Modern America: A History of a Conservative Subculture* (Grand Rapids, MI: Eerdmans, 1984), 19.

41. Bratt, *Dutch Calvinism in Modern America*, 150–154; Bratt, "The Dutch Schools," in *Reformed Theology in America: A History of Its Modern Development*, ed. David Well (Grand Rapids, MI: Baker, 1997), 146.

42. For example, Kuyper, "Blurring of the Boundaries."

43. As will hopefully become apparent herein, but note well that the presupposition of Kuyper's entire common grace project is that there is an antithesis between good and evil. If not, what would common grace presume to explain? Kuyper, *De Gemeene Gratie*, 2.5–9.

44. As, for example, D. A. Carson does following the lead of Bratt; Carson, *Christ and Culture Revisited* (Grand Rapids, MI: Eerdmans, 2008), 215.

45. Kuyper, *De Gemeene Gratie*, 2.10.

46. Ibid., 2.11.

47. Houkes helpfully makes this distinction between the *Hervormden* and Kuyper's group. Houkes, *Christelijke Vaderlanders*, 277, but see Houkes's entire conclusion, 271–280.

48. Kuyper, *De Gemeene Gratie*, 2.261.

49. Kuyper, "Common Grace," 194.

50. Ibid., 196–197.

51. Ernst Troeltsch, *The Social Teaching of the Christian Churches*, trans. Olive Wyon, vol. 1, Library of Theological Ethics (Louisville, KY: Westminster/John Knox, 1960), 331.

52. Kuyper, "Common Grace," 176.

53. Ibid., 172.

54. Kuyper, *De Gemeene Gratie*, 2.278.

55. Ibid., 2.15.

56. Kuyper, "Common Grace," 167–168.

57. Kuyper, *De Gemeene Gratie*, 1.11–47.

58. For example, from 1870, Kuyper, "De Naam in de Heilige Schrift," in *Uit het Woord. Stichtelijke Bijbelstudiën*, vol. 1 (Amsterdam: J.A. Wormser, n.d.), 15.

59. Kuyper, *De Gemeene Gratie*, 2.28; Kuyper, "Common Grace," 174.

60. Kuyper, "Common Grace," 168.

61. Kuyper, *De Gemeene Gratie*, 1.222; Kuyper, "Common Grace," 168. Here is a key instance where the term *special* as a translation of *particulier* is confusing, and I have amended Bratt's translation accordingly.

62. Kuyper, *De Gemeene Gratie*, 2.52.

63. Ibid., 2.268–283.

64. Kuyper, "Common Grace," 191–193.

65. Kuyper, *De Gemeene Gratie*, 2.242–243.

66. Ibid., 2.245.

67. Ibid., 2.246.

68. Ibid., 3.111, 127.

69. Kuyper, "Common Grace," 197, italics in original.

70. G. J. Schutte, *Het Calvinistisch Nederland: Mythe en Werkelijkheid* (Hilversum: Verloren, 2000), 155.

71. Cf. Kuyper, "Calvinism: Source and Stronghold of Our Constitutional Liberties (1874)," in *Abraham Kuyper: A Centennial Reader*, ed. Bratt (Grand Rapids, MI: Eerdmans, 1998), 296.

72. *Pace* Koch, *Biografie*, 197.

73. For example, in 1873 Kuyper, "De Uitverkiezing," in *Uit het Woord. Stichtelijke Bijbelstudiën*, vol. 2, *Uit het Woord* (Amsterdam: J.A. Wormser, n.d.), 127.

74. NB Jeroen Koch notes that Kuyper changed his perspective on the nation from viewing it as a Reformed nation to a plural one in which his Reformed group was one part. Jeroen Koch, "Abraham Kuyper tussen Gereformeerde Natie en Gereformeerde Zuil," *Tijdschrift voor Geschiedenis* 120 (2007).

75. Kuyper, *Tweeërlei Vaderland* (Amsterdam: J.A. Wormser, 1887), 10.

76. Stellingwerf, "Het Arcanum van Abraham Kuyper," in *Geboekt in Eigen Huis: Werken van Abraham Kuyper Aanwezig in de Bibliotheek van de Vrije Universiteit*, ed. Stellingwerf (Amsterdam: VU Uitgeverij, 1987), 31. *Pace* Sean Lucas and Carson, who say that Kuyper failed to distinguish between the church and the world. It might not have been the distinction that Carson and Lucas would wish, but Kuyper consistently separated church and world, in theory, and more also. Lucas, "Southern Fried Kuyper? Robert Lewis Dabney, Abraham Kuyper, and the Limitations of Public Theology," *Westminster Theological Journal* 66 (2004): 200; Carson, *Christ and Culture Revisited*, 215.

77. Kuyper, *Tweeërlei Vaderland*, 20–21.

78. Ibid., 35.

79. Kuyper, "Common Grace," 174. Cf. Kuyper, *De Gemeene Gratie*, 2.243.

80. Kuyper, *De Gemeene Gratie*, 247.

81. Kuyper used the term *life-system* as an English equivalent to the German *Welt-anschauung*, which Peter Heslam equates with the more recent term *worldview*. Peter S. Heslam, *Creating a Christian Worldview: Abraham Kuyper's Lectures on Calvinism* (Grand Rapids, MI: Eerdmans, 1998), 88–89; Kuyper, *Lectures on Calvinism* (Grand Rapids, MI: Eerdmans, 1931), 9–40; David K. Naugle, *Worldview: The History of a Concept* (Grand Rapids, MI: Eerdmans, 2002).

82. Arie Molendijk suggests that Weber and Troeltsch depended on Kuyper for their concept of Calvinism. Kuyper named historians Robert Fruin and R. C. Bakhuizen van den Brink as his influences. Molendijk, "Neo-Calvinist Culture Protestantism: Abraham Kuyper's *Stone Lectures*," *Church History and Religious Culture* 88 (2008), 235–250; Kuyper, *Lectures on Calvinism*, 14–15.

83. Kuyper, *Lectures on Calvinism*, 15.

84. Ibid., 17.

85. Ibid., 20–21.

86. Ibid., 26–28.

87. Heslam, *Creating a Christian Worldview*, 88.

88. Molendijk, "Neocalvinistisch cultuurprotestantisme: Abraham Kuypers *Stone Lectures*," *Documentatieblad voor de Nederlandse Kerkgeschiedenis na 1800* xxix (2006); Molendijk, "Neo-Calvinist Culture Protestantism: Abraham Kuyper's *Stone Lectures*," 235–250.

89. Kuyper, *Lectures on Calvinism*, 31. Also: "The church has to retire to the domain of *particular* grace, and that exempted from her rules lies the wide and free domain of 'common grace'" (129).

90. Ibid., 42.

91. Ibid., 62.

92. Kuyper, *De Gemeene Gratie*, 254.

93. Compare Abraham Kuyper, *Confidentie: Schrijven aan den Weled. Heer J.H. van der Linden* (Amsterdam: Höveker & Zoon, 1873), 52; Kuyper, *Lectures on Calvinism*, 22, 47.

94. Compare "Wedergeboorte en Bekeering" and *De Leer der Verbonden* to the *Lectures*. Kuyper, *De Leer der Verbonden*, vol. 5, Uit Het Woord. Stichtelijke Bijbelstudiën (Kampen: Kok, 1909); Kuyper, *Lectures on Calvinism*; Kuyper, "Wedergeboorte en Bekeering," in *Uit Het Woord. Stichtelijke Bijbelstudiën*, vol. 3 (Amsterdam: Höveker & Wormser, n.d.).

95. Kuyper, *Lectures on Calvinism*, 67, italics in original.

96. Cf. Kennedy, *Stad op een Berg*, 52–53; George Harinck and Lodewijk Winkeler, "De Negentiende Eeuw," in *Handboek Nederlandse Kerkgeschiedenis*, ed. Herman J. Selderhuis (Kampen: Kok, 2006), 688.

97. Petrus Antonius van Leeuwen, *Het Kerkbegrip in de Theologie van Abraham Kuyper* (Franeker: Wever, 1946), 270.

98. Cf. J. Douma, *Algemeene Genade: Uiteenzetting, Vergelijking en Beoordeling van de Opvatting van A. Kuyper, K. Schilder, en Joh. Calvijn over 'Algemeene Genade'* (Goes: Oosterbaan & Le Cointre, 1976), 64–66; Heslam, *Creating a Christian Worldview*, 134–135.

99. Kuyper, "Common Grace," 194–195, italics in original.

100. Ibid., 200.

101. It is misleading to say that Kuyper thereby puts the Christian school or press on the "plane of special grace," as David VanDrunen does. Kuyper repeatedly warns against confusing the organic church with the field of common grace, in any scenario. This was, after all, his criticism of the national church. Say rather that Kuyper overestimates Christians' ability to thoroughly Christianize any sphere, church, state, school, or otherwise. David VanDrunen, "Abraham Kuyper and the Reformed Natural Law and Two Kingdoms Traditions," *Calvin Theological Journal* 42 (2007): 297; Kuyper, *De Gemeene Gratie*, 2.253–255; Kuyper, "Common Grace," 200.

102. The classic English-language study of pillarization is Arend Lijphart, *Politics of Accommodation: Pluralism and Democracy in the Netherlands* (Berkeley: University of California Press, 1968).

103. George Harinck, *Waar Komt het VU-Kabinet Vandaan? Over de Traditie van het Neocalvinisme* (Amstelveen: EON, 2007), 5.

104. W. Balke, *Gunning en Hoedemaker: Samen op Weg* ('s-Gravenhage: Boekencentrum, 1985), 62–66.

105. Cf. Houkes, *Christelijke Vaderlanders*.

106. Douma, *Algemeene Genade*, 64.

107. Kuyper, "Common Grace," 197.

108. Cf. Casanova, *Public Religions in the Modern World*, 7; Peter Berger et al., *Religious America, Secular Europe? A Theme and Variations* (Aldershot: Ashgate, 2008).

109. Kuyper, *Tweeërlei Vaderland*, 30.

110. Casanova, *Public Religions in the Modern World*, 70.

Bibliography

Aalders, Maarten. *125 Jaar Faculteit Der Godgeleerdheid Aan De Vrije Universiteit*. Meinema: Zoetemeer, 2005.

Abma, G. "Hoe Neutraal Is Neutraal? Hoedemaker En De Politiek." In *Hoedemaker Herdacht*, edited by G. Abma and Jan De Bruijn, 188–215. Baarn: Ten Have, 1989.

"Algemeen Reglement Voor Het Bestuur Der Hervormde Kerk in Het Koningrijk Der Nederlanden." (1816), http://www.kerkrecht.nl/main.asp?pagetype=Literat uur&item=90&subitem=.

Anderson, Clifford Blake. "A Canopy of Grace: Common and Particular Grace in Abraham Kuyper's Theology of Science." *Princeton Seminary Bulletin* 24 (2003): 123–140.

Appelius, J. C. *Brief Behelzende De Voornaamste Gronden, En De Byzondere Mening Van De Hedendaagsche Nieuwe Lere Der Sacramenten: Neffens De Voornaamste Bewyzen, Tegen Dezelve: Als Ook Eene Oplossing Van Hare Voornaamste Tegenwerpingen*. Groningen: Wed. I. Spandaw, 1768.

Augustijn, Cornelis. "Kerk En Godsdienst 1870–1890." In *De Doleantie Van 1886 En Haar Geschiedenis*, edited by Wim Bakker, 41–75. Kampen: Kok, 1986.

Augustijn, Cornelis. "De Spiritualiteit Van De Dolerenden." In *Abraham Kuyper: Vast En Verandelijk: De Ontwikkeling Van Zijn Denken*, edited by Cornelis Augustijn and Jasper Vree, 183–199. Zoetermeer: Meinema, 1998.

Augustijn, Cornelis. "Kuypers Theologie Van De Samenleving." In *Abraham Kuyper: Vast En Veranderlijk*, edited by Cornelis Augustijn and Jasper Vree, 24–53. Zoetermeer: Meinema, 1998.

Augustijn, Cornelis and Jasper Vree, eds. *Abraham Kuyper: Vast En Veranderlijk: De Ontwikkeling Van Zijn Denken*. Zoetermeer: Meinema, 1998.

Austin, John L. *How to Do Things with Words*. Oxford: Oxford University Press, 1962.

Bacote, Vincent E. *The Spirit in Public Theology: Appropriating the Legacy of Abraham Kuyper*. Grand Rapids, MI: Baker Academic, 2005.

Balke, W. *Gunning En Hoedemaker: Samen Op Weg*. 's-Gravenhage: Boekencentrum, 1985.

Bavinck, H. "Review of *Tractaat Van De Reformatie Van Der Kerken*, by Abraham Kuyper." *De Vrije Kerk* 9 (1883): 542–575.

"The Belgic Confession." In *The Creeds of Christendom*, vol. 3, edited by Philip Schaf, 383–436 Grand Rapids, MI: Baker, 1993.

Benedict, Philip. *Christ's Churches Purely Reformed: A Social History of Calvinism*. New Haven, CT: Yale University Press, 2002.

Berger, Peter. "Secularization Falsified." *First Things*, no. 180 (2008): 23–27.

Berger, Peter, Grace Davie, and Effie Fokas. *Religious America, Secular Europe? A Theme and Variations*. Aldershot: Ashgate, 2008.

Blei, Karel. *The Netherlands Reformed Church, 1571–2005*. Translated by Allan J. Janssen, The Historical Series of the Reformed Church in America. Grand Rapids, MI: Eerdmans, 2006.

Blei, Karel. "Volkskerk." In *Christelijke Encyclopedie*, edited by George Harinck, Wim Berkelaar, Albert de Vos and Lodewijk Winkeler, 1819. Kampen: Kok, 2006.

Bolt, John. *A Free Church, a Holy Nation: Abraham Kuyper's American Public Theology*. Grand Rapids, MI: Eerdmans, 2000.

Bolt, John. "The Vandrunen-Kloosterman Debate on 'Natural Law' and 'Two Kingdoms' in the Theology of Herman Bavinck." *Bavinck Society Discussion* (2010), http://bavinck.calvinseminary.edu/wp-content/uploads/2010/06/Discussion_1_VanDrunen-Kloosterman_debate.pdf.

Bonhoeffer, Dietrich. *Sanctorum Communio: A Theological Study of the Sociology of the Church*, edited by Wayne Whitson Floyd Jr. Vol. 1, Dietrich Bonhoeffer Works. Minneapolis: Fortress, 1998.

Bos, David. *In Dienst Van Het Koninkrijk: Beroepsontwikkeling Van Hervormde Predikanten in Negentiende-Eeuws Nederland*. Amsterdam: Bert Bakker, 1999.

Bowlin, John R. "Some Thoughts on Doing Theology in Public." *Princeton Seminary Bulletin* 28 (2007): 235–243.

Bratt, James. "Abraham Kuyper's Public Career." *Reformed Journal* 37 (1987): 9–12.

Bratt, James. "The Dutch Schools." In *Reformed Theology in America: A History of Its Modern Development*, edited by David Well, 146. Grand Rapids, MI: Baker, 1997.

Bratt, James D., ed. *Abraham Kuyper: A Centennial Reader*. Grand Rapids, MI: Eerdmans, 1998.

Bratt, James. *Abraham Kuyper: A Biography*, unpublished, 2004.

Bratt, James. "The Context of Herman Bavinck's Stone Lectures: Culture and Politics in 1908." *Bavinck Review* 1 (2010): 4–24.

Bratt, James D. *Dutch Calvinism in Modern America: A History of a Conservative Subculture*. Grand Rapids, MI: Eerdmans, 1984.

Bratt, James D. "Abraham Kuyper: Puritan, Victorian, Modern." In *Religion, Pluralism, and Public Life: Abraham Kuyper's Legacy of the Twenty-First Century*, edited by Luis E. Lugo, 3–21. Grand Rapids, MI: Eerdmans, 2000.

Brinkman, Martien E. and Cornelis van der Kooi. "Het Calvinisme Van Kuyper En Bavinck." In *Het Calvinisme Van Kuyper En Bavinck*, edited by Martien E. Brinkman and Cornelis van der Kooi, 7–21. Zoetermeer: Uitgeverij Meinema, 1997.

Budziszewski, J., ed. *Evangelicals in the Public Square: Four Formative Voices on Political Thought and Action*. Grand Rapids, MI: Baker Academic, 2006.

Burke, Edmund. *Reflections on the Revolution in France*, edited by F. G. Selby. New York: McMillan, 1890.

"The Canons of the Synod of Dort." In *The Creeds of Christendom*, edited by Philip Schaff, 550–597. New York: Harper & Brothers, 1905.

Cantor, Norman. *The American Century: Varieties of Culture in Modern Times*. New York: Harper Collins, 1997.

Carson, D. A. *Christ and Culture Revisited*. Grand Rapids, MI: Eerdmans, 2008.

Casanova, José. *Public Religions in the Modern World*. Chicago: University of Chicago Press, 1994.

Chadwick, Owen. *From Bossuet to Newman: The Idea of Doctrinal Development*. Cambridge, UK: Cambridge University Press, 1957.

Conser, Walter H., Jr. *Church and Confession: Conservative Theologians in Germany, England, and America, 1815–1866*. Macon, GA: Mercer University Press, 1984.

Cox, Jeffery. *The English Churches in a Secular Society*. New York: Oxford University Press, 1982.

Cramer, J. "Vrijmaking Der Kerk, Waardoor? En Wanneer?" *Stemmen voor Waarheid en Vrede* 7 (1870): 392–410.

de Bres, Guido. "The Belgic Confession (1561)." In *Creeds and Confessions of Faith in Christian Tradition*, edited by Jaroslav Pelikan and Valerie Hotchkiss, 405–426. New Haven: Yale University Press, 2003.

de Bruijn, Jan. "Philippus Jacobus Hoedemaker: Een Biografische Schets." In *Hoedemaker Herdacht*, edited by G. Abma and Jan De Bruijn, 11–29. Baarn: Ten Have, 1989.

de Bruijn, Jan. *Abraham Kuyper: Een Beeldbiografie*. Amsterdam: Bert Bakker, 2008.

Doedes, J. I. *De Leer Der Zaligheid: Volgens Het Evangelie*. Utrecht: Kemink en Zoon, 1868.

Douglas, Mary. "Judgments on James Frazier." *Daedelus* 107 (1978): 151–164.

Douma, J. *Algemeene Genade: Uiteenzetting, Vergelijking En Beoordeling Van De Opvatting Van A. Kuyper, K. Schilder, En Joh. Calvijn over 'Algemeene Genade'*. Goes: Oosterbaan & Le Cointre, 1976.

Doyle, Dennis M. "Möhler, Schleiermacher, and the Roots of Communion Ecclesiology." *Theological Studies* 57, no. 3 (1996): 467–480.

Dr. Kuyper in De Caricatuur. Amsterdam: Van Holkema & Warendorp, 1909.

Dulles, Avery. *Models of the Church*. New York: Doubleday, 1987.

Finke, Roger and Rodney Stark. *The Churching of America, 1776–2005: Winners and Losers in Our Religious Economy*, 2d ed. New Brunswick, NJ: Rutgers University Press, 2005.

Flinterman, R.A. "Toorenenbergen, Johan Justus Van." In *Biografisch Lexicon Voor De Geschiedenis Van Het Nederlands Protestantisme*, edited by D. Nauta, A. de Groot, J. Van den Berg, F. R. J. Knetch, and G. H. M. Posthumus Meyjes, 421–424. Kampen: Kok, 1983.

Gellner, Ernest. *Nations and Nationalism*. Ithaca, NY: Cornell University Press, 1983.

Gerrish, B. A. "Continuity and Change: Friedrich Schleiermacher on the Task of Theology." In *Tradition and the Modern World: Reformed Theology in the Nineteenth Century*, 13–48. Chicago: University of Chicago Press, 1978.

Ginther, James. "The Church in Medieval Theology." In *The Routledge Companion to the Christian Church*, edited by Gerard Mannion and Lewis Mudge, 48–62. London: Routledge, 2008.

Graafland, C. "De Doop Als Splijtzwam in De Gereformeerde Gezindte." In *Rondom De Doopvont*, edited by Willem van 't Spijker, 446–497. Goudriaan, The Netherlands: De Groot, 1983.

Gunning, J. H., Jr. *Lijden En Heerlijkheid*. Amsterdam: B. van den Land, 1875.

Gunning, J. H., Jr. "Antwoord Aan Dr. A. Kuyper Van J. H. Gunning (1876)." In *De Weg Ter Godzaligheid*, 56–57. Zwolle: J. P. van Dijk, 1877.

Haight S.J., Roger. *Christian Community in History: Historical Ecclesiology*, vol. 1. New York: Continuum, 2004.

Haight S.J., Roger. *Christian Community in History: Comparative Ecclesiology*, vol. 2. New York: Continuum, 2005.

Haight S.J., Roger. "Comparative Ecclesiology." In *The Routledge Companion to the Christian Church*, edited by Gerard Mannion and Lewis Mudge, 387–401. New York: Routledge, 2008.

Harinck, George. "Een Leefbare Oplossing: Katholieke En Protestantse Tradities En De Scheiding Van Kerk En Staat." In *Ongewenste Goden: De Publieke Rol Van Religie in Nederland*, edited by Marcel ten Hooven and Theo de Wit, 106–130, notes 316–318. Amsterdam: Sun, 2006.

Harinck, George. "'Men Zal Met Een Serieuze Analyse Moeten Beginnen.' Jasper Vree En Abraham Kuyper." *Documentatieblad voor de Nederlandse Kerkgeschiedenis na 1800* 29 (2006): 51–60.

Harinck, George. *Waar Komt Het Vu-Kabinet Vandaan? Over De Traditie Van Het Neocalvinisme*. Amstelveen: EON, 2007.

Harinck, George and Gerard Dekker. "The Position of the Church as Institute in Society: A Comparison between Bonhoeffer and Kuyper." *Princeton Seminary Bulletin* 28, no. 1 (2007): 86–98.

Harinck, George and Lodewijk Winkeler. "De Negentiende Eeuw." In *Handboek Nederlandse Kerkgeschiedenis*, edited by Herman J. Selderhuis, 597–721. Kampen: Kok, 2006.

Hart, D. G. *Defending the Faith: J. Gresham Machen and the Crisis of Conservative Protestantism in Modern America*. Baltimore: Johns Hopkins University Press, 1994.

Havinga, Andreas. "Church Authorities Not to Discipline Dutch 'Atheist' Pastor." *Ecumenical News International* (2009), http://www.eni.ch/featured/article.php?id=2861.

Heppe, Heinrich. *Reformed Dogmatics: Set out and Illustrated from the Sources*. Translated by G. T. Thomsom. Edited by Ernst Bizer. Grand Rapids, MI: Baker, 1950.

Heslam, Peter S. *Creating a Christian Worldview: Abraham Kuyper's Lectures on Calvinism*. Grand Rapids, MI: Eerdmans, 1998.

Heslam, Peter S. "Review of *Abraham Kuyper: Een Biographie*, by Jeroen Koch." *Documentatieblad voor de Nederlandse Kerkgeschiedenis na 1800* 65 (2006): 69–71.

Hobsbawn, Eric. *The Age of Revolution, 1789–1848*. Cleveland: World, 1962.

Hobsbawn, Eric. *Nations and Nationalism since 1780: Programme, Myth, Reality*. Cambridge, UK: Cambridge University Press, 1990.

Hoedemaker, Philip J. "De Kerk En De Staat Onder Het Oude Verbond." *Troffel en Zwaard* 1 (1898): 142–162.

Hoedemaker, Philip J. *Artikel Xxxvi: Onzer Nederduitsche Geloofsbeleidenis Tegenover Dr. A. Kuijper Gehandhaafd*. Amsterdam: J.H. van Dam, 1901.

Hoedemaker, Philip J. *Dr. A. Kuyper in Tegenspraak Met Groen Van Prinsterer; Een Waarschuwend Woord Voor De Verkiezingen in Juni 1891 Door Een Hervormd Predikant*. Amsterdam: Egeling, 1891.

Hoedemaker, Philip J. *Heel De Kerk En Heel Het Volk!: Een Protest Tegen Het Optreden Der Gereformeerden Als Partij, En Een Woord Van Afscheid Aan De Confessioneele Vereeniging*. Sneek: J. Campen, 1897.

Hoedemaker, Philip J. "Kerk En Staat in Israel." *Troffel en Zwaard* 1 (1898): 208–237.

Holifield, E. Brooks. *Theology in America: Christian Thought from the Age of the Puritans to the Civil War*. New Haven, CT: Yale University Press, 2003.

Houkes, Annemarie. *Christelijkevaderlanders: Godsdienst, Burgerschap, En De Nederlandse Natie (1850–1900)*. Amsterdam: Wereldbibliotheek, 2009.

Kamphuis, J. *Een Eeuwig Verbond*. Haarlem: Uitgeverij Vijlbrief, 1984.

Kärkkäinen, Veli-Matti. *An Introduction to Ecclesiology: Ecumenical, Historical and Global Perspectives*. Downers Grove, IL: InterVarsity, 2002.

Kennedy, James C. *Stad Op Een Berg: De Publieke Rol Van Protestantse Kerken*. Zoetermeer: Boekencentrum, 2009.

Kennedy, James C. "Dutch Political Developments and Religious Reform." In *Political and Legal Perspectives*, edited by Keith Robbins, 117–145. Leuven: Leuven University Press, 2010.

"Kerkberoerte Te Amsterdam." *De Nederlandsche Spectator* 2 (1886).

Knight, Frances. *The Church in the Nineteenth Century*, I.B. Tauris History of the Christian Church. London: I.B. Tauris, 2008.

Kobes, Wayne A. "Sphere Sovereignty and the University: Theological Foundations of Abraham Kuyper's View of the University and Its Role in Society." Ph.D. diss., Florida State University, 1993.

Koch, Jeroen. *Abraham Kuyper: Een Biografie*. Amsterdam: Uitgeverij Boom, 2006.

Koch, Jeroen. "Abraham Kuyper Tussen Gereformeerde Natie En Gereformeerde Zuil." *Tijdschrift voor Geschiedenis* 120 (2007): 524–533.

Krabbendam, Hans. "Zielenverbrijzelaars En Zondelozen: Reacties in De Nederlandse Pers Op Moody, Sankey, En Pearsall Smith, 1874–1878." *Documentatieblad voor de Nederlandse Kerkgeschiedenis na 1800* 34 (1991): 39–55.

Kselman, Thomas. "The Varieties of Religious Experience in Urban Modern France." In *European Religion in the Age of the Great Cities, 1830–1930*, edited by Hugh McLeod, 165–190. London: Routledge, 1995.

Kuyper, Abraham. "A Pamphlet on the Reformation of the Churches (Trans. Herman Hoeksema)." *Standard Bearer* vols. 54–63 (1978–1987).

Kuyper, Abraham. "Aan Ds. J. H. Gunning." In *De Weg Ter Godzaligheid*, 33–38. Zwolle: J. P. van Dijk, 1875.

Kuyper, Abraham. *Abraham Kuyper's Commentatio (1860): The Young Kuyper about Calvin, a Lasco, and the Church*, edited by Jasper Vree and Johan Zwaan. Vol. 2, Brill's Series in Church History. Leiden: Brill, 2005.

Kuyper, Abraham. *Afwerping Van Het Juk Der Synodale Hierarchie*. Amsterdam: J.A. Wormser, 1886.

Kuyper, Abraham. "Calvinism and Confessional Revision." *Presbyterian and Reformed Review* 2 (1891): 369–399.

Kuyper, Abraham. "Calvinism: Source and Stronghold of Our Constitutional Liberties (1874)." In *Abraham Kuyper: A Centennial Reader*, edited by James Bratt, 279–322. Grand Rapids, MI: Eerdmans, 1998.

Kuyper, Abraham. "Confidentially (1873)." In *Abraham Kuyper: A Centennial Reader*, edited by James Bratt, 45–61. Grand Rapids, MI: Eerdmans, 1998.

Kuyper, Abraham. "Common Grace (1895–1901)." In *Abraham Kuyper: A Centennial Reader*, edited by James Bratt, 165–201. Grand Rapids, MI: Eerdmans, 1998.

Kuyper, Abraham. "Complot En Revolutie." In *Het Conflict Gekomen*. Amsterdam: J.H. Kruyt, 1886.

Kuyper, Abraham. *Confidentie: Schrijven Aan Den Weled. Heer J.H. Van Der Linden*. Amsterdam: Höveker & Zoon, 1873.

Kuyper, Abraham. "Conservatism and Orthodoxy: False and True Preservation (1870)." In *Abraham Kuyper: A Centennial Reader*, edited by James D. Bratt, 65–85. Grand Rapids, MI: Eerdmans, 1998.

Kuyper, Abraham. *Dat De Genade Particulier Is*. Vol. 4, Uit Het Woord. Stichtelijke Bijbelstudiën. Kampen: Kok, 1909.

Kuyper, Abraham. "De Autonomie Der Gemeente." *De Standaard*, September 20, 1874.

Kuyper, Abraham. "De Doopskwestie." *De Heraut*, October 7, 1870, 2.

Kuyper, Abraham. "De Eeredienst Der Hervormde Kerk En De Zamenstelling Van Haar Kerkboek." In *Geschiedenis Der Christelijke Kerk in Nederland, in Tafereelen*, edited by B. ter Haar and W. Moll, 87–113. Amsterdam: Portielje & Zoon, 1869.

Kuyper, Abraham. "De Eerste Kerkvergadering of De Vestiging Onzer Hervormde Kerk, En De Strijd Om Haar Zelfstandig Bestaan, 1550–1618." In *Geschiedenis Der Christelijke Kerk in Nederland in Tafereelen*, edited by B. ter Haar and W. Moll, 71–86. Amsterdam: G. Portielje & Zoon, 1869.

Kuyper, Abraham. *De Gemeene Gratie*. 3 vols. Kampen: Kok, 1931–1932.

Kuyper, Abraham. "De Heelen En De Halven." *De Standaard*, June 17, 1885.

Kuyper, Abraham. *De Kerkelijke Goederen*. Amsterdam: H. Höveker, 1869.

Kuyper, Abraham. *De Leer Der Onsterfelijkheid En De Staatsschool*. Amsterdam: H. de Hoogh, 1870.

Kuyper, Abraham. *De Leer Der Verbonden*. Vol. 5, Uit Het Woord. Stichtelijke Bijbelstudiën. Kampen: Kok, 1909.

Kuyper, Abraham. "De Menschwording Gods: Het Levensbeginsel Der Kerk (1867)." In *Predicatiën, in De Jaren 1867 Tot 1873, Tijdens Zijn Predikantschap in Het Nederlandsch Hervormde Kerkgenootschap, Gehouden Te Beesd, Te Utrecht, En Te Amsterdam*, 253–275. Kampen: Kok, 1913.

Kuyper, Abraham. "De Naam in De Heilige Schrift." In *Uit Het Woord. Stichtelijke Bijbelstudiën*. Amsterdam: J.A. Wormser, n.d.

Kuyper, Abraham. "De Ontwikkeling Der Pauselijke Macht Onder Nicolaas I." In *Kuyper Archief*, 300. Amsterdam: Historisch Documentatiecentrum voor het Nederlands Protestantisme (1800-heden), 1859.

Kuyper, Abraham. "De Openbare Godsvereering En Het Bestaan Der Kerk, December 3, 1864." In *Archief Kuyper*. Amsterdam: Historisch Documentatiecentrum voor het Nederlands Protestantisme.

Kuyper, Abraham. "De Sleutelen." In *Uit Het Woord. Stichtelijke Bijbelstudiën*, 39–87. Amsterdam: J.A. Wormser, n.d.

Kuyper, Abraham. "De Sleutelmacht." In *Uit Het Woord. Stichtelijke Bijbelstudiën*, 89–121. Amsterdam: J.A. Wormser, n.d.

Kuyper, Abraham. "De Spitse Der Openbaring." In *Uit Het Woord. Stichtelijke Bijbelstudiën*, 261–279. Amsterdam: J. A. Wormser, n.d.

Kuyper, Abraham. "De Uitverkiezing." In *Uit Het Woord. Stichtelijke Bijbelstudiën*, 123–198. Amsterdam: J.A. Wormser, n.d.

Kuyper, Abraham. "De Wedergeboorte, May 1, 1864." In *Kuyper Archief*. Amsterdam: Historisch Documentatiecentrum voor het Nederlands Protestantisme, 1864.

Kuyper, Abraham. *De Zegen Des Heeren over Onze Kerken: Rede Ter Inleiding Op Het Gebed Voor Het Samenkomen Der Gereformeerde Kerken in Generale Synode Gehouden in De Noorderkerk Te Middelburg, Op 10 Augustus 1896*. Amsterdam: J.A. Wormser, 1896.

Kuyper, Abraham. *Drie Kleine Vossen*. Kampen: J.H. Kok, 1901.

Kuyper, Abraham. "Dr. Kuyper's Democracy." In *A Free Church, a Holy Nation: Abraham Kuyper's American Public Theology*, edited by John Bolt, 481–482. Grand Rapids, MI: Eerdmans, 2001.

Kuyper, Abraham. *E Voto Dordraceno: Toelichting Op Den Heidelbergschen Catechismus*. 4 vols. Kampen: J.H. Kok, 1892–1895.

Kuyper, Abraham. "Een Wandel in 'T Licht: De Grondslag Van Alle Gemeenschap in De Kerk Van Christus, August 9, 1863." In *Archief Kuyper*. Amsterdam: Historisch Documentatiecentrum voor het Nederlands Protestantisme, 1863.

Kuyper, Abraham. "Eenheid: Rede, Ter Bevestiging Van Een Dienaar Des Woords, Gehouden 31 Augustus 1873 in De Nieuwe Kerk Te Amsterdam." In *Predicatiën, in De Jaren 1867 Tot 1873, Tijdens Zijn Predikantschap in Het Nederlandsch Hervormde Kerkgenootschap, Gehouden Te Beesd, Te Utrecht, En Te Amsterdam*, 413–444. Kampen: Kok, 1913.

Kuyper, Abraham. *Encyclopaedie Der Heilige Godgeleerdheid*. 3 vols. Amsterdam: J.A. Wormser, 1894.

Kuyper, Abraham. "Geworteld En Gegrond (1870)." In *Predicatiën, in De Jaren 1867 Tot 1873, Tijdens Zijn Predikantschap in Het Nederlandsch Hervormde Kerkgenootschap, Gehouden Te Beesd, Te Utrecht, En Te Amsterdam*, 325–351. Kampen: Kok, 1913.

Kuyper, Abraham. *Grace Is Particular*. Translated by Marvin Kamps. Granville, MI: Reformed Free Publishing Association, 2001.

Kuyper, Abraham. "Heidelbergsche Catechismus, Zondag 21, De Kerk, Februari 7, 1864." In *Archief Kuyper*. Amsterdam: Historisch Documentatiecentrum voor het Nederlands Protestantisme.

Kuyper, Abraham. "Heidelbergsche Catechismus, Zondag 21, De Kerk, Februari 7, 1864." In *Archief Kuyper*. Amsterdam: Historisch Documentatiecentrum voor het Nederlands Protestantisme, 1864.

Kuyper, Abraham. "Heilsfeit En Heilswoord." In *Uit Het Woord. Stichtelijke Bijbelstudiën*. Amsterdam: J.A. Wormser, n.d.

Kuyper, Abraham. "Het Gemeenschapleven Der Menschheid, Einddoel Van Jezus' Kerk En Middel Harer Ontwikkeling, December 11, 1865." In *Kuyper Archief*. Amsterdam: Historisch Documentatiecentrum voor het Nederlands Protestantisme.

Kuyper, Abraham. "Humanisme En Christendom, November 26, 1865." In *Archief Kuyper*. Amsterdam: Historisch Documentatiecentrum voor het Nederlands Protestantisme.

Kuyper, Abraham. *Het Conflict Gekomen*. Amsterdam: J.H. Kruyt, 1886.

Kuyper, Abraham. "Het Gemeenschapleven Der Menschheid, Einddoel Van Jezus' Kerk En Middel Harer Ontwikkeling, December 11, 1865." In *Kuyper Archief*. Amsterdam: Historisch Documentatiecentrum voor het Nederlands Protestantisme, 1865.

Kuyper, Abraham. "Het Mystieke Lichaam Van Christus." *Zondagsblad (van De Standaard)* 1875.

Kuyper, Abraham. *'Het Rede Op Het Volksgeweten': Rede Ter Opening Van De Algemeene Vergadering Der 'Vereeniging Voor Christelijk Nationaal-Schoolonderwijs,' Gehouden Te Utrecht, Den 18 Mei 1869.* Amsterdam: B.H. Blankenberg Jr., 1869.

Kuyper, Abraham. "Humanisme En Christendom, November 26, 1865." In *Archief Kuyper.* Amsterdam: Historisch Documentatiecentrum voor het Nederlands Protestantisme, 1865.

Kuyper, Abraham. *Ijzer En Leem: Rede Ter Inleiding Op Het Gebed Voor De Eenige Hoogschool Hier Te Lande, Die Op Gods Woord Gegrond Staat.* Amsterdam: J.H. Kruyt, 1885.

Kuyper, Abraham. "Individualisme En Kerk, September 26, 1868." In *Archief Kuyper.* Amsterdam: Historisch Documentatiecentrum voor het Nederlands Protestantisme, 1868.

Kuyper, Abraham. "It Shall Not Be So among You (1886)." In *Abraham Kuyper: A Centennial Reader,* edited by James Bratt, 125–140. Grand Rapids, MI: Eerdmans, 1998.

Kuyper, Abraham. *Kerkvisitatie Te Utrecht in 1868 Met Het Oog Op Den Kritieken Toestand Onzer Kerk.* Utrecht: J.H. van Peursem, 1868.

Kuyper, Abraham. *Lectures on Calvinism.* Grand Rapids, MI: Eerdmans, 1931.

Kuyper, Abraham. "(Letter to the Editor)." *De Bazuin* 46 1895.

Kuyper, Abraham. "Locus De Ecclesia." In *Dictaten Dogmatiek.* Grand Rapids, MI: J.B. Hulst, n.d.

Kuyper, Abraham. "Locus De Foedere." In *Dictaten Dogmatiek.* Grand Rapids: B. Sevensma, 1910.

Kuyper, Abraham. "(Main Points of Ecclesiology)." *De Heraut,* December 4, 1884.

Kuyper, Abraham. "Modernism: A *Fata Morgana* in the Christian Domain (1871)." In *Abraham Kuyper: A Centennial Reader,* edited by James Bratt, 87–124. Grand Rapids, MI: Eerdmans, 1998.

Kuyper, Abraham. "Pietje Baltus (*De Standaard,* March 30, 1914)." In *Abraham Kuyper: A Centennial Reader,* edited by James Bratt, 58–59. Grand Rapids, MI: Eerdmans, 1998.

Kuyper, Abraham. "Practijk in De Bediening." In *Practijk Der Godzaligheid.* Kampen: J. H. Kok, 1909.

Kuyper, Abraham. *Ons Program (Met Bijlagen).* Amsterdam: J.H. Kruyt, 1879.

Kuyper, Abraham. "Referaat over De Belijdenis (1870)." In *Revisie Der Revisie-Legende,* 56–68. Amsterdam: J.H. Kruyt, 1879.

Kuyper, Abraham. "Review of J. I. Doedes, *De Heid. Cat. In Zijne Eerste Levensjaren, 1563–1567, Hist. Bibliogr. Nalezing, Met 26 Facsimilé's.*" In *Godgeleerde Bijdragen Voor 1867,* 403–422. Utrecht: Kenmink en Zoon, 1867.

Kuyper, Abraham. *Separatie En Doleantie.* Amsterdam: J.A. Wormser, 1890.

Kuyper, Abraham. *Soevereiniteit in Eigen Kring. Rede Ter Inwijding Van De Vrije Universiteit, Den 20sten Oktober 1880 Gehouden, in Het Koor Der Nieuwe Kerk Te Amsterdam.* Amsterdam: J.H. Kruyt, 1880.

Kuyper, Abraham. "Sphere Sovereignty (1880)." In *Abraham Kuyper: A Centennial Reader*, edited by James Bratt, 461–490. Grand Rapids, MI: Eerdmans, 1998.

Kuyper, Abraham. *Stellingen in Den Professorenkrans Der "Vrije Universiteit."* 1884.

Kuyper, Abraham. "The Blurring of the Boundaries (1892)." In *Abraham Kuyper: A Centennial Reader*, edited by James Bratt, 363–402. Grand Rapids, MI: Eerdmans, 1998.

Kuyper, Abraham. *Tractaat Van De Reformatie Der Kerken, Aan De Zonen Der Reformatie Hier Te Lande Op Luther's Vierde Eeuwfeest Aangeboden.* Amsterdam: Höveker & Zoon, 1883.

Kuyper, Abraham. "Tweede Annexe: Referaat over De Belijdenis." In *Revisie Der Revisie Legende.* 56–68. Amsterdam: J.H. Kruyt, 1879.

Kuyper, Abraham. *Tweeërlei Vaderland.* Amsterdam: J.A. Wormser, 1887.

Kuyper, Abraham. "Uniformity: The Curse of Modern Life (1869)." In *Abraham Kuyper: A Centennial Reader*, edited by James Bratt, 19–44. Grand Rapids, MI: Eerdmans, 1998.

Kuyper, Abraham. "(Untitled Series on Baptism and the Visible Church)." vols. 519–533. *De Heraut* 1887–1888.

Kuyper, Abraham. "Van Het Kerkelijk Ambt." *De Heraut* 1887–1888.

Kuyper, Abraham. "Van De Kerk." *De Heraut* 1919–1920.

Kuyper, Abraham. *Het Conflict Gekomen: Vredelievden in De Besturen*, vol. 3. Amsterdam: J.H. Kruyt, 1886.

Kuyper, Abraham. "Vrijheid: Bevestigingsrede Van Dr. Ph. S. Van Ronkel (1873)." In *Predicatiën, in De Jaren 1867 Tot 1873, Tijdens Zijn Predikantschap in Het Nederlandsch Hervormde Kerkgenootschap, Gehouden Te Beesd, Te Utrecht, En Te Amsterdam*, 395–411. Kampen: Kok, 1913.

Kuyper, Abraham. *Vrijmaking Der Kerk.* Amsterdam: H. de Hoogh, 1869.

Kuyper, Abraham. *Wat Moeten Wij Doen: Het Stemrecht Aan Ons Zelven Houden of Den Kerkeraad Machtigen? Vraag Bij De Uitvoering Van Art. 23 Toegelicht.* Culemborg: A.J. Blom, 1867.

Kuyper, Abraham. "Wedergeboorte En Bekeering." In *Uit Het Woord. Stichtelijke Bijbelstudiën*, 1–60. Amsterdam: Höveker & Wormser, n.d.

Kuyper, Abraham, ed. *Aan De Kerkeraden Der Nederduitsche Hervormde Gemeenten in Nederland.* Utrecht: Kemink en Zoon, 1868.

Langman, H. J. *Kuyper En De Volkskerk: Een Dogmatisch-Ecclesiologische Studie.* Kampen: Kok, 1950.

Lijphart, Arend. *Politics of Accommodation: Pluralism and Democracy in the Netherlands.* Berkeley: University of California Press, 1968.

Lucas, Sean Michael. "Southern Fried Kuyper? Robert Lewis Dabney, Abraham Kuyper, and the Limitations of Public Theology." *Westminster Theological Journal* 66 (2004): 179–201.

Mackay, James H. *Religious Thought in Holland during the Nineteenth Century.* London: Hodder and Stoughten, 1911.

Marsden, George M. "Introduction: Reformed and American." In *Reformed Theology in America*, edited by David Wells, 1–12. Grand Rapids, MI: Baker, 1997.

Marsden, George M. "Christianity and Cultures: Transforming Niebuhr's Categories." *Insights: The Faculty Journal of Austin Seminary* 115 (1999): 4–15.

Martin, David. "Comparing Different Maps of the Same Ground." In *Reflections on Sociology and Theology*. 74–88. Oxford: Clarenden Press, 1997.

Marty, Martin E., and Edith L. Blumhofer. N.d. "Public Religion in America Today." http://divinity.uchicago.edu/martycenter/research/publicreligion_today.shtml.

McLeod, Hugh. *Secularization in Western Europe, 1848–1914*. New York: St. Martin's, 2000.

McManners, John. "Enlightenment: Secular and Christian (1600–1800)." In *The Oxford Illustrated History of Christianity*, edited by John McManners, 267–299. Oxford: Oxford University Press, 1990.

Moberly, R. C. *Ministerial Priesthood: Chapters (Preliminary to a Study of the Ordinal) on the Rationale of Ministry and the Meaning of Christian Priesthood*, 2d ed. London: John Murray, 1910.

Molendijk, Arie L. "'Mine': The Rhetorics of Abraham Kuyper." *Journal for the History of Modern Theology/Zeitschrift für Neuere Theologiegeschichte* 15 (2008): 248–262.

Molendijk, Arie L. "Neo-Calvinist Culture Protestantism: Abraham Kuyper's *Stone Lectures*." *Church History and Religious Culture* 88 (2008): 235–250.

Molendijk, Arie L. "Neocalvinistisch Cultuurprotestantisme: Abraham Kuypers *Stone Lectures*." *Documentatieblad voor de Nederlandse Kerkgeschiedenis na 1800* 29 (2006): 5–19.

Mouw, Richard J. "Baptism and the Salvific Status of Children: An Examination of Some Intra-Reformed Debates." *Calvin Theological Journal* 41 (2006): 238–254.

Mudge, Lewis. "Searching for Faith's Social Reality." *Christian Century*, September 22 1976, 784–787.

Naugle, David K. *Worldview: The History of a Concept*. Grand Rapids, MI: Eerdmans, 2002.

Nauta, D. *De Verbindende Kracht Van De Belijdenis Schriften: Verhandeling over De Formulierkwestie in De Negentiende Eeuw in Nederland*. Kampen: Kok, 1969.

Nevin, John Williamson. *The Anxious Bench*. Chambersburg: Publication Office of the German Reformed Church, 1844.

Niebuhr, H. Richard. *The Social Sources of Denominationalism*. New York: Henry Holt and Company, 1929.

Nijenhuis, W. "De Nederlandse Hervormde Kerk En De Doleantie." In *De Doleantie Van 1886 En Haar Geschiedenis*, edited by Wim Bakker, O. J. de Jong, Willem van 't Spijker, and L. J. Wolthuis, 178–202. Kampen: Kok, 1986.

Noll, Mark. *The Old Religion in the New World: The History of North American Christianity*. Grand Rapids, MI: Eerdmans, 2002.

Noll, Mark. *The Civil War as a Theological Crisis*. Chapel Hill: University of North Carolina, 2007.

"Notulen, April 10, 1880." In *Archief Curatoren, Ingekomen Stukken*. Amsterdam: Historisch Documentatiecentrum voor het Nederlands Protestantisme, 1880.

Oberman, Heiko. "Calvin's Legacy: Its Greatness and Limitations (Revised Version of the Kuyper Lectures, 1986, Free University of Amsterdam)." In *The Two Reformations: The Journey from the Last Days to the New World*, edited by Donald Weinstein, 116–168. New Haven, CT: Yale University Press, 2003.

"'Particulier' In De Geïntegreerde Taal-Bank." December 11 (2007–2009), http://gtb.inl.nl/iWDB/search?actie=article&wdb=WNT&id=M052414&lemmodern=particulier.

Pauw, Amy Plantinga. "Practical Ecclesiology in John Calvin and Jonathan Edwards." In *John Calvin's American Legacy*, edited by Thomas J. Davis, 91–110. New York: Oxford University Press, 2010.

Pelikan, Jaroslav. *Credo: Historical and Theological Guide to Creeds and Confessions of Faith in the Christian Tradition*. New Haven, CT: Yale University Press, 2003.

Pierson, Allard. *Dr. A. Pierson Aan Zijne Laatste Gemeente*. Arnhem: D.A. Thieme, 1865.

Puchinger, George. *Abraham Kuyper: De Jonge Kuyper (1837–1867)*. Franeker: Weaver, 1987.

Puchinger, George. *Abraham Kuyper: His Early Journey of Faith*. Translated by Simone Kennedy. Edited by George Harinck. Amsterdam: VU Press, 1998.

Rasker, A. J. *De Nederlandse Hervormde Kerk Vanaf 1795*. Kampen: Kok, 1974.

Rauwenhoff, L. W. E. "De Kerk." *Theologisch Tijdschrift* 1 (1867): 1–37.

Rullmann, J. C. *De Strijd Voor Kerkherstel in De Nederlandsch Hervormde Kerk Der Xixe Eeuw*. Amsterdam: W. Kirchner, 1915.

Rullmann, J. C. *Kuyper-Bibliographie*. 3 vols. 's-Gravenhage: Js. Bootsma, 1923–1940.

Schaeffer, J. C. *De Plaats Van Abraham Kuyper in "De Vrije Kerk."* Amsterdam: Buijten & Schipperheijn, 1997.

Schleiermacher, Friedrich. *Brief Outline of the Study of Theology*. Translated by William Farrer. London: T&T Clark, 1850.

Schleiermacher, Friedrich. *The Christian Faith*. New York: T&T Clark, 1999.

Schutte, G. J. *Het Calvinistisch Nederland: Mythe En Werkelijkheid*. Hilversum: Verloren, 2000.

Skinner, Quentin. *Visions of Politics: Regarding Method*, Vol. 1. Cambridge, UK: Cambridge University Press, 2002.

Smilde, E. *Een Eeuw Van Strijd over Verbond En Doop*. Kampen: Kok, 1946.

Smith, James K. A. *Introducing Radical Orthodoxy: Mapping a Post-Secular Theology*. Grand Rapids, MI: Baker Academic, 2004.

Stark, Rodney and William S. Bainbridge. "Of Churches, Sects, and Cults: Preliminary Concepts for a Theory of Religious Movements." *Journal for the Scientific Study of Religion* 18, no. 2 (1979): 117–133.

Steeman, Theodore M. "Church, Sect, Mysticism, Denomination: Periodological Aspects of Troelsch's Types." *Sociological Analysis* 36 (1975): 181–204.

Stellingwerf, Johannes. "Het Arcanum Van Abraham Kuyper." In *Geboekt in Eigen Huis: Werken Van Abraham Kuyper Aanwezig in De Bibliotheek Van De Vrije Universiteit*, edited by Johannes Stellingwerf, 13–47. Amsterdam: VU Uitgeverij, 1987.

Stellingwerff, Johannes. *Dr. Abraham Kuyper En De Vrije Universiteit*. Kampen: Kok, 1987.

Sykes, Stephen. *The Identity of Christianity: Theologians and the Essence of Christianity from Schleiermacher to Barth*. Philadelphia: Fortress, 1984.

Taylor, Charles. *A Secular Age*. Cambridge, MA: Harvard University Press, 2007.

Thorkildsen, Dag. "Scandanavia: Lutheranism and National Identity." In *The Cambridge History of Christianity: World Christianities C. 1815–1914*, edited by Sheridan Gilley and Brian Stanley, 342–358. Cambridge: Cambridge University Press, 2006.

Trapman, J. "Allard Pierson En Zijn Afscheid Van De Kerk." *Documentatieblad voor de Nederlandse Kerkgeschiedenis na 1800* 19 (1996): 15–27.

Troeltsch, Ernst. *The Social Teaching of the Christian Churches*. Translated by Olive Wyon. Vol. 1, Library of Theological Ethics. Louisville, KY: Westminster/John Knox, 1960.

Troeltsch, Ernst. *The Social Teaching of the Christian Churches*. Translated by Olive Wyon. Vol. 2, Library of Theological Ethics. Louisville, KY: Westminster/John Knox, 1960.

Van Dale Groot Woordenboek: Engels-Nederlands, Nederlands Engels Version 2.1. Van Dale Lexicographie, Utrecht/Antwerpen.

van den Berg, C. H. W. "De Ontstaangeschiedenis Van De Doleantie Te Amsterdam." In *De Doleantie Van 1886 En Haar Geschiedenis*, edited by W. Bakker, O. J. de Jong, Willem van 't Spijker, and L. J. Wolthuis, 76–105. Kampen: J.H. Kok, 1986.

van den Berg, C. H. W. "Kuyper En De Kerk." In *Abraham Kuyper: Zijn Volksdeel, Zijn Invloed*, edited by Cornelius Augustijn, J. H. Prins, and H. E. S. Woldring, 146–178. Delft: Meinema, 1987.

van den Berg, J. "Oplossing Der Kerk in De Maatschappij? Modernen, Ethischen En De Toekomstvisie Van Richard Rothe." In *Ad Interim: Opstellen over Eschatologie, Apocalyptic En Ethiek*, edited by T. Baarda, J. Firet, and G. Th. Rothuizen, 151–167. Kampen: Kok, 1976.

van der Borght, Eduardus. *Theology of Ministry: A Reformed Contribution to an Ecumenical Dialogue*. Studies in Reformed Theology. Leiden: Brill, 2007.

van der Schee, Willem. "Kuyper's Archimedes Point: The Reverend Abraham Kuyper on Election." In *Kuyper Reconsidered: Aspects of His Life and Work*, edited by Cornelis van der Kooi and Jan de Bruijn, 102–110. Amsterdam: VU Uitgeverij, 1999.

van Egmond, A. "Kuyper's Dogmatic Theology." In *Kuyper Reconsidered: Aspects of His Life and Work*, edited by Cornelis van der Kooi and Jan de Bruijn, 85–94. Amsterdam: VU Uitgeverij, 1999.

van Eijnatten, Joris and Fred van Lieburg. *Nederlandse Religiegeschiedienis*. Hilversum: Verloren, 2005.

van Gelderen, J. "Op Weg Naar De Vereniging Van 17 Juni 1892." In *De Vereniging Van 1892 En Haar Geschiedenis*, edited by L. J. Wolthuis and Jasper Vree, 35–80. Kampen: Kok, 1992.

van Leeuwen, Petrus Antonius. *Het Kerkbegrip in De Theologie Van Abraham Kuyper*. Franeker: Wever, 1946.

van Rooden, Peter. "Secularization in the Netherlands." *Kirchliche Zeitschrift* 11 (1998): 34–41.

van Rooden, Peter. "Long-Term Religious Developments in the Netherlands, C. 1750–2000." In *The Decline of Christendom in Western Europe, 1750–2000*, edited by Hugh McLeod and Werner Ustorf, 113–129. Cambridge, UK: Cambridge University Press, 2003.

van Spanning, H. "Hoedemaker En De Antirevolutionairen." In *Hoedemaker Herdacht*, edited by G. Abma and Jan De Bruijn, 234–245. Baarn: Ten Have, 1989.

van Tijn, Theo. *Twintig Jaren Amsterdam: De Maatschappelijke Ontwikkeling Van De Hoofdstad, Van De Jaren '50 Der Vorige Eeuw Tot 1876*. Amsterdam: Scheltema & Holkema, 1965.

Van Til, Cornelius. *Common Grace and the Gospel*. Nutley: Presbyterian and Reformed, 1977.

van Toorenenbergen, A. "De Kerk." *Waarheid in Liefde* (1867): 513–568.

Vanden Berg, Frank. *Abraham Kuyper*. Grand Rapids, MI: Eerdmans, 1960.

VanDrunen, David. "Abraham Kuyper and the Reformed Natural Law and Two Kingdoms Traditions." *Calvin Theological Journal* 42 (2007): 283–307.

Veenhof, Jan. "Geschiedinis Van Theologie En Spiritualiteit in De Gereformeerde Kerken." In *100 Jaar Theologie: Aspecten Van Een Eeuw Theologie in De Gereformeerde Kerken in Nederland (1892–1992)*, edited by Martien E. Brinkman, 14–95. Kampen: J.H. Kok, 1992.

Veenhof, Jan. "A History of Theology and Spirituality in the Dutch Reformed Churches (Gereformeerde Kerken), 1892–1992." *Calvin Theological Journal* 28 (1993): 266–297.

Velema, Willem H. *De Leer Van De Heilige Geest Bij Abraham Kuyper*. 's-Gravenhage: Van Keulen, 1957.

Volf, Miroslav. *After Our Likeness: The Church as the Image of the Trinity*. Grand Rapids, MI: Eerdmans, 1998.

Vos, G. J. *Het Keerpunt in De Jongste Geschiedenis Van Kerk En Staat: De Eerste Bladzijde Der Tweede Afscheiding*. Dordrecht: J.P. Revers, 1887.

Vree, Jasper. "Abraham Kuyper in De Jaren 1848–1874: Een Briljante, Bevlogen Branie." *Documentatieblad voor de Nederlandse Kerkgeschiedenis na 1800* 29 (2006): 27–49.

Vree, Jasper. "De Drie Formulieren Van Enigheid: Een Vondst Van Abraham Kuyper." *Historisch Tijdschrift GKN* 13 (2007): 3–17.

Vree, Jasper. "De Herziening Van Het Hervormde Algemeen Reglement (1846–1852)." In *Om De Toekomst Van Het Protestantse Nederland. De Gevolgen Van De*

Grondwetsherziening Van 1848 Voor Kerk, Staat En Maatschappij, edited by G. J. Schutte and Jasper Vree, 22–63. Zoetermeer: Meinema, 1998.

Vree, Jasper. "Gunning En Kuyper: Een Bewogen Vriendschap Rond Schrift En Kerk in De Jaren 1860–1873." In *Noblesse Oblige: Achtergrond En Actualiteit Van De Theologie Van J. H. Gunning Jr.*, edited by Theo Hettema and Leo Mietus, 62–86. Gorinchem: Ekklesia, 2005.

Vree, Jasper. "'Het Reveil' En 'Het (Neo-)Calvinisme' in Hun Onderlinge Samenhang (1856–1896)." In *Abraham Kuyper: Vast En Veranderlijk: De Ontwikkeling Van Zijn Denken*, edited by Cornelis Augustijn and Jasper Vree, 54–85. Zoetermeer: Meinema, 1998.

Vree, Jasper. "Historical Introduction." In *Abraham Kuyper's Commentatio (1860): The Young Kuyper about Calvin, a Lasco, and the Church*, 7–66. Leiden: Brill, 2005.

Vree, Jasper. "Hoe De Citadel Onstand: De Consolidatie Der Vereniging 1892–1905." In *Abraham Kuyper: Vast En Veranderlijk, De Ontwikkeling Van Zijn Denken*, edited by Cornelis Augustijn and Jasper Vree, 200–242. Zoetermeer: Meinema, 1998.

Vree, Jasper. *Kuyper in De Kiem: De Precalvinistische Periode Van Abraham Kuyper, 1848–1874*. Hilversum: Uitgeverij Verloren, 2006.

Vree, Jasper. "More Pierson and Mesmer, and Less Pietje Baltus: Kuyper's Ideas on Church, State, and Culture During the First Years of His Ministry (1863–1866)." In *Kuyper Reconsidered: Aspects of His Life and Work*, edited by Cornelis van der Kooi and Jan de Bruijn, 299–309. Amsterdam: VU Uitgeverij, 1999.

Vree, Jasper. "Organisme En Instituut: De Ontwikkeling Van Kuypers Spreken over Kerk-Zijn (1867–1901)." In *Abraham Kuyper: Vast En Veranderlijk: De Ontwikkeling Van Zijn Denken*, 86–108. Zoetermeer: Meinema, 1998.

Vree, Jasper. "Palingenesie Bij Abraham Kuyper: Een Levensproces Dat Door Heel De Schepping Gaat." In *Protestants Nederland Tussen Tijd En Eeuwigheid*, 154–171. Zoetermeer: Meinema, 2000.

Vree, Jasper. "Petrus Hofstede De Groot and the Christian Education of the Dutch Nation (1833–1861)." *Nederlands Archief voor Kerkgeschiedenis* 78 (1998): 70–93.

Vree, Jasper. "The Marnix-Vereeniging: Abraham Kuyper's First National Organization (1868–89)." *DRCH* 84 (2004): 388–475.

Vree, Jasper. "'Want Hij Weet Wat Maaksel Wij Zijn, Gedachtig Zijnde Dat Wij Stof Zijn': Het Publieke En Het Persoonlijke Geloofsleven Van P. Hofstede De Groot." In *De Kunst Van Het Ontfermen. Studies Voor Gerben Heitink*, edited by Alma Lanser, Jelle van Nijen, Ciska Stark, and Sake Stoppels, 147–169. Kampen: Kok, 2003.

Vulsma, R. F. *Burgerlijke Stand, Bevolkingsregister En Genealogie*. Naarden: Boekencentrum, 1968.

Wacker, Grant. *Heaven Below: Early Pentecostals and American Culture*. Cambridge, MA: Harvard University Press, 2001.

Weber, Max. *The Theory of Social and Economic Organization*, edited by Talcott Parsons. New York: Free Press, 1947.

Welch, Claude. *Protestant Thought in the Nineteenth Century, 1799–1870*, Vol. 1. New Haven, CT: Yale University Press, 1972.

Welch, Claude. *Protestant Thought in the Nineteenth Century, 1870–1914*, Vol. 2. New Haven, CT: Yale University Press, 1985.

Wintle, Michael. *Pillars of Piety: Religion in the Netherlands in the Nineteenth Century, 1813–1901*, Occasional Papers in Modern Dutch Studies. Hull: Hull University Press, 1987.

Wintle, Michael. *An Economic and Social History of the Netherlands, 1800–1920: Demographic, Economic, and Social Transition*. Cambridge, UK: Cambridge University Press, 2000.

Witte, John, Jr. *The Reformation of Rights: Law, Religion, and Human Rights in Early Modern Calvinism*. Cambridge, UK: Cambridge University Press, 2007.

Wolterstorff, Nicholas. "Abraham Kuyper on Christian Learning." In *Educating for Shalom: Essays on Christian Higher Education*, edited by Clarence W. Joldersma and Gloria Goris Stronks, 199–225. Grand Rapids, MI: Eerdmans, 2004.

Wolterstorff, Nicholas. "Abraham Kuyper (1827–1920)." In *The Teachings of Modern Protestantism, on Law, Politics, and Human Nature*, edited by John Witte Jr. and Frank S. Alexander, 29–69. New York: Columbia University Press, 2007.

Wood, John Halsey, Jr. "Church, Sacrament, and Society: Abraham Kuyper's Early Baptismal Theology, 1859–1874." *Journal of Reformed Theology* 2 (2008): 275–296.

Wood, John Halsey, Jr. "Going Dutch in the Modern Age: Abraham Kuyper's Struggle for a Free Church in the Nineteenth-Century Netherlands." *Journal of Ecclesiastical History*, 2012.

Wood, John Halsey, Jr. "Theologian of the Revolution: Abraham Kuyper's Radical Proposal for Church and State." In *Kingdoms Apart: Engaging the Two Kingdoms Perspective*, edited by Ryan McIlhenny, 155–171. Presbyterian and Reformed, 2012.

Wuthnow, Robert. *After the Baby Boomers: How Twenty- and Thirty-Somethings Are Shaping the Future of American Religion*. Princeton, NJ: Princeton University Press, 2007.

Young, William. "Historic Calvinism and Neo-Calvinism." *Westminster Theological Journal* 36 (1974): 48–64, 156–173.

Zwaan, Johan. "Sociale Bewogenheid in Een Jeugdwerk Van Abraham Kuyper." In *Een Vrije Universiteitsbibliotheek: Studies over Verleden, Bezit En Heden Van De Bibliotheek Der Vrije Universiteit*, edited by Johannes Stellingwerf, 203–219. Assen: Van Gorcum, 1980.

Zwaanstra, Henry. "Abraham Kuyper's Conception of the Church." *CTJ* 9 (1974): 149–181.

Index